THE FARMER'S WIFE GUIDE TO GROWING A GREAT GARDEN—
and Eating from It, Too!

THE FARMER'S WIFE GUIDE TO GROWING A GREAT GARDEN— and Eating from It, Too!

GROWING, STORING, FREEZING, AND COOKING YOUR OWN VEGETABLES + 250 RECIPES AND SERVING IDEAS!

WRITTEN AND ILLUSTRATED BY

Barbara Doyen

M. EVANS AND COMPANY, INC.
NEW YORK

M. Evans and Company, Inc.
216 East 49th Street
New York, New York 10017

Library of Congress Cataloging-in-Publication Data

Doyen, Barbara.
    The farmer's wife guide to growing a great garden and eating from it, too!
: storing, freezing, and cooking your own vegetables / by Barbara Doyen.
      p. cm.
    Includes bibliographical references (p.).
    ISBN 0-87131-974-8
    1. Vegetable gardening. 2. Vegetables. 3. Cookery (Vegetables) I. Title:
Growing a great garden, and eating from it, too. II. Title.
SB321 .D72 2002
635—dc21   2002020246

Book design by Rik Lain Schell

Printed in the United States of America

9 8 7 6 5 4 3 2 1

Contents

To my husband, The Farmer (also known as Bob Doyen),
who talked me into becoming The Farmer's Wife.

"THE WEALTH OF MAN STARTS WITH FOOD PRODUCED FROM THE SOIL."

—Arnie Waldstein

WHY GARDEN?

First of All, It's Fun!

I can't wait to jump out of bed in the spring and summer to view my garden each morning. I get great joy in seeing the progress of each row of beans, each tomato plant. And that joy stays with me throughout my hectic business day.

Great Eating!

Home-grown vegetables taste much better than anything you can buy, because they are fresh—you can harvest them at their peak of ripeness and be eating them in minutes in your kitchen. Commercial growers often can't harvest at the peak of flavor because their produce would spoil during shipping.

Uncommon Delights!

You can grow special varieties not available in stores. You'll never be bored, because every year you can try different varieties to add new taste treats to your repertoire.

Minimize Chemicals in Your Diet

You'll know exactly what was used on your produce for insect control, fertilizer, etc. Since you have a choice, you can select products that are wholesome for your body and for the environment.

Reduce Your Food Bills!

You can save a lot of money, although this is just a bonus for many people. I must confess that I'd be growing a garden even if this were not the case.

Get Fit!

Instead of doing boring exercises or "gerbilling," as The Farmer calls it, on an indoor treadmill, you'll be laboring outdoors with a purpose. And you'll be rewarded with a trimmer figure and great food to eat, as well!

Beautify Your Yard!

Gardening adds interest to the landscape, whether you merely squeeze some vegetable plants into your flower beds or window planters, or have whole areas dedicated just to food production. As I work each day at my computer, I get great enjoyment from looking out of my home-office windows at my gardens spread out on the lawn like vast quilts. Most vegetable plants are quite attractive, and gardens can be designed to complement any landscape.

Great Nutrition!

Commercially grown produce is harvested when it has the maximum ability to ship well, which means it's usually not completely ripened and therefore not at the peak of its nutritional content. Add the lag time for shipping, as well as any processing that's done to enhance the appearance or keeping ability of the produce, and you've lost a lot of nutrients. With homegrown produce, you can harvest at the peak of ripeness and be eating your produce fresh out of the garden in minutes, thus increasing the nutrients available to your body.

Also, did you know that tomatoes harvested on a sunny day have more vitamin C than tomatoes picked on a cloudy day? It's an easy way to give yourself a nutrition boost, but only when you grow your own!

On the farm, since we're so subject to the whims of our environment, we're always looking for signs of what nature has in store for us. By the end of summer, we notice that wild animals are already preparing for winter. If winter is going to be especially cold or long, the animals will have thicker pelts than usual, develop more body fat, and will somehow know to hibernate in deeper holes or shelters with greater protection from the elements. Even the caterpillar fur varies in thickness from year to year. What signals these adjustments? It has to come from their attunement to nature. I suspect that one day we'll find that eating locally grown food helps our bodies adapt to the conditions in the season to come. It's another reason to garden at least part of our own food!

Mental Health!

Gardening is an antidote to depression. Instead of bemoaning the dreary winter weather, you'll be spending the months studying gardening catalogues and books. You can draw up plans for new beds, and redesign old beds. You can start seedlings and dream of their promise as you watch them grow and develop. In the summer, there is always something to do outside, giving us purpose, and our gardens are constantly changing, lending endless variety to our lives.

Spiritual Health!

There is something about having your hands in the soil, planting a seed or a seedling, and nurturing its growth that's profoundly fulfilling. It connects us to the source of our existence and puts us in harmony with the rhythms of nature.

Our life comes from the earth, yet many never come into contact with the earth. We live in cement cities, in high-rises far above the land. Or we live in sterile houses surrounded by yards tended by a lawn service and nursery-planted landscaping pruned and groomed by specialists. We have public parks, but they're removed from our living and working spaces, and we do nothing personally to care for them. Literally and figuratively too many of us are no longer "grounded."

With bare hands, grasp a handful of soil. Don't recoil from it, feel the life it contains: beneficial bacteria, worms, insects, seeds—it's just brimming with potential, full of nature's vitality. It is our origin, and we need to touch it, to feel our roots, to connect with our true being.

Although most of our population is far removed from living and working on real farms, it is my sincere hope that no matter where you live and work, this book will encourage you to come in contact with your own soil, to feel the joy and satisfaction of having a hand in creating your own delicious, nourishing food.

GARDEN NOTES

I always said I'd never marry a farmer. So, of course, that's just what I did!

But The Farmer had to work hard to convince me, trying numerous persuasive sales pitches. I knew he was serious when he offered to stop harvesting for two whole days during perfect weather to move me to the farm. That just isn't done: Farmers don't take time off, because of the urgency of getting their crops in before winter. Still, I resisted.

Then he said, "Just think, if you married me and moved to the farm, you could have all the gardens and orchards you want." That did it. So, after our wedding, The Farmer got on his tractor and started tearing up strips of sod for my gardens. (He also promised all the pets I wanted, but that's another story!)

I am passionate about vegetables, of every kind. I started growing things that The Farmer had never heard of, let alone tasted. For instance, I prepared many kinds of cooked greens: spinach, Swiss chard, beet tops, and kale, and I diligently put up the excess. The Farmer said we were the only family in the county, maybe even the state, with four kinds of silage in the freezer. (For those who don't know, silage is chopped green plant material stored and fed to livestock during the winter.) I grew so many vegetables, that we bought extra freezers to hold them all.

Even a diversity of vegetables can get boring after a while. I became creative at developing new recipes, to keep meals interesting for me to prepare and my family to eat, and finding ways to make all sorts of vegetables appealing to children. Some of these are included here.

During the years the children were still at home, my gardens supplied every bit of our produce, which we enjoyed fresh from spring through fall, and which I stored or froze for all our winter needs. With the help of this book, you can do it, too. It's fun. It's easy. It's nutritious and delicious! Try it!

Everyone Can Grow a Garden!

What if your yard is too small? Even if you lack room for a dedicated garden, you can add vegetable plants to your flower beds or landscaping. If space is really at a premium, go vertical—grow vining plants on trellises, fences, or walls. Vegetables are adaptive, and many of the plants are quite attractive, too.

What if you don't have any yard at all? Window boxes provide gardening opportunities for growing vegetables right along with flowers. Or try container gardening on a patio, deck, terrace, or rooftop. High-rise apartment gardeners are able to produce an astonishing number of crops in containers. So long as you have sunlight, provide good drainage (by placing pebbles in the bottom of the pot), use good potting soil, select varieties appropriate for the size of the container, and water daily, you can't go wrong.

To this Farmer's Wife, there is nothing like a nice garden patch outdoors, or better yet, several of them! If you lack yard space, look around. Many communities have garden plots for rent, or perhaps you have a friend or neighbor with room for a backyard garden in exchange for some vegetables.

WHAT TO LOOK FOR WHEN SELECTING YOUR GARDEN SPOT:

- Level ground. If your terrain slopes, plant crosswise to the slope or install terraces.
- At least six hours of sun a day; more is better. Avoid planting near trees or structures that will block the sunlight.
- Good soil, or soil that can be amended. (See how in "Preparing the Soil," below.)

- A space free of obstacles such as underground cables, water lines, large rocks, etc.
- Avoid a low area, where pockets of cold air settle. You can spot these by studying where early morning frost accumulates.
- Avoid choosing a site where water drains and accumulates. Or provide for a drainage system, which probably will require professional help, or raise the ground level by bringing in soil.
- A convenient source of water nearby for watering, and hoses or other means to get the water to the garden.
- Easy access so that you can get in and out of the garden, and you'll be able to carry in tools and compost and haul out quantities of vegetables and garden refuse.

NOTE: If you'll be enclosing your garden space with a fence, be sure you install an entry gate, or even a double gate, if you'll be bringing a wheelbarrow or a garden tractor into the space. Two gates opposite each other make driving equipment through the garden easier.

Preparing the Site

Now that you've decided on your planting area, you probably need to clear it off before you can begin gardening. The ground can't be planted until you remove the plant material already growing there. In the old days, farmers used teams of horses or oxen for this; today we use tractors.

Trees and shrubs will require heavy equipment and you probably should get some professional help for these. Everything else you can handle yourself. Here are some methods:

SMOTHERING. If you have some lead time, this is a great way to kill plants, roots and all, but it doesn't happen overnight. It takes a while to be effective. For some plants, like grass, it takes only a few days; for really stubborn plants, like Canadian thistles, it takes up to two years! Since all plants need air, smothering eventually works to kill everything. You lay down a tarp, old carpeting, black plastic, or thick layers of newspapers or magazines, and weigh it down with bricks, cement blocks, old boards, etc. If you have selected a new garden spot in the fall, mow it off and lay down whatever you've chosen as a barrier. By spring, your plot should be ready.

CHEMICAL SPRAYS. These kill everything in two weeks, and I do mean everything. If even the smallest drop touches a leaf, the whole plant dies, so be very careful as you're applying the spray, and be sure to do it on a calm day to avoid wind drift. Chemicals can be dangerous, so follow the label instructions carefully and protect yourself as directed.

HAND DIGGING. This is a lot of work, especially when you're doing an entire garden plot! If you'll be gardening where you've got sod, you can dig it out and even plant it elsewhere, if you wish. If you live in a city, you can probably rent a machine that will accomplish this task, but around here it's done with a flat shovel. First slice down into the ground in parallel straight lines the width of the shovel, sort of like cutting the rows in a sheet cake. Then do a crosswise cut, and slide the shovel below the grass roots, just like inserting a cake server. Remove the square chunk of sod to a wheelbarrow, wagon, or truck. To lighten your load, you can shake off much of the dirt that clings to the roots before loading it.

NOTE: At this writing, we just finished using the shovel technique to prepare the space for a new strawberry bed that had to be readied in a hurry, and I must warn you that this is hard physical labor! The good news is that you can reuse the sod. I planted ours in an area where the lawn had winter killed. Do this right before several days of rain and you won't have to water it!

TILLING. You can rent a machine, but if you continue gardening, you'll want to own one of your own. Tilling breaks up any remaining roots and aerates the soil nicely. It's good to cover the garden area, going back and forth and then going over it all a second time, up and down, crisscrossing your original rows. You may need to wait a few days and repeat the process, mixing in any needed amendments. (See "Preparing the Soil," below.)

NOTE: I bought a portable, heavy-duty tiller that weighs only twenty pounds but does a great job, even on my large gardens. The Farmer frowned when I ordered it, because he thought it was too small and lacking in horsepower—keep in mind, his "garden" covers 1,000 acres, and his tractors are huge! For a long time I resisted buying a tiller, and then The Farmer recommended that I get a large expensive one—but I am very happy with mine and use it all over the farmstead. Even The Farmer is impressed. (See "Sources" for information.)

COMBINATION APPROACH.

Many people use a combination, first digging out the sod, or smothering it or using chemicals, and then tilling. This is a good method for eliminating the underground root systems on weeds, such as quack grass, that have the ability to regrow from very tiny segments.

Preparing the Soil

Austrian friends invited me to dinner at their charming home nestled on a mountainside in the Alps. The view was breathtakingly spectacular. My hosts were the village's medical doctor and his wife, who knew that I was from the United States, but not exactly where. When they introduced me to their fifteen-year-old son, he announced that he wanted to become a farmer in Iowa, because that's where you find the best soil in the world! When he learned that I was from Iowa, he suddenly took a great interest in speaking with me!

Indeed, we are blessed with the best topsoil in the world. We can grow almost anything in it, provided our growing season is long enough to mature the crop before frost. Knowing how wonderful our soil is, some Iowa gardeners who must relocate to another state, haul truckloads of our rich black dirt right along with their furniture, which is very expensive, indeed!

Far better, though it takes time, would be to work with the soil in their new location, mixing in lots of compost and, if a source can be found, well-rotted manure, making it rich and fertile.

On a trip to Texas, I visited an area that had such poor soil that it wouldn't even support many weeds. Yet some people had used this same soil to create beautiful, productive gardens. I asked one gardener how she did it, and her answer was just what I've said here: mix in lots of compost over several years. But just when her soil was getting really fertile, she sold her house—and took her dirt with her. A tractor with a bucket loaded it into trucks and transferred it to her new home a few blocks away. She assured me that it is a very common practice and expected by the new owners.

So don't be discouraged if you're not starting out with wonderful soil. You can fix it!

HOW TO IMPROVE YOUR SOIL

First, you need to understand what soil does, besides anchoring plants to the ground. Soil allows plant roots to get three important things: water, air, and nutrients. Let's look at different soil types:

LOAM SOIL is the best for most purposes, because it is well aerated and holds moisture. It's full of humus, or decayed material, which provides nutrients to the soil. The humus is renewed every time farmers till under last year's crop residue (which is compost) or spread livestock manure (which is also decayed plant material, if you think about it). The year a fire burned across The Farmer's fields, we lost not only the crops, but also the valuable plant material that enriches our soil. Loam is what we have here in Iowa.

CLAY SOIL holds moisture and lacks air, so plants drown. To correct this problem, greatly increase the humus in the clay by adding lots of compost, manure, peat moss, or rotted leaves to the soil and thoroughly tilling it together when the clay is somewhat dry and crumbly. If the clay gets greasy during rains, you can add sand to make it more friable, but do this only if you intend to water during dry spells. Otherwise the clay will get brick-hard and plant roots won't be able to penetrate it.

SANDY SOIL gives the roots plenty of air, but it doesn't hold water and dries out quickly, so the plants die of thirst. It is also lacking in nutrients. The solution: increase humus by adding lots of compost, manure, peat moss, or rotted leaves to the soil and thoroughly tilling it together.

Do you see a pattern here? No matter what soil type you start out with, you'll improve it by adding manure and/or compost. This not only adds nutrients, but it conditions the soil, adding to its ability to hold moisture and air, and making it easier for the roots to grow. You can recognize fertile soil that's high in organic matter, because it will be a nice deep brown color or even black.

So, what about this wonderful compost stuff?

Compost

It was called the pig bucket. In days of old, every farmwife had one in her kitchen. At meal time, onion peelings, apple cores, corn shucks, or any kind of food scraps (except animal or dairy, which went to the cats and dogs) were put into the pig bucket. Periodically, it would be emptied by tossing the contents over the fence into the pigpen, and the pigs relished eating them. There was no hurry about emptying the pig bucket until it became full; there is no odor problem so long as you don't add any liquids or animal or dairy products.

Although we no longer have pigs, we still have a pig bucket. It still gets filled with all manner of food scraps except animal or dairy products. It is still periodically emptied, but now we dump the contents onto the ground where it decomposes into humus, often called compost, with the aid of bacteria and fungus. You can place a layer of compost under any plant that needs a boost. You can leave the compost on the surface, where it will slowly releases its nutrients, or you can lightly turn it under with your tiller to speed the nutrients' absorption and add aeration to the soil.

Plant material breaks down into compost faster if it's chopped into pieces. Leaves, weeds, hay, and even the contents of the pig bucket can be run over with a lawn mower—which easily chops them up. For best results, don't layer the material too deep before mowing it, especially if you have a small mower. Place the material on the ground three or four feet away from your compost pile and let the mower thrown it onto the pile for you.

Much has been written about how hot the compost pile must get, how often you need to turn it, when to water it, how high to make the pile. If you have room, find an out-of-sight place to dump your kitchen and garden refuse right on the ground, up to three feet deep. Stir it with a pitchfork once a week, and water it occasionally, if you're having a dry spell. That's all there is to it. The compost is ready to use when it's dark and crumbles easily in your hand.

If your yard isn't large enough to hide a compost pile, which does look unsightly, you can buy a compost bin that makes quick work of the composting process. You'll find you need two of them, though— one to collect new material in, and the other to process it. Once the compost has been processed, pour it out on the garden and lightly till it into the soil at any time. Then that bin will be ready to start a new batch.

Weeds can be composted, but not if they've set seeds, unless your compost pile gets hot, or you'll risk spreading viable seeds in the garden. Also avoid composting plants that are diseased or harboring insect pests.

In late fall, clean off the garden and shovel the compost (as well as manure, if it's available) in a layer over the garden; it doesn't matter if it's completely decomposed. Just till it under and the compost will break down by spring, adding nutrition to the soil. You may not need any other fertilizer.

NOTE: Save and recycle all eggshells directly into your garden because they'll add valuable nutrients. I prefer to place them in between the rows of vegetables, and turn them under with my tiller. In the winter, keep a separate bucket under your kitchen sink just to collect the eggshells. If the bucket gets too full, just mash the shells with a meat mallet and there will be room for many more.

OTHER SOURCES OF COMPOST: Many communities have set up centers to create compost from plant debris and leaves that are saved and collected instead of being burned or buried. Gardeners can load it and take it home, sometimes for free, sometimes for a donation.

SOURCES OF MANURE: If you have a farm friend, you might be able to get wonderful manure for your garden; be aware that this is a valuable resource for farmers' own fields, and so you should offer to pay for it. Other possible sources of manure include horse stables and zoos. Remember that raw manure is fine only on bare gardens and it takes weeks to break down. Only use well-rotted manure near plants, because raw manure will burn the roots, usually killing them.

NOTE: Do not use human, cat, or dog feces, as there is the danger of disease transmission if it hasn't been fully and properly aged. It is often contamination from human waste that causes digestive problems in undeveloped countries.

Planning Your Garden

It's a good idea to map out your garden. It's fun, it's a great antidote to bad winter weather, it will save you lots of time later, and you won't run out of room before you get everything planted.

Always date and save your garden maps; I suggest storing them in a large three-ring binder you can name *My Garden Book.*

CHOOSING VEGETABLE VARIETIES

Under each listing, I've included only a few of the many dozens, hundreds, or sometimes even thousands of varieties available for each vegetable. In the "Sources" section in the back of this book, you can find information about locating many more varieties, and even where to purchase them via mail-order or online.

Keep notes in your three-ring garden book about the varieties you're trying, and later be sure to record the results. You might even save the tags on your purchased seedlings, or the empty seed packages, for further reference.

Unless I say otherwise in the listing, most vegetables are grown as annuals, and must be replanted every year. If you are planting hybrid varieties, the seeds in the vegetables you harvest should not be saved and planted the next year.

Leftover purchased seeds might be viable for germination the following year, or longer, if they are kept dry. Be sure to write the year on the packet, if it isn't already there. I recommend storing the packets of seeds in heavy-duty plastic zipper freezer bags; many of these have a built-in label you can write on with a permanent marker. Buy enough bags for all your vegetable types, placing multiple varieties of each type in one bag. Organize the bags alphabetically in a box or container for quick access.

Testing Seed for Germination

In the days before hybrids, when farmers handpicked their fields, they saved their best-looking ears of corn to plant the next year. Late the next winter, the farmer would shell off some kernels from each of the ears into a bucket. He'd stir the kernels up to get a good sampling, then count out 100 kernels. These would be wrapped in a damp cloth, placed in a warm spot, and kept evenly moist. A week or ten days later, the farmer would unwrap the cloth and count how many kernels had germinated, or rather, count how many had not germinated. This number would be subtracted from the original 100 kernels to give the percent of germination. This information would aid the farmer in knowing how densely to plant the kernels, in order to maximize the crop production. For instance, if only 50 percent of the seed germinated, then he would plant 50 percent more seeds to make up for the loss. If germination was very low, he'd repeat the test. If it was still low, he'd try to buy some new seed from a neighbor, because his wasn't any good.

Today, The Farmer uses only hybrid seed for his crops. There are many hybrids available, each having different characteristics. Some do well despite too-wet ground; some perform better during droughts (this means The Farmer must guess which kind of weather we'll be having!). Some hybrids mature quickly, which is useful if you're facing a short growing season. The Farmer might need these if he is unable to get the seed in the ground early enough, perhaps due to a late winter, or perhaps because hail killed the crop he planted and now he's trying to replant it. These are only some of the characteristics.

There are companies that specialize in producing seeds for farmers to buy, and they test-germinate them in laboratories as well as plant test plots in Hawaii, Puerto Rico, or even South America, during our winters. Based on what they learn from these controlled tests, the seed companies give farmers very specific information, like how many thousand seeds of a particular variety should be planted per acre, and what the seed count is per bag.

Any vegetable seed you buy from a reputable nursery will be labeled, stating that it was grown for the current year, and you can rely on it to germinate well. If you are considering using leftover seed that's more than a year old, or that hasn't been properly stored, you might want to count out a few seeds and wrap them in a damp cloth or paper towel, and check on the germination rate, the way farmers used to do.

CROP ROTATION

On my trip to the southern Caribbean island of Montserrat (before the volcano blew and made it uninhabitable), some locals were very eager to show me their tiny corn patches. To create the planting area, they'd searched the jungle to find a small, flat spot and hacked away the growth with machetes. The soil looked rich, but they used inferior seed; they did nothing to maintain or improve the soil; and they didn't rotate their crops. As soon as the harvest was complete, they removed and burned the old stalks and immediately planted more corn, growing several crops per year. Their corn plants never grew much above waist height and produced tiny ears, whereas at home, our corn is at least as tall as a person and has ears at least eight inches long. Eventually, they abandoned the spot and sought another, which was not easy on a mountainous island.

As you plan your garden, you should allow for crop rotation. It's a good idea to avoid growing any vegetable on soil where any member of its family grew in the previous two or even three years. Why? Because related vegetables tend to deplete the same nutrients, they tend to harbor the same diseases, and they attract the same problem insects.

Vegetable Families

The following are detailed in the listings in this book.

THE BEAN FAMILY. All kinds of beans and peas. Members of this family add valuable nutrients to the soil, so they can precede any crop.

THE BEET FAMILY. Spinach, Swiss chard, beets.

THE CABBAGE FAMILY. Cabbage, Brussels sprouts, kale, cauliflower, broccoli, kohlrabi, radishes. All members of this family are heavy feeders; if possible, precede with members of the bean family and mix in lots of compost.

THE LETTUCE FAMILY. All types of lettuce.

THE ONION FAMILY. All types of onions, garlic, asparagus.

THE SQUASH FAMILY. Summer squash and zucchini, winter squash and spaghetti squash, pumpkins, cucumbers. When planting members of the squash family, I recommend also avoiding ground where any melons grew previously. Follow with members of the bean family, if possible.

THE PARSLEY FAMILY. Carrots, parsnips.

THE POTATO FAMILY. Potatoes, tomatoes, eggplants, sweet and hot peppers. Follow with members of the bean family, if possible.

OTHERS THAT ARE UNRELATED. Corn, okra, sweet potato.

NOTE: To aid you in rotating the crops, always keep a map of where you planted what, and be sure to date each listing. Store these in your three-ring garden binder for future reference.

YOUR GARDEN CALENDAR

Important numbers for you to know:

- Your zone number
- Your average last frost date in the spring
- Your average first frost date in the fall
- The length of your growing season

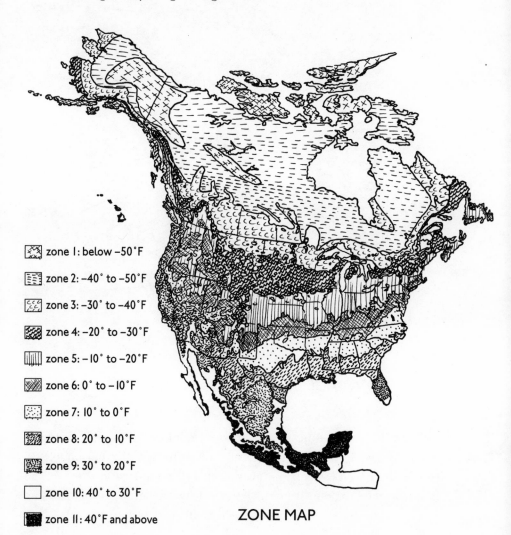

zone 1: below −50°F

zone 2: −40° to −50°F

zone 3: −30° to −40°F

zone 4: −20° to −30°F

zone 5: −10° to −20°F

zone 6: 0° to −10°F

zone 7: 10° to 0°F

zone 8: 20° to 10°F

zone 9: 30° to 20°F

zone 10: 40° to 30°F

zone 11: 40°F and above

ZONE MAP

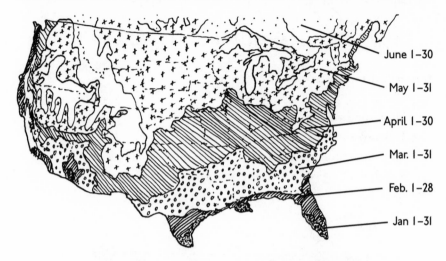

AVERAGE DATE OF LAST SPRING FROST

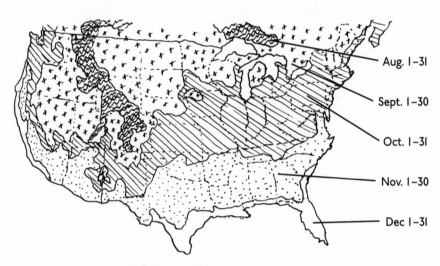

AVERAGE DATE OF FIRST WINTER FROST

To get your zone number and frost date information, consult maps, ask a knowledgeable gardener, or call your local Extension office. Count the days between the average last frost date and the average first frost date to determine the length of your average growing season.

These numbers will help you answer all sorts of questions:

- What plant varieties should I grow in my area? You wouldn't want to plant a vegetable that takes 120 days to harvest when your average growing season is only 90 days.
- When should I start my seedlings indoors? If you begin too early, the plants might exceed the size of their pots or become too mature to adjust well to being transplanted.
- When do I plant seeds or seedlings outdoors? Too early, and the seeds or seedlings might die; too late, and they may not have time to produce before winter.
- When can I sow a second crop in the summer? You'll need to count backward from the average first frost date to determine this. You wouldn't want to plant a second crop you'll never harvest.
- When do I harvest my late crops? Many crops won't survive past a fall frost, so you'll want to plan for them to mature prior to this date.

Once you know your average last frost date, you can mark it on your gardening calendar and start counting backward for the following dates:

THE NUMBER OF WEEKS TO START SEEDLINGS BEFORE THE AVERAGE LAST FROST DATE IN YOUR AREA

Ten or more weeks:
- Asparagus
- Kale
- Onions

Six to ten weeks:
- Broccoli
- Brussels sprouts
- Cabbage
- Cauliflower
- Kohlrabi
- Lettuce
- Tomatoes

Five to eight weeks:
• Eggplant

Three to eight weeks:
• Peppers

Four weeks:
• Okra

Three to four weeks:
• Sweet potatoes (slips)

Two to three weeks:
• Cucumbers

WHEN TO TRANSPLANT SEEDLINGS INTO THE GARDEN

Four to six weeks before the average last frost date in your area:
• Kale
• Kohlrabi
• Lettuce
• Onions

Two to four weeks before the average last frost date in your area:
• Broccoli
• Brussels sprouts
• Cabbage
• Cauliflower

After the average last frost date in your area:
• Asparagus
• Cucumbers
• Eggplant
• Okra
• Peppers
• Sweet potatoes
• Tomatoes

NOTE: Just because you've reached your average last frost date, that does not guarantee that there will not be more frosts in your area. Do not plant a frost-sensitive plant when your weather is still freezing, even if you've surpassed that magic frost-free date. Similarly, if you are having a very early, warm spring, you might be able to plant frost-sensitive plants much sooner. You need to use common sense and understand that this information is only a guideline.

WHEN TO DIRECT-SEED VEGETABLES

As soon as the ground can be worked in the spring:
- Asparagus (crowns)
- Beets
- Carrots
- Kale
- Kohlrabi
- Lettuce
- Onions (seeds, sets, plants)
- Shallots
- Parsnips
- Peas
- Potatoes
- Radishes
- Spinach
- Swiss chard

After the average last frost date for your area:
- Beans
- Corn
- Cucumbers
- Eggplant
- Okra
- Peppers
- Pumpkins
- Soybeans
- Summer squash
- Winter squash
- Zucchini

In midsummer for a fall crop:
- Beets
- Broccoli
- Brussels sprouts
- Cabbage
- Carrots
- Cauliflower
- Corn
- Kale
- Kohlrabi
- Lettuce
- Peas
- Radishes
- Spinach
- Swiss chard

Seedlings

Purchased seedlings are a great time-saver. But there are reasons you might want to start your own seedlings: It's fun, it's cheaper than buying seedlings, and you can get unusual varieties not available in stores.

TIPS FOR STARTING YOUR OWN SEEDLINGS

- Start them indoors the specified number of weeks before your average last frost date.
- Use peat pots, if possible, because you plant the pots along with the seedling.
- Use a purchased potting mix. It's specially designed to start seedlings; it's inexpensive and timesaving; and you'll avoid problems with insects, disease, and weeds.
- Fill the peat pots with soil and lightly firm it.
- Place the peat pots on plastic trays. Since I grow my seedlings indoors and can't allow the water to drain out onto the floor the way you can in a greenhouse, I've purchased about three dozen inexpensive plastic cat litter boxes just for this purpose. One box will hold between twenty-four and

fifty peat pots, depending on the size. I've raised many thousands of seedlings in these boxes. They can be reused year after year, once they've been rinsed with a mild bleach solution; this disinfects them and prevents plant diseases.

- Trickle or spray water over the pots and the soil to moisten them. Be patient, it will take a while for the water to be absorbed. If using nondraining trays, put about ½ inch of water in the bottom of the tray after you've filled it with closely spaced peat pots. The pots and soil should be moist before planting them.

- For quick and easy planting, use a dull pencil to poke a hole in the firmed soil to the proper planting depth, insert the seed, and use the pencil to close the hole. For small seeds, place them on the surface and use the pencil to press them into the soil. There are devices to help control fine seeds, or you can pour the seed out from a folded index card.

- To ensure germination, some gardeners like to plant two seeds per pot and then thin back to one seedling by pinching off the other.

- Cover the seedling pots with plastic film, which you should remove as soon as the sprouts have emerged.

- Keep the pots evenly moist, preferably by bottom watering. Once the seeds have sprouted, don't let the pots get soggy. In a few days, you'll know from experience how much water to use. Check the trays daily; do not allow the pots to dry out.

- Since some types of seeds do better with bottom heat, gardeners place the trays in a warm place, like on top of the refrigerator. You can purchase heat mats for this purpose, but be sure to follow instructions to avoid electric shock. Remove the tray from the heat as soon as the seeds have germinated.

- Once the seeds have germinated, you need to be sure that they get plenty of light, either sunlight from a big south-facing window, or artificial light. You can purchase wonderful ready-made lighting systems equipped with special plant-growing lights that range in size from small tabletop units for hobby gardeners to multi-tiered wheeled models for the serious gardener (see "Sources"). When using artificial light, keep making adjustments so that the lightbulbs are always about two inches above the seedlings, for maximum benefit. Seedlings that aren't getting enough light get long and spindly as they try to grow closer to the light source.

Artificial lighting systems

Don't plant your seedlings outdoors too soon. Follow the recommendations under each vegetable listing for the appropriate planting time. Before transplant, you'll need to harden off your seedlings, to lessen the shock of being outside, or they will die, or else their growth will be set back greatly.

HOW TO HARDEN OFF YOUR SEEDLINGS:

- Start one or two weeks before the transplant date.
- Find a protected place outdoors. The plants should not get any wind, and they should never get cold. I place my seedling trays on a cement patio on the south, right against the house. The cement warms in the sun and radiates heat to the seedlings, which is good in our cool spring weather. Protect the seedlings from the cat herd and other outdoor pets and wildlife!

- Start by placing the seedlings outdoors in a partially shady spot, gradually moving them into direct sunlight.
- The potting soil dries out quicker outdoors; be sure the seedlings have adequate moisture. Check on this several times a day, and water as needed. A garden hose with a misting nozzle makes outdoor watering easy. By now I have transferred all the peat pots into trays that have mesh bottoms for good drainage, so I can water generously, knowing that any excess water will run off.
- The first day, leave the seedlings outside only a couple of hours, then return them to your house or greenhouse. Gradually increase the time they're outside, as the seedlings toughen up, until they are spending the whole day in the sun. Eventually, allow them to stay out day and night, still in the protected place, but under your watchful eye so that you'll be ready to bring them inside if harsh weather threatens.

NOTE: Since the number of seedlings I plant outside runs into the thousands each year, it's rather a nuisance to be transferring the individual trays in and out for the hardening process. Last year, The Farmer came up with a better plan. He designed a sixteen-foot-long flat wagon with a mesh bottom, which he had built for my birthday. Now I can place all my seedling trays on this wagon and use my garden tractor to pull it into the sun each day, and I can back it into a shed for protection. I can water all the seedlings directly on the wagon, because the mesh allows the excess to run right through. If I want to, I can pull the wagonload of seedlings directly to my planting area. I was so thrilled to get it—what a great gift for a gardener!

Planting the Garden—The Farmer's Wife Way

Although there are any number of ways to arrange your vegetable plants, the typical farmer's wife's garden is a rectangle, a miniature version of The Farmer's fields. Farmers admire nice, orderly crop rows and pay attention to how straight each other's rows are.

Somehow, we farmers' wives just sort of follow their lead in our garden plots. It's been handed down from generations past, and now that I have tried many methods, I'm back to gardening with straight full rows. It's the tradition for a reason—it's the most efficient way to manage a garden, and it looks neat and tidy.

START IN EARLY SPRING, when the soil is ready to be worked. When you squeeze a handful of garden soil and it crumbles, instead of sticking together in a ball, you can begin!

PREPARE THE SEED BED. Sprinkle the eggshells you saved all winter on top of the soil. Add a layer of well-rotted manure or compost, if desired. Then till the entire garden to mix in the nutrients and fluff up the soil for aeration. Once the soil is tilled, don't step on it except between the rows, after the markers are in place.

GATHER YOUR SUPPLIES. The materials you'll need are very minimal:

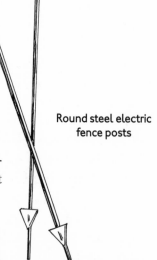

Round steel electric fence posts

- **A hoe.** A good garden hoe has a sturdy wood or synthetic handle. The business end, from the shank on down, should be made of all one piece of sturdy metal. A basic hoe will perform several garden tasks, but as you get more involved in gardening, you may wish to purchase several types. One has a pointed tip that's good for opening rows for seed. Another has the points at the sides and sharpened top and bottom edges—this is used for weeding by slicing or sliding it back and forth just beneath the surface.
- **Stakes** to mark the ends of rows. Go to a farm-and-ranch supply store and buy round steel electric fence posts, and while you're at it, buy some of the insu-

lators, too (see "Wildlife Protection").
These are inexpensive and so easy to use—
and they make great garden stakes.

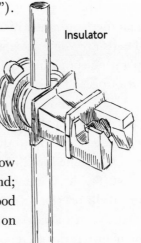

Insulator

- **String.** Use carpenter's string, because
it's not elastic, and it won't rot. Get
the brightest color you can find—mine
is fluorescent pink—so that it is easy to
see against the soil. Attach a length of
string longer than your longest garden row
to a piece of wood sharpened at one end;
wind the string on the other end of the wood
like a spool. Tie a two- or three-inch loop on
the loose end of the string.
- **Seeds and seedlings.** Be sure to guard both against the wind.
- **Covers.** Gallon cans or gallon-sized plastic milk jugs, both
with the bottoms removed, will protect the young seedlings
as they adjust to the transplanting.
- **Black or clear plastic** sheets are sometimes laid on the soil
to warm it prior to planting or transplanting. Clear plastic
actually can warm the soil more than the opaque black.
Black plastic can be left in place after planting, and some
gardeners transplant certain seedlings into slits in the black
plastic. Never leave clear plastic on the soil after the seeds
have germinated.

Start planting! This is the fun part! I so look forward to doing this
each spring. The anticipation of it gets me through many a winter
storm!

- **First, set your row markers in place.** If you're using the
electric fence posts I recommended, this is easy—just push
them into the ground with your foot on the triangular metal
vane at the base. If you are using wooden stakes, you'll probably need to hammer them into place.

Like The Farmer, I like to have straight, parallel rows that are
spaced two and a half feet (thirty inches) apart. We both feel this is

the optimum spacing; it gives the plants plenty of room for the tops and the roots, and my tiller is small enough to work between the rows. There are some exceptions to this spacing; for example, if you are planting sprawling vine crops or you want to make wide plant rows to save space. The specifics are detailed under each vegetable listing.

I like to allow about one foot of border all around the garden so that I can run the tiller in this perimeter all summer to maintain a tidy edge right up to the lawn. If this appeals to you, line up all your row posts one foot in from the garden edge.

NOTE: As you are positioning your posts, be careful that you do not walk on the soft soil or you'll compact it. After you've set the posts, you can walk in the spaces between them, but not where you'll be planting the seed.

- Now, for the string. Loop the end over one steel post and let it slide to the ground. Unwind the string from the stake and pull it across the garden in a straight line. Wrap the string two or three times around the steel post at the other end and insert the sharpened end of the stake in the ground. There is no need to tie the string, it will stay securely.
- Using the string as a guide, drag the tip of your hoe in the ground from post to post, making a planting trench or furrow as deep as is needed for the seeds. (See the individual vegetable listings for information.) You might have to go over the row several times to get the correct depth.
- Following your garden plan, place the seeds in the furrow, spacing them as directed for each type of plant. The brightly colored string contrasts nicely with the soil and is easy to see as a guide.
- Using your hoe, gently cover the seeds using the raised dirt alongside the row. Press downward gently with the back of the hoe to firm the soil in place. This also makes the furrow surface just a bit lower, which keeps moisture in the trench, conserving water when hand-watering and encouraging germination.
- Make a notation of the crop planted and the date on your garden plan.

- Pull the string stake up and unwrap the string from the steel post. Lay the stake on the ground at this end of the row. Remove the loop from the post on the other end and place it on the next steel post so that you can start another row.
- If you are planting seedlings, you don't need to make a furrow. Just follow the string, spacing the plants as recommended.
- When you are finished with the planting, keep the soil evenly moist; this will probably require daily watering, using a fine mist so that you don't wash the soil away from the seeds. This is one time you don't have to water deeply, you just need to keep the soil wet so that the seeds absorb the moisture and sprout and grow into plants.

NOTE: The steel fence posts can be removed after the seeds have sprouted and you can see where the rows are. They are very easy to remove—just gently rock them back and forth a bit and pull up. Or, leave them in all summer and attach plastic bags at the top to repel wildlife (see "Wildlife Protection").

HOW TO PLANT SEEDLINGS

- First, generously water the pots.
- If possible, do the transplanting on an overcast day, just before several days of rain. This will prevent transplant shock and save you from watering chores!
- As you are planting, protect the trays of seedlings from the wind.
- Follow your garden map, and plant the seedlings in neat rows. Jot down the planting date on the map.
- Make a small planting hole with a hand trowel.
- If you have a problem with cutworms, which chew through the stems of seedlings, use cutworm collars that extend one inch below the soil and one or two inches above it. You can use the cardboard rolls from paper towels or toilet tissue, cut into two- or three-inch lengths and slit, to slide the stems inside. Or simply wrap a strip of newspaper around the stems.

- Insert the peat pot to the proper planting depth as indicated in the vegetable listings, fill in any remaining space in the hole, and firm the soil around the seedling.
- Make sure the entire peat pot is under the soil, or else break off the rim. If any peat protrudes, it will wick water away from the roots, killing the young seedling.
- Place a gallon can with both ends removed over the seedling for one or two weeks. Or use a plastic gallon-sized milk jug with the cap removed and the bottom cut out. Press the can or jug into the soil so that it won't blow away or be knocked over by cats or dogs. NOTE: As you are saving your gallon milk jugs, string them onto a wire loop. This makes them easier to store and to carry.
- Water the transplants daily until the seedlings are doing well. By then the roots will have grown outside of the peat pots into the garden soil, which doesn't dry out as quickly as your potting soil did.

NOTE: To make watering easier, some of the vegetable listings suggest perforating a plastic gallon milk jug along the sides and bottom with a nail and burying it with the seeds or seedlings. Leave the top two inches of the jug above the ground, and you can fill the jug with your garden hose. This makes an inexpensive drip irrigation system, and it's a great way to direct the moisture to the roots as well as conserve water. The latter is important to farmers who are concerned about their well running dry.

Care

THINNING. Most direct-seeded vegetables are planted a little thicker than you want them to end up growing. Why? To allow for those seeds that might not germinate. With seed from reputable dealers, you can get by spacing the seeds farther apart, so that you are doing less thinning. If you notice that you are missing a plant, it's pretty easy to poke another seed into the ground.

COVERING FOR FROST. If your tender garden plants are being threatened by a late frost, just cover them with old sheets, blankets, or even old shirts. You can purchase lengths of a filmy fabric designed for this purpose. You can even buy hoops to insert in the ground and cover with fabric, to make protective tunnels.

Seedlings covered by milk jugs will be fine without additional cover, although you might want to put the caps back on. Seedlings protected by gallon cans might be at risk. Cover them with cloth, or if the seedling is still small enough, you can put board scraps across the top.

COVERING FOR SHADE. Some crops quit producing, or even die, when the sun gets too hot in midsummer. To prevent this, you can install inexpensive hoop tunnels over the rows and cover them with a mesh shade cloth designed to allow rain and air to pass through, yet block part of the harsh sunlight. The hoops come in all sizes, from some that barely cover one- or two-foot-tall rows, to hoops large enough for a person to stand under.

COVERING FOR INSECTS. If you have a crop that's bothered by insects, one way to avoid the problem is to provide a barrier over the plants. There are fabrics designed to keep insects out, which are spread over the crops like a big blanket, or you can drape the fabric over the hoops already mentioned. This works great for crops like cabbage, that produce vegetables without fertilization. For crops like squash, you will have to remove the barrier long enough for bees to pollinate the flowers, or else you'll have to hand-pollinate them.

WATERING. The garden needs even moisture; although a little wilting during the heat of the day is normal, if the plants remain wilted the next morning, they need a drink. It's better to do a deep watering once every week or ten days that moistens the soil to a depth of six or eight inches, than light watering more often. Light watering encourages shallow root development, and shallow roots dry out faster.

If your garden is small, you can water by hand, using a watering can or a garden hose with a spray attachment. There are many other methods for watering, including elaborate drip-irrigation systems, which work well for some but are not very practical for me. The easiest and cheapest method of watering a large garden is to use a sprinkler device that attaches to your hose. These can be adjusted to set a spray pattern that matches the dimensions of your garden, and they can even be placed on timers. It takes about four hours for our system to equal one inch of rain—you can test yours by placing containers within the drip area. The overhead methods have a downside—they take the most water; the drip systems take the least.

Water early in the day, so that the plants' leaves have a chance to dry in the sun, avoiding the disease problems caused by lingering moisture.

If the garden doesn't receive enough moisture, the plants might not bloom, or they might drop their blossoms. Too little moisture when the young vegetables are developing can give them a bitter taste—maybe you've noticed this in store-bought vegetables, especially carrots.

WEEDING. Through the years, I've tried many approaches to weed control. One way to keep the weeds down is to cover the ground with mulch. I did this on my gardens for ten years, with excellent results. Mulch presents some advantages: You can walk in the garden rows without compacting the soil or getting your feet muddy, and if the mulch is thick enough, it keeps weeds down between the rows, although you'll still have to do some weeding by hand within the rows.

I use mulch on many of my perennial flower beds and around fruiting trees and bushes. Although I am a devoted Ruth Stout fan (she originated the year-round mulch system), I've largely given up the practice on my vegetable gardens. Why?

- In the spring, mulch keeps the soil cold far too long, requiring you to go to the trouble to remove all the mulch—which is a big job with my large gardens—and then replace it. Plus, you're fighting weeds in the exposed areas.
- The best way to increase fertility is mixing the manure or compost *into* the soil—not laying it on top of the soil. Mulch prevents you from doing this, so you either have to layer it on top of the mulch, which greatly slows down getting the nutrients into the soil, or you have to pull the mulch back in both spring and fall, mix in the compost, and return the

mulch—more labor, and it can be difficult to do if the mulch has crusted.

- Mulch helps keep the roots cool (for those plants that prefer this) and it holds in moisture—but, if the soil underneath it is dry, or you have a year where you're getting only light rain, or no rain, mulch prevents the available moisture from penetrating to the soil. It also makes watering more difficult unless you are using a drip irrigation method installed beneath the mulch. If you're having a year with too-frequent rains, mulch can keep the soil too soggy.
- Exposing the garden soil directly to the hot summer sun is nature's way of dealing with insects and disease organisms, and the heat can even kill weed seeds in the top layer.

For all these reasons, I've done an about-face and returned to the traditional Farmer's Wife method, which is actually much less work than any other approach, if you have a small tiller.

I love my tiller! I can set the tines for my deeper spring and fall tilling, turning under manure and compost and chopping up the previous year's roots in no time. I set the tines for shallow tilling throughout the summer, so that I can lightly go over my garden every week or two without disturbing the plant roots. This not only keeps the weeds down, but it aerates the soil and prevents crusting, so that any rain can easily penetrate the soil to the benefit of the roots. I can till all of my gardens in less than an hour, and it's the quickest and easiest method of weeding I've ever used. Plus, the gardens always look neat and tidy. Even The Farmer is impressed with my clean crop rows!

Cape Cod hand weeder

For those small areas where hand weeding is required, I recommend the Cape Cod hand weeder—it works quickly and efficiently.

TYING PLANTS TO SUPPORTS. As discussed in detail under each vegetable listing, some garden plants need to be supported because their stems aren't strong enough to hold the plant upright, especially when it's producing a crop. You'll need to use something to attach the plant stems to the support. I strongly recommend using pantyhose strips, because they will stretch and "give" as the plant grows, unlike wire, which can cut into the plant and even strangle it. Other materials for attaching plants to supports include cloth strips, twine, and special Velcro strips designed for garden use.

INSECT AND DISEASE PROBLEMS. The two are related, because not only do insects harm the crop directly, but their chewing opens up the plant, making it susceptible to airborne disease organisms, and insects can also transmit disease by carrying it on their bodies.

Please understand that all bugs aren't harmful to the garden. There are many insects that benefit us, and we don't want to eliminate them along with the harmful insects. Don't be quick to use strong chemicals that kill all insects indiscriminately. Many environmentally friendly products, like insecticidal soaps that handle aphids and other bugs, are available now, and BT takes care of worms and caterpillars without making them dangerous to birds that later eat them.

You can purchase natural products to treat plant insects and diseases (see "Sources"), or you can try making your own.

- A homemade insecticidal soap can be made by adding 3 tablespoons of a mild dishwashing soap (not the kind with degreaser) to a gallon of water. Stir it up and spray the plants thoroughly; wait an hour or two and then rinse it off. You will probably need several applications for bad infestations. NOTE: I use this in the fall when I want to pot up and bring some outdoor plants inside before a frost.
- Baking soda spray works on anthracnose, blights, and mildew and is a general fungicide. In one quart of warm water, combine 1 teaspoon of baking soda and 1 teaspoon of vegetable oil or mild liquid dishwashing soap (not the kind with degreaser). Shake often while spraying, and be sure to get the tops and bottoms of leaves.

- A 50-50 solution of skim milk and water combats mildews, especially on cucumbers, tomatoes, and squash.
- Hydrogen peroxide, the 3 percent solution commonly available in stores, can be sprayed on plants for bacterial and fungal problems. If the problem is confined to a few large leaves, you can dip several cotton balls in the peroxide and wipe the leaves with it.

Although many people fear them, bees, bumblebees, and wasps are our friends. Not only do they pollinate our crops, but they eat the larvae of insect pests. But their population has seriously declined, unfortunately, due to a harmful bee parasite and due to humans' use of pesticides. Unless someone has a severe allergy, don't reach for a chemical spray when you see them—we can coexist peacefully. If you remain calm and don't interfere with them, they will totally ignore you, rarely attacking unless provoked. You might even want to encourage them by using bee attractants in your garden and installing bumblebee houses—both are available at local nurseries or from garden supply and garden product catalogues. See the "Sources" section.

Insects and diseases that are troublesome in one part of our country may not even exist in another. I've listed solutions for a few problems that might be common to many areas. If you run into trouble, consult a trusted nursery or call your local Extension office. You might want to consult a copy of the Gardens Alive! catalogue, which not only describes various problems with photos, but offers safe solutions as well (see "Sources").

Wildlife Protection

One year I was having trouble with rabbits, which were eating off almost everything in my main garden almost as soon as it came out of the ground! I feared our wonderful Australian Shepherd dog, who had always done a great job of keeping the rabbits away, was getting too old to keep up.

So, I had The Farmer build a fence around my very large main garden. He did a great job, too, even installing gates at opposite ends so that I could drive a tractor and wagon through a path he made through the center. He even buried the fencing six inches deep to keep the rabbits from tunneling into the garden. Our dog watched sadly from outside the fence.

But it didn't stop the rabbits! In fact, they were more active than ever before! Every morning I was dismayed anew to see how my lovely garden had been decimated. When I suggested to The Farmer that maybe he hadn't made the fence tall enough, he just laughed and said that rabbits couldn't jump that high. Finally, I discovered what had happened: We'd fenced the rabbits inside!

The best-ever solution: Through the years, I've had problems with many kinds of animals and have tried most of the recommended remedies. But I've found one thing to be quick, easy, inexpensive, completely harmless to wildlife, and extremely effective: plastic bags, the type you get from the store when you buy groceries. Tie these bags to posts around your garden, and you'll never be bothered with any wildlife!

I recommend using electric fence posts and insulators, which you can find at a farm-and-ranch supply store. They have a triangular

metal vane at the bottom that makes it easy to push the post into the ground with your foot. Slide the insulator on the top and tighten it, and then you can tie the handles of the plastic bag to the insulator using a double or triple knot. The electric fence posts double as row markers at planting time. They are very easy to reposition, too: Just loosen the post by waving the top back and forth, parallel to the metal vane, and pull it out.

Here's how the bags repel animals and birds: They are lightweight and usually will stay filled with air, like soft balloons. They move in the slightest breeze. Animals don't know what the bags are, and even if they get brave enough to come near the bags, the bags' movement seems erratic and unpredictable, spooking them. The bags make a subtle crackling sound, which the animals hear from a distance, keeping them away.

How successful are the bags? Our sweet corn was always raided by raccoons and deer, no matter what we tried, until I used this trick. I placed the bags a third of the way down the electric fence posts, and put the posts on the ends of every other row of corn, and never lost a single ear! Now, that's success!

Moles are actually beneficial animals, because they eat grubs, not plant roots. Try using bacillus to eliminate the grubs, and the moles will go elsewhere. Or try this formula from Doc and Katy Abraham in the newsletter for The Hobby Greenhouse Association: 1 part castor oil and an equal part liquid detergent, plus a little warm water. Beat this into a foam. To use it, stir 2 or 3 tablespoons into a watering can of warm water and pour it over the soil where the moles are troublesome. Repeat the dousing until the moles leave.

Harvest

Many vegetables are harvested at the immature stage, for example, broccoli, summer squash, and okra; others, like pumpkins and winter squash, are harvested only after they are mature. The days to maturity given on seed packets or with purchased seedlings give you only an approximate idea of when to expect the first harvest. Variations in climate, soil, and moisture conditions can greatly affect the first harvest date. Each vegetable entry describes what to look for when the vegetable is ready to harvest and how to harvest it. Each vegetable variety listed indicates the number of days until harvest. If you are starting with seedlings, this date reflects the number of days from transplanting the seedling outdoors until harvest; otherwise, it's the number of days from the time the seed is planted outdoors.

Once the plant has become productive, it's important to keep up with the harvest. Why?

- To encourage more blooms and more vegetables. If there is even one overripe vegetable, many plants stop blooming and concentrate their energy on maturing the seeds.
- To lengthen the life of the plant. After a plant has produced mature seeds, it often dies. Continuous harvest prolongs not only the production, but the life span of the plant.
- To avoid attracting insects to overripe, and perhaps rotting, vegetables.

Postharvest

CLEAR OFF THE GARDEN

- By hand, remove the largest plants, like squash vines, that will be troublesome to till. If they are healthy, these can be composted. You should burn any plant material that looks diseased or that is harboring insect pests. If you're not allowed to burn it, dispose of it with your trash.

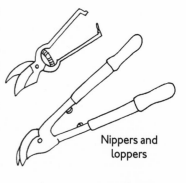

Nippers and loppers

- If desired, you can leave the sweet corn stalks in the garden for peas or beans to climb the next year. Otherwise, remove them, either by pulling out the plants after they have died, or else cut them off at the ground using the corn knife, nippers, or loppers.

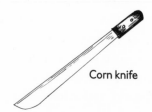

Corn knife

- Clear off any weeds that might have gotten by you and gone to seed. You don't want to have a bigger infestation next season.
- Remove any black plastic used to control weeds and warm the soil, to allow the soil to breathe.
- Pull out the electric fence posts or other row markers.
- Mow off any remaining plant material. There is no need to remove it by hand. Aim the mower so that it throws the material back onto the garden, where it will become humus over the winter.

NOURISH THE SOIL

Place a layer of manure, compost, or even fall leaves on the garden. This material does not have to be rotted, because it will decompose by spring.

TILL THE SOIL THOROUGHLY

Do this when the ground is not too wet; if you squeeze a handful of dirt and it stays in a ball, it is too wet. Tilling it wet will not only be hard on you and your tiller, but it will be harmful to the soil. Wait until the ground is dry enough that tilling works it up nicely.

To make fall tilling easy, start by going parallel to the crop rows. Go up and down the rows, tilling the entire surface, slightly overlapping each swath. Then, till the entire plot a second time, going at right angles to the first direction. By now, you'll notice that most of the compost and crop residue has been mixed into the soil, and the garden will be full of soft ridges. Last, till around the perimeter of the garden, leaving neat and tidy edges. That's all there is! This doesn't take long, even in a large garden.

The Farmer plows under his crop residue every fall, to break up the current crop's root systems and to prevent the dead plant material from blowing away, losing his humus for the next year. His big equipment can do the job in one tilling, so he goes across, not parallel to, the crop rows.

Turning the soil, whether in a garden or in a large field, adds aeration and brings the dry, dead plant material into contact with the moist earth; both aid in the decomposition process. Rain, ice, and snow all do their part to help, and by spring, the ground is soft and fertile, ready for a new crop!

My Garden Book

Growing up, I was in 4-H, an Extension-sponsored organization, for youth living on farms or in town to do all sorts of home, garden, or farm-related projects. One of the requirements was to keep careful, written records of each project from start to finish. Our projects were judged at county fairs, and the top ribbon-winners would progress to the state fair for further judging competitions. When our projects were finished, we had to turn in our record books for evaluation. This was good training, because it taught us not only to plan out anything we wanted to do, and to keep records as we worked on the project, but also to evaluate the completed project. Was it worthwhile? Fun? Cost-effective? Time-effective? Did it satisfy the objective going in? What would you do differently? Do you want to do it again? What were the problems you faced? What steps did you take to solve any problems you had?

Throughout this text, I've mentioned keeping your gardening records in a large three-ring binder. Part of keeping your gardening records was creating your own garden calendar, with details about the planting dates, the expected harvest dates, frost date information, etc.

Now that all your outdoor work is done, this would be a great time to add more information to your garden record book. Include notes about what vegetables you liked and disliked this year, garden ideas for next year, new vegetables you want to try growing, etc. If you haven't already done so, be sure you map out where you planted what this year, so that you can rotate the crops next year. You might even want to keep a few photos of your efforts.

Putting information into your garden book should be an ongoing process. Throughout the winter, as you study seed catalogues and place your orders, as you dream up your new garden map, all these things can be stored in one central place—in your record book. As you plant the garden, keep a clipboard and a pencil with you—I place mine in a five-gallon bucket along with my cordless two-line phone—and quickly jot down what you've planted and where, making sure to date it.

Later, count forward on your garden calendar the number of days it will take before the anticipated first harvest. This is especially useful to new gardeners; those of us with many gardening years under our belt know the rhythms of nature and when to expect the first green beans, the first tomato, etc.

All this information will greatly aid you as you plan and create next year's garden. It might seem like it takes time to make your records, but it really saves time in the long run. Keep up your garden book— you'll be glad you did!

KITCHEN NOTES

It's a great day when you begin eating all of your vegetables fresh from the garden—you can just walk out the door at mealtime and make your selection!

Harvest and Storage Tips

For best results:

- Harvest produce at the peak of ripeness.
- As you harvest, keep the vegetables protected from sun.
- Use the produce right away. Either eat it, store it, or give it away.
- When buying seeds or seedlings, select varieties listed as "long-keepers" or "good freezers" for storage.

Leafy vegetables are subject to wilt. Get them to the house quickly and place them in cold water for hydration. Drain most—but not all—of the moisture off the leaves before storing.

Some vegetables, like corn, beans, and peas, will quickly loose their sweetness as their sugars turn to starch. Eat them soon after harvest or get them chilled right away to slow down the conversion process.

Preparation Tips

- Use cold water to wash the vegetables.

- As much as possible, try to retain the skins because of the added nutrients.
- Save all peelings, cores, and other plant material for the compost pile. Keep a bucket under the sink to collect this material.
- Save your eggshells and put them directly in the garden to add nutrients to your soil and, thus, to your food. In the winter I keep a plastic bucket under the sink to store the eggshells until the weather cooperates, occasionally mashing the shells with a meat mallet to conserve space.

Serving Ideas

Many garden vegetables can be served raw, as an appetizer, perhaps with a dip.

CHOICES FOR A DIP BASE:
- 1 cup sour cream
- ½ cup sour cream plus ½ cup cream cheese.
- 1 cup cottage cheese, drained and blended smooth.
- 1 cup cottage cheese plus ¼ cup buttermilk, blended together
- 1 cup plain yogurt

CHOICES FOR SEASONING THE DIP BASE:
- Snipped chives
- 1 tablespoon dried parsley flakes, 1 teaspoon salt, ⅟₁₆ teaspoon garlic powder
- 1 teaspoon vinegar, 1 teaspoon garlic salt, 2 tablespoons bacon bits, added just before serving
- 1 tablespoon dry onion soup mix plus 1 teaspoon instant beef bouillon granules

TIPS FOR COOKING VEGETABLES:
- Don't overcook! Vegetables should be cooked only to the tender-crisp stage. Cooking beyond this stage causes vegetables to become mushy and to loose color and valuable nutrients.

- Use as little water as possible. Nutrients get dissolved in water, and if you drain the vegetables, these nutrients are discarded along with elements that give the vegetables flavor.
- Skin (if you must) and cut up the vegetables just before cooking them. This also helps preserve nutrients.
- Cook vegetables uncovered or only partially covered to prevent discoloration. Do not use baking soda in the water to preserve the color. It harms the flavor and makes the vegetables mushy.
- If your water is alkaline, white and red vegetables might discolor. To prevent this, just add a teaspoon of lemon juice or vinegar to the cooking water. This is not necessary for tomatoes, because they are naturally acidic.
- Cook vegetables just before serving them. Keeping vegetables hot on the stove while preparing the rest of the meal causes overcooking and loss of nutrients and color.

How to Cook Vegetables

BOILING

This method is appropriate for any vegetable.

Use as little water as possible. For most vegetables, like green beans or carrots, I put no more than ½ inch of water in the bottom of the smallest saucepan that will hold the vegetables. This means that many of the vegetables will be sitting above the water and will actually be steam-cooked.

Some vegetables should be placed in water and then heated on the stove; others should be placed in the water after it's heated to boiling. Here is a general guideline:

- Vegetables that grow below the ground (potatoes, sweet potatoes, parsnips, etc.) should be placed in cool water and then heated. Put tap water into the cooking pan and then add the vegetables as you peel them, cut them up, etc.

- Vegetables that grow above the ground (green beans, summer squash, tomatoes, etc.) should be placed in boiling water. Heating the water before adding the vegetables preserves nutrients. Bring the water just to a boil, add the vegetables, reduce heat to a low simmer, and place a lid on the pan.

A tight-fitting lid will keep the steam heat inside the pan, further reducing the need for water, reducing the cooking time, and retaining nutrients—but do not overcook. With experience, you will know how much water to start out with so that very little remains when the vegetables are just tender-crisp, and still brightly colored.

Many farmwives like to lightly salt the cooking water, although I do not do this.

Rather than throwing away any leftover liquid, which contains nutrients, try to incorporate it into a casserole or soup.

STEAMING

Boil water in one pan. On top of it, place a tightly lidded perforated pan holding the vegetables. The steam rises through the perforations and cooks the vegetables. The bottom pan should be no more than half full of water, and the water should not touch the vegetables or the bottom of the steamer insert.

This method takes a bit longer than the boiling method, but it does the best job of preserving the vegetable's nutrients and color.

BAKING

This is the preferred method for whole vegetables like potatoes, winter squash, and pumpkins, but it can also be used for sliced potatoes, whole onions, carrots, beets, and squash. Carrots, beets, and potatoes can also be shredded before baking.

The vegetables are baked in their skins, which preserves nutrients, moisture, and flavor. Be sure to prick the skin once or twice to allow an escape for pent-up steam. Or, if the vegetables aren't whole, add a little water to the pan for moisture and be sure that the pan is tightly lidded or sealed with aluminum foil to keep the vegetables moist and allow them to steam.

Generally, the oven is set at 350 to 400 degrees F and the vegetables are baked until tender.

BROILING

This method is used for sliced vegetables, like potatoes, eggplant, onions, or tomatoes. You place the vegetables on a greased broiler rack and brush them with olive oil or melted butter. Place the rack about 3 inches below the heating element. Often the vegetables will need to be turned and brushed with butter or oil and returned to the broiler to cook the other side.

This method is quick and easy and convenient, too, because the vegetables can be placed alongside a steak or other piece of meat. Using a convection-broiler is even quicker and easier than a straight broiler oven.

Be sure to watch the broiler closely—it's easy to burn the food.

STIR FRY METHOD WITH OIL

Slice, dice, or shred the vegetables, as desired. A combination of mixed vegetables is especially good for this method. For suggestions, see below.

Coat the bottom of a wok or large skillet with olive or other cooking oil. Turn the burner to high heat and quickly toss in and vigorously stir the vegetables, reducing the heat to medium if necessary, stirring constantly. The vegetables will cook quickly and retain their bright colors. They are done when lightly browned and crisp-tender. Serve immediately.

STIR FRYING WITH LIQUID

Slice, dice, or shred the vegetables, as desired. Using a large skillet, heat a small amount (perhaps a few tablespoons) of water, broth, or other liquid to a simmer. Add the vegetables, reduce heat to a low simmer, and cover the pan with a tightly fitting lid. Or, forego the lid and keep the heat at a strong simmer as you stir the vegetables constantly, adding a little liquid if the pan goes dry before the vegetables are crisp-tender. The goal is to have the liquid run out just as the vegetables are ready to serve.

GRILLING

Chop the vegetables into chunks and either thread them on a skewer, toss them in a cast-iron skillet, or place them into one of the special perforated grilling pans.

You must use olive oil: Brush it on the skewered vegetables; generously coat the bottom of the cast-iron skillet before adding the vegetables; or, when using the perforated pan, shake the vegetables with olive oil in a tightly covered plastic container to coat all sides.

Larger vegetables, like sliced eggplant, can be placed directly on the grill without the skewer or pan.

Turn, shake, or stir the vegetables as they cook.

Remove the vegetables from the grill when they are lightly browned, and serve them immediately.

A basic recipe for basting any grilled vegetable:

Cut the vegetables into chunks, thread them on skewers, combine the following, and baste the vegetables frequently with the mixture until they are done:

1/3 cup olive oil
2 tablespoons red wine vinegar
1/4 teaspoon salt (or less)
1/8 teaspoon pepper

How to Dress Up Vegetables

LEMON: Serve vegetables topped with a splash of fresh-squeezed lemon juice for a bit of pizzazz that sharpens the vegetable flavors.

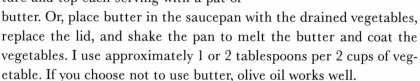

BUTTER: After the vegetables have been cooked, drain off the excess moisture and top each serving with a pat of butter. Or, place butter in the saucepan with the drained vegetables, replace the lid, and shake the pan to melt the butter and coat the vegetables. I use approximately 1 or 2 tablespoons per 2 cups of vegetable. If you choose not to use butter, olive oil works well.

CREAM CHEESE: Vegetables are great when topped with a pat of cream cheese. This can be done on individual servings or you can place the cream cheese in the lidded saucepan with the drained vegetables—this will melt the cheese and a quick stir will coat the vegetables when serving.

HERBS AND SPICES: Each vegetable listing suggests complementary herbs and spices.

If you are using the dried form, try approximately ¼ teaspoon per 2 cups of vegetable. This can be added as you are doing either of the stir-frying methods above. Otherwise, add the dried herbs to the melted butter and serve as described.

Fresh herbs and spices can be minced fine and sprinkled over cooked vegetables just prior to serving. Or, they can be added directly to melted butter or as you do either stir-fry method. Remember to use three times as much fresh as dried herbs, so that for every 2 cups of vegetable, you would use approximately ¾ teaspoon of fresh herbs, adjusting up or down to taste.

Herbs chopped very fine allow the flavoring oils to escape into the vegetables.

OTHER FLAVORINGS: All vegetables are compatible with minced green or regular onion, chives, scallions, parsley, sliced black olives, sliced mushrooms, or freshly ground black pepper, so these aren't listed individually.

All the vegetables taste great topped with shredded or thinly sliced cheese, which can be added to each individual serving or spread on top of an ovenproof dish containing vegetables and placed under the broiler for a few seconds.

VEGETABLE COMBINATIONS can be a refreshing change of pace and a colorful blend of color and texture. Try cooking these together:
- Green peas and pearl onions
- Cauliflower and green peas
- Cauliflower and red sweet pepper
- Carrots and green peas
- Limas and carrots
- Broccoli and carrots
- Carrots and green beans
- Tomatoes and zucchini
- Okra and tomatoes
- Corn and green peas

STIR-FRIED VEGETABLE BLENDS can include almost any homegrown vegetable, depending on what is available. Try any of the following together: Carrots, green or red sweet peppers, broccoli, cauliflower, onions, green beans, leftover sweet corn cut off the cob, etc. For a bit of zip, stir in a little grated lemon or orange zest before serving.

For **QUICK CREAMED VEGETABLES,** put 1 cup or more of heavy cream in an open saucepan or small skillet. Simmer on low without stirring till thickened to the consistency of a sauce. To season the sauce, add salt and pepper to taste (white pepper looks nicer than the specks of black pepper) or a pinch of curry powder or one of the other herbs or spices mentioned in the vegetable listings. Pour the cream over warm, well-drained vegetables and serve. Very easy—and wonderful!

By the way, farmwives of previous generations didn't worry about using cream or butter and neither do I. With a ready supply from their milk cows, farmwives used fresh cream and butter to make all kinds of wonderful food. I'm back to thinking they were healthier as a result!

What to Do with Leftovers

Frugal farmwives have always been loath to waste food, including little dabs of leftover vegetables. Refrigerate them in a covered container, and you can later:

- Toss them, cold, in a lettuce salad.
- Combine them with the next meal's cooked vegetable for a color and texture combination.
- Stir several leftover vegetables into chicken or beef broth for soup, adding seasonings suggested with the vegetables. The vegetable cooking water can be added to the broth for a boost in flavor and nutrients.
- Add leftover vegetables to a casserole for a one-pot meal.

General Notes and Procedures for Putting Up Vegetables

Canning is the traditional farm method for preserving foods. My mother and her mother used to can hundreds of quart jars of produce, and I remember how pretty they looked in our basement storage room. The wonderful taste of home-canned goods is unbeatable.

Traditionally, the farmwife would do the canning in her summer kitchen—a separate one-room building on the farmstead—to keep the heat from canning away from the main house. With the advent of central air-conditioning, few farms have a summer kitchen now, yet in my canning days, the house would heat up faster than our air-conditioning could keep up. So The Farmer bought a supplemental window unit for the kitchen, which helped, but was a hassle to put in every summer and take out every fall. No matter what, canning is hot, time-consuming, and hard work! Sadly, I no longer have the time to do it.

But I've found a great alternative to canning—freezing. It's fast, easy, and doesn't heat up the house. It also preserves more nutrients in the food and nearly matches canning for flavor and texture, if done correctly.

Specific directions for freezing are listed under each vegetable. In general, most vegetables need to be blanched, that is, cooked just a little, in order to inactivate enzymes that cause a deterioration in color, texture, or flavor and to preserve nutrients. Do not overcook or the vegetables suffer loss of flavor, texture, and nutrients. You want to cook them just long enough to make the color look brighter than it did when the vegetables were raw, but you want the vegetables to retain their crispness, not be crisp-tender as they would be for eating. There are three ways to blanch vegetables.

BLANCHING IN BOILING WATER

The fastest method for freezing a large quantity.

- Put a fairly large kettle of water on your biggest burner and bring to a boil. A kettle that is lined with a metal basket is ideal (see note below). Otherwise, you will need a colander and a second large heatproof pot.
- While the water is coming to a boil, fill a bowl or your kitchen sink with ice cold water; an empty milk jug that has been filled with water and frozen works very well for keeping the water chilled. Open a large terry towel on the counter by the sink.

- When the water comes to a boil, dump in the prepared vegetables and begin the timing as soon as the water returns to a boil. Stir often.
- When the timing is complete, immediately remove the vegetables from the boiling water, either by pulling out the basket, scooping them out with a large slotted ladle, or by straining the vegetables in the colander, catching the water in the second pot. This water can be reused for the next batch.
- Immediately plunge the vegetables into the ice-cold water in the sink. If using a basket, dunk the basket up and down in the water, allow the water to drain out of the basket, and overturn the chilled vegetables onto the terry towel.
- Allow the vegetables to dry or blot them with another towel. Then place them in freezer containers or plastic bags, squeeze out excess air, seal, and freeze. I like to use self-sealing bags because they will lay flat and stack well, conserving freezer space. If the plastic is thin, use double-bagging.
- Repeat these steps to blanching the rest of the vegetables, adding more water to the kettle as needed. Replace the water if it gets too cloudy. Always use fresh water when switching to a new vegetable variety.

STEAM BLANCHING

For me, this is a little more time-consuming than the boiling method, because it's hard to find a steamer that holds enough to efficiently process the quantities I freeze. But vegetables maintain the best color and flavor by steaming and it's the method of choice for freezing asparagus, which blanches well in a fish steamer.

- Bring water to boil in the steamer pot (see note below). Check that the water does not touch the bottom of the steamer basket.
- Place vegetables in the steaming basket and cover with the lid. Start timing when the lid is in place, increasing the boiling time listed in the individual vegetable chapters by 50 percent.

- Plunge the steamer basket into icy cold water.
- Follow the remaining directions above, in the boiling method of blanching.

NOTE: Use nonreactive kettles and steamers when blanching vegetables to avoid changes in color and flavor. Avoid using aluminum, brass, copper, iron, zinc, or chipped enameled pans.

MICROWAVE BLANCHING

This is my least favorite method. Although it's easy, I feel that the microwave harms the texture and flavor of vegetables. If you wish to try this method, follow the microwave manufacturer's directions. It may take some experimenting to determine exactly how long to microwave each type of vegetable in your particular model.

BLANCHING AT HIGHER ALTITUDES: You probably already know that water boils at a lower temperature if you live at a higher altitude. Just increase the blanching time a little. You want the vegetables to be brighter colored than when raw, but you want them to retain their crispness, as discussed above.

FREEZER PACKAGING

PLASTIC BAGS: Overall, when freezing vegetables, I prefer heavy plastic bags that are self-sealing (as opposed to using a wire twist tie) because they lie flat, conserving freezer space; the food freezes quickly, because it's spread out flat; it's easy to eliminate air as you seal the package; the bags are disposable, eliminating cleanup for reuse; and they are inexpensive. I recommend placing the filled bags on cookie sheets or in cake pans until they are frozen so that you don't end up with awkward shapes that are hard to store.

RECYCLED CARTONS: Another option are the cartons you get when you buy yogurt, cottage cheese, sour cream, etc. Clean the cartons thoroughly before use for freezing. These cartons are an especially good choice for anything with liquid, like tomato sauce. Leave

½ to 1 inch of headspace for expansion when the liquid freezes. Best of all—these cartons are free, and you are recycling instead of throwing away a resource. The only downside: The cartons are usually round and don't conserve freezer space as well as if they were square.

FREEZER CONTAINERS: You can purchase reusable plastic freezer containers that are made in a square shape to maximize freezer space. These recyclable cartons must be washed by hand and stored for reuse. The biggest downside? When putting up dozens or hundreds of packages, as I do, purchased freezer containers become costly.

VACUUM SEALING: Air in the package causes oxidation, which causes food to deteriorate in the freezer. One way to eliminate even more air than is possible for you to squeeze out of the package by hand is to purchase a vacuum-seal machine. To use this machine, you usually have to purchase special plastic sleeving material. You fill the plastic with the desired quantity of prepared produce, and the machine sucks out the remaining air and heat-seals the end of the plastic, usually in one operation. I've done this and it works well, although the machine didn't stand up to much use. Perhaps the machines have been improved since I last tried them.

THAWING AND PREPARING FROZEN VEGETABLES

Most vegetables can be cooked without first thawing. They will retain nutrients and have better texture and flavor if they are cooked straight from the freezer. The exceptions:

- Corn on the cob should be completely thawed before being cooked.
- Greens, like Swiss chard, spinach, and beet tops, should be partially thawed and separated so that you're not cooking one solid chunk.
- Any vegetable that has been previously cooked (not blanched) should be partially thawed. Examples: mashed potatoes, winter squash or pumpkin puree, etc.

Once they have thawed, use the vegetables right away. Do not refreeze the vegetables.

For the best texture, do not boil at high temperatures; hard boiling ruins frozen vegetables.

NOTE: Eating vegetables that have been properly frozen for eight to twelve months is not harmful, but the quality might suffer.

ASPARAGUS IN THE GARDEN

We're always excited by our first asparagus harvest, because it's our earliest fresh, homegrown vegetable each spring. It's so much more flavorful than anything you can buy in the store! It's far more tender, too, because asparagus toughens the longer the delay between harvest and eating.

The stem of the plant is the part that is eaten. Asparagus has a large, deep root structure that sends up shoots in the spring. These can be harvested for about a month. Then the spears should be allowed to grow so that the asparagus can replenish itself for the next year.

Raising your own patch is easy, and once established, asparagus can be harvested year after year, one of only a few perennial vegetables.

LOCATION: Since the spears develop into lovely fernlike fronds about five to six feet tall, and female plants later have berries that turn bright red, asparagus makes a lovely background for flowers, perhaps along a rustic fence. Allow three feet spacing between the asparagus and the flower bed. Do consider your location carefully, as it will be permanent and last many years.

GROWING RANGE: Asparagus will grow anywhere (except perhaps the Deep South), so long as it can go dormant during the winter months.

SOIL REQUIREMENTS: Asparagus prefers a loose soil but tolerates a wide variety of soils so long as drainage is good.

MOISTURE: Asparagus needs plenty of water the first year. Once the asparagus bed is established, asparagus is adaptable to drought because the roots are so deep. Ideally, the bed should receive two inches of water every two weeks during a dry period. Asparagus likes to be moist, but never soggy.

LIGHT: Asparagus likes full sun but can tolerate just a little shade, if necessary.

PLANTING ASPARAGUS FROM SEED: Start the seeds indoors twelve to fourteen weeks prior to transplant time.

- To ensure that the seeds are free of disease, soak them for two minutes in one part liquid laundry bleach plus four parts water. Rinse the seeds well in cool water.

- Soak the seeds in water for one or two days before planting.
- Plant the seeds half an inch deep in peat pots with a commercial potting soil mixture.
- Place the pots in a sunny window or apply bottom heat. The seeds will germinate in two to three weeks.
- The seedlings will need twelve to fourteen hours of light daily, so you might have to supplement with artificial light.
- A weak application of a complete fertilizer, like 15-15-15, can be used every four weeks at no more than half the recommended rate. Using more than that favors the top growth when you want to encourage the root growth. Be careful not to get any of the fertilizer on the tops.
- Plant the seedlings in the garden when they are about twelve inches tall, about two to four weeks after the frost-free date. Space them six inches apart in soil that has never grown asparagus.
- When the seedlings bloom, check the blossoms under a magnifying glass. The male plants have larger and longer blossoms than the female plants. Eliminate the female plants.
- The following year, dig up the remaining male seedlings and transfer them to a permanent bed, spaced twelve inches apart in rows at least three feet wide.
- Adequate moisture is critical to the developing asparagus both in the pots and after transfer to the garden.

Advantages: Starting asparagus from seed is cheaper and it reduces the chance of disease. (Although I've never had a problem with diseases from crowns purchased from reputable sources, and I've planted a lot of asparagus.) Some experts say that asparagus started from seed lives longer and produces more spears.

Disadvantages: Starting asparagus from seed is time-consuming, and it will delay the harvest by at least one year.

PLANTING ASPARAGUS FROM CROWNS: Plant the asparagus outdoors in early spring as soon as the ground can be worked.

- Plant the crowns without delay, as soon as possible after you get them, in early spring, if possible.
- Select a planting site where asparagus has not grown previously.
- Use a tiller to thoroughly loosen the soil, mix in well-rotted manure or fertilizer, and dig furrows about eight inches deep. Space the rows at least three feet apart.
- Place the crown head buds up in the furrow on a two-inch mound of soil, spreading the roots horizontally in the row. Adjust the crown so that it is six to eight inches deep in the furrow, and cover the crown with one or two inches of soil. Firm the soil to anchor the roots.
- Water in the furrows after planting.
- As the asparagus grows, periodically use a hoe to knock some dirt into the furrow. Cover the stems, but do not bury the airy foliage. As the summer progresses, the furrows will be filled in and level.
- Adequate moisture is essential to establishing the crowns. Be sure to water at least to a depth of eight inches each week, if rainfall is insufficient.
- Sprinkle well-rotted manure in the furrows at planting time, or purchase a fertilizer mix for asparagus and apply it during the summer according to the package directions.

Advantage: Crowns can be harvested after two years, and their root systems become established much quicker.

ONGOING CARE:

- **Tilling:** During the early summer, occasionally use a tiller between the rows to keep the weeds down and for aeration and increased moisture penetration until the ferny tops are full grown and impassable. Don't do anything to damage the tops, because this will reduce the next year's crop, maybe even jeopardizing the crowns' ability to survive the winter.

    In the fall, even after the tops have died and been removed, the stems remaining in the ground might be tough; do not till over the crowns in the fall because the blades might catch these stems and damage the crowns.

    In late winter, before the roots have come out of hibernation, the entire bed should be tilled to loosen the soil for aeration and moisture penetration. To be on the safe side, don't till more than four or five inches deep over the crowns, although they can probably withstand deeper tilling. (Late one winter, I decided to get rid of one of my large established beds due to a persistent thistle problem, so The Farmer used his big tractor and field machinery to till it rather deeply. To my amazement, the asparagus came up better than ever, and the thistle problem was under control!)

- **Mowing:** Asparagus should be allowed to grow until the tops have died and turned yellow. The dead tops are attractive even through the winter, and can be removed by hand early the following spring. Since I have several large beds that tend to look unkempt, The Farmer mows off the dead fronds in late fall.

- **Mulching:** Although I've maintained both mulched and unmulched beds for years (using the same asparagus variety), I've found it's far better not to mulch asparagus. Mulch prolongs dormancy and significantly shortens the harvest period. Since the asparagus roots are so deep, rain cannot get to them through a layer of mulch, and it's unnecessary to waste resources watering established asparagus beds. With a small power tiller, an unmulched asparagus bed is little trouble.

VARIETIES INCLUDE:

- **Mary Washington**, a very reliable asparagus that is resistant to asparagus rust.
- **Jersey King**, which is supposed to be an all-male variety.
- **Jersey Giant**, which is good for colder climates and is disease resistant.
- **Jersey Knight**, which is good for warmer climates.
- **UC157**, which was specially developed for milder winter climates like those in the Pacific Coast, the Southwest, and the South.
- **Purple Passion** or **Sweet Purple**, which has purple spears that are larger and sweeter than traditional asparagus. It turns green when cooked.

NOTE: Asparagus plants are either male or female and require bees to transfer the pollen to the female flowers, which develop into berries. Male plants produce the most and the largest stalks for eating, and are the longest-lived, so it is worthwhile to concentrate on mostly male hybrid varieties.

YIELD: With good care, each crown can give you up to two dozen spears per harvest season.

HARVESTING: Select stalks that have tightly closed tips and are at least as thick as a pencil or better; male spears can get as thick as the base of your thumb. (Contrary to what some say, the thicker spears are very tender and not at all woody when they're homegrown.) They will be seven to ten inches in length, sometimes even longer. Although some gardeners cut the stem, I recommend that you reach more than halfway down the stalk and snap it off—it will break at just the right place, where the stem becomes too tough to eat. Leave the tough bottom stub on the plant.

Once the spears start coming, be sure to check the plants every day or two, or they will mature too much for harvest.

NOTE: Do not harvest any spears for the first two years if you've planted asparagus crowns, not for at least three years if you've started the asparagus from seed. Harvesting sooner than this can dwarf the plants and permanently reduce the bed's yield and vigor. Here's a good rule of thumb: After the bed is old enough to eat from, the first harvest should last for only one or two weeks, and the second harvest only two or three weeks the following spring.

Always allow the bed to grow freely from late spring until the fronds die back in late fall.

Harvesting the bed heavily for too long a period can kill the roots. A friend who rented out her house lost her well-established bed because the renters harvested it to death. Some spears need to be allowed to grow so that photosynthesis occurs, which gets carbohydrates to the roots to survive through winter and to have the energy to send up new shoots in the spring.

Asparagus in the Kitchen

The very first fresh vegetable in the spring, asparagus can be used as a side dish or in soups, salads, and casseroles.

STORING: Wrap asparagus in plastic and refrigerate, if you'll be using it soon. Or else place the cut ends in water and refrigerate for later use, if you're waiting to harvest enough for a meal. Otherwise, freeze it right away. Remember that asparagus gets tougher the longer it is stored.

FREEZING: Freeze asparagus as soon as you can after the harvest to prevent the spears from getting tough.

- Wash in cold water and cut off ends, if they aren't tender. (These ends can be pureed and added to cream soups, etc.)

- Cut into lengths to fit into freezer bags.
- Blanch about two minutes, cool, and drain.
- Pack in freezer bags or containers. If leaving the stalks in four- or five-inch lengths, alternate the heads to pack them better. Seal, label and date, and freeze.

EATING ASPARAGUS

PREPARING: Rinse in cold water and drain. Cut into pieces, if desired. Although some people peel the stalks, I find it entirely unnecessary.

FLAVORING: Asparagus goes well with basil, celery seed, ground mustard, dill weed, marjoram, nutmeg, oregano, tarragon, lemon juice and zest, mustard seed, sesame seed, tarragon, parsley, butter, bacon, mushrooms, almonds, salt and pepper, and cheeses like Gruyere and Parmesan.

Plain melted butter is wonderful on asparagus, or add the following to the butter:

- chopped hazelnuts or cashews
- capers
- any of the seasonings listed above

Top chilled cooked asparagus with mayonnaise or sour cream. Sprinkle with snipped chives.

COOKING: Methods include steaming, boiling, grilling, frying, baking. To boil or steam the long asparagus stalks, use a fish steamer.

NOTE: For best flavor and nutrition, cook only until bright green and crisp-tender; do not overcook.

Sauteed Asparagus

This is probably the easiest—and best—preparation method. Just heat some olive oil or butter in a skillet and add the asparagus spears. Saute them until they're bright green and tender-crisp. If desired,

reserve the tender tips to add to the pan after the thicker, lower portions of the spears are partially cooked.

Easy Creamed Asparagus with Eggs

We love this!
Prepare boiled or steamed asparagus. Top with warm, sliced hard-
boiled eggs. Over this pour thickened cream and sprinkle on a little
paprika or cheddar cheese. (To thicken cream, just put 1 cup of heavy
whipping cream in a small saucepan and simmer a few minutes without stirring.) Very easy and delicious!

Easy Asparagus with Almonds

Prepare boiled or steamed asparagus. Thicken cream and stir in a little shredded cheddar cheese to melt. Pour over the asparagus and top
with slivered almonds.

Easy Asparagus with Cheese

Steam or boil asparagus until tender-crisp. Drizzle with melted butter and sprinkle with grated cheese, like Gruyere or Parmesan. Place
under the broiler for a few seconds until the cheese is softened.

Asparagus and Strawberry Salad

1. Cut asparagus into 1- or 1½-inch pieces. Cook in boiling water or
   steam until tender-crisp. Do not overcook! Cool.
2. Serve asparagus on a bed of lettuce, top with fresh halved strawberries.
3. Sprinkle with raspberry vinaigrette dressing.
4. Top with slivered or sliced almonds. Serve.

BEANS IN THE GARDEN

Along with corn and squash, beans were a staple to the natives of North and South America since prehistoric times. They grew well in a variety of climates, and the seeds were easily transported, so they were soon distributed all over the world by the early explorers.

Beans are easy to grow and it's fun to try the many varieties!

TYPES OF BEANS:

- **Snap beans** are eaten pods and all when the seeds are still immature. They are also called string beans, green beans, French beans, and garden beans. The diameter is the width of a pencil or less for the beans to be tender and have the best flavor. The pods might be flat or swollen with immature seeds, and they can be colors other than the usual green, including purple, yellow, even speckled. Snap beans are a short-season crop that can be grown nearly everywhere.
- **Green shell beans,** like limas, are grown for their immature seeds, which are shelled out of the pods in the green stage. A longer-season crop.
- **Dry beans,** like kidney and pinto beans, are grown for their mature seeds, which become hard and dry at the end of the growing season. They are left in the garden until the pods

73

are dry and brittle and will crack open to release the mature beans. The longest-season beans, especially for the larger varieties, like limas.

All three types of beans are available on two types of bean plants:

- **"Bush"** beans are self-supporting and usually grow eighteen to twenty-four inches tall. They can be harvested sooner than pole beans and will produce for a long time given the right conditions.
- **"Pole"** beans are twining vines that must have the support of stakes or a trellis. The beans are larger than snap beans, they have a more pronounced "bean" flavor, and they produce for a long period. They require a longer growing season and take a longer time before the first harvest, but they take up less garden space and you don't have to bend over to pick them! Besides the regular green beans, pole beans include green shell beans like limas and baby limas, and even some unusual varieties like yard-long beans, which are tasty when picked under eighteen inches in length, but which will, indeed, grow to be a yard long.

LOCATION: Since beans benefit the soil by adding nitrogen, try to plant beans in the garden where corn, a heavy nitrogen feeder, grew the previous year. Although you can plant beans on ground where beans grew previously, rotating crops is the ideal because it prevents or discourages disease and insect problems.

NOTE: Beans are self-pollinating, so you don't have to worry about cross-pollination unless you plan to save the seed for next year, in which case it would be a good idea to separate varieties by at least fifty feet.

NOTE: Young children enjoy pole bean wigwams or teepees in the yard. Anchor several poles at least six feet long in the ground in a circle formation. Tie the poles together at the top. Plant pole beans at the base of the poles and train them to cover the structure. Children can easily harvest the beans because they'll be hanging inside the teepee.

Snap beans are usually grown in the garden in rows and never need staking.

Pole beans need support and cling to the support by coiling. They can be grown along a tall fence or trellis, or you can place a row of stakes at least six feet tall (better yet, eight to ten feet tall) in the garden every twelve inches, or you can tie three tall stakes together at the top and anchor them in the ground for a sturdy support. The tripod is the ideal choice if you live in an area with strong wind. Put the supports in place prior to planting the beans.

GROWING RANGE: Snap and green shell beans can be grown almost everywhere. Dry beans need a longer growing season, especially the larger-seeded varieties.

SOIL REQUIREMENTS: Beans tolerate a wide range of soils but prefer fertile, well-drained soil. The soil should be somewhat loose during germination or the beans will have a tough time emerging, especially if a crust forms on the surface. Tilling will break up the soil. After germination, the beans don't mind heavy soil, but it should be kept tilled to allow moisture to be absorbed.

MOISTURE: Keeping the soil moist (but not soggy) aids the germinating bean plant as it pushes up through heavy soil.

Beans should have one inch of water per week. If you get less rainfall than that, you will need to water. If you regularly get more rainfall than that, you need to add sand to your soil or else grow the beans in raised beds for drainage.

NOTE: Try to water at the base of the plants, avoiding splashing the water on the leaves. If using an overhead sprinkler, water early in the day so that the moisture evaporates from the leaves quickly, to avoid disease transmission.

NOTE: Farmers avoid walking in wet beans because it can transmit a disease called rust.

LIGHT: Full sun. Part shade reduces yields.

PLANTING SEASON: Do not plant any beans until after the last frost date for your area. The soil must be warm for the beans to germinate; the seeds will quickly rot in cold soil. Also, late frosts are very hard on bean plants.

In areas with cold winters, pole beans should be planted in the spring, but bush beans can be planted from late spring until mid-summer. Since the plants suffer during extremely hot weather and the beans are tough and less flavorful, I recommend planting a second crop in midsummer. Or stagger your planting at two-week intervals for a continuous harvest.

In the South, all types of beans can be grown almost year-round.

HOW TO PLANT:

All beans: Plant the seeds one inch to one and a half inches deep and four to six inches apart (depending on variety) in rows spaced two and a half feet apart.

Bush beans germinate in a week; pole beans take about two weeks, depending on conditions.

You'll find that garden beans don't all germinate. Rather than planting them thicker to compensate and then culling every other plant, I prefer to space them properly at the outset. It's no problem to poke a bean seed into the ground where I'm missing a plant or two.

If your soil is less than ideal, consider buying bean innoculate powder from the nursery or garden catalogue and treat the seed according to the directions on the package. The powder is made up of beneficial soil microbes that aid the beans in converting the nitrogen in the air into a usable form. The same innoculate can be used on peas.

Pole beans: Plant the seed after the supports are in the ground. One or two bean vines can grow up each pole, or one plant can grow every six inches along a fence. It's best to overplant pole beans; you can thin the beans later by cutting off the unwanted plants. By the way, you can mix pole bean varieties in a row and you'll still get a "true" crop because they are self-pollinating.

NOTE: Although unnecessary with most beans, large, flat lima-type seeds should be planted with the "eye" facing down. They'll grow much better since they're already heading in the right direction. Otherwise, the newly germinated bean could die before it gets out of the ground.

ONGOING CARE:

- **Tilling.** If the tiller throws a little soil onto the lower plant stems, they will develop additional roots.
- **Weeding.** The tiller takes care of most weeds; hand weeding in the rows is only necessary till early summer when the bean canopy discourages weed seed from germinating.
- **Watering,** as necessary, especially during bloom time. If the bean plants get too dry, they will quit producing new pods,

and the existing pods will get tough and lose flavor. If the bean pods stay unusually small or curl into C shapes, the plant needs water.

- Harvesting snap and green shell beans frequently to stimulate the plant to produce more beans.
- Directing pole bean vines to their support. Once there, they'll latch on and grow all by themselves. Gardeners usually train the vines to grow in a clockwise spiral.
- Staying out of the beans when they are wet, as this can spread disease.

NOTE: If the plants have blossoms but don't develop bean pods, the likely cause is heat stress. If this happens regularly in your area, either plant shorter-season beans to avoid the hottest days of summer, or use succession planting, so that there will be beans blooming when the heat abates. But don't give up on the beans that stop production. After the hottest part of the summer is past, they will produce again until fall frost kills the plants.

VARIETIES INCLUDE:
- **Early Contender**, one of many snap bush bean varieties, produces a crop ahead of most others. It withstands the heat and is good for cooking, canning, and freezing. 49 days.
- **Royal Burgundy** or **Purple Queen** snap bush bean, which, as the name implies, has purple pods that turn green when the beans are cooked. This meaty bean has exceptional flavor and is especially easy to harvest because the purple pods are easy to spot. 50 days.
- **Golden Wax** or **Golden Butterwax** snap bush beans have bright yellow pods that are easy to spot for harvest. Be sure to harvest the beans when they are young and tender as yellow beans are not at all good when overripe. 56 days.
- **Limas** require a long growing season and are not suitable for Canada or the northern United States, unless you're growing the bush type of baby limas. They need warmer temperatures, tolerate heat well, and shouldn't be planted until two or more weeks after snap beans because the plants can't tol-

erate even a hint of frost. 65 to 75 days.

- **Scarlet Runner beans,** a vine type that needs a sturdy support because it grows up to ten feet in length. The attractive flowers are bright red and the bean seeds are red and black. They require pollination from bees or hummingbirds. If your summers are hot, over 90 degrees, the flowers will not set beans until the temperature begins dropping for fall. Harvest the pods when they are flat, before the beans inside start to swell. They can be grown on teepee or wigwam supports. 70 days for pods; 115 days for dry beans.

YIELD: Snap beans vary greatly in yield, depending on moisture, soil conditions, and the variety chosen. Speaking very generally, you might expect to harvest five to ten pounds per ten-foot row.

Bush-type green shell or dry beans yield about half that of snap beans, perhaps three to six pounds per ten-foot row.

Pole beans produce about three times the crop of bush beans planted in the same space.

HARVESTING: Snap beans are best picked young, when the pod is tender and tasty and the beans are still too small to fill out the pod. Check the plants at least every other day so that they don't get too mature; remove overly mature beans from the plants and discard. Keeping the plant harvested encourages production. Be careful not to damage the plants or knock off the blossoms during harvesting.

Green shell beans are harvested while the beans are full sized but the pods are still immature, or "green" and soft, but before there is any sign of yellowing or browning.

NOTE: Harvest snap and shell beans frequently. The beans taste best when young and tender, and the plants will be stimulated to blossom and keep producing beans. Be careful not to damage the plants when harvesting; hold the bean in one hand and the stem in the other and snap apart.

Dry beans are not harvested until the leaves have yellowed and withered and the pods are brittle and the beans inside are dry. Don't delay harvest or the pods might split open or shatter, spilling the beans on the ground.

Beans in the Kitchen

STORING: Snap and green shell beans can be stored, unwashed, in open plastic bags in the refrigerator in the crisper drawer.

Dry beans, if completely dry, can be stored in jars or plastic bags at room temperature. They will keep a long time.

FREEZING SNAP BEANS:
- Tender, young pods with small beans freeze the best.
- Wash in cold water, trim ends, cut to desired length or to fit freezer containers.
- Blanch 3 minutes. Cool and drain.
- Pack in freezer containers or bags. Seal, label and date, and freeze.

FREEZING GREEN SHELL OR LIMA BEANS:
- The beans should still be in the green stage.
- Shell out of the pods, rinse in cold water.
- Blanch small beans 1 minute, medium beans 2 minutes, large beans 3 minutes. Cool and drain.
- Pack in freezer containers or bags. Seal, label and date, and freeze.

FREEZING DRY SHELLED BEANS: These can be frozen after they're cooked. Place them in freezer containers. Seal, label and date, and freeze.

To prevent moth or weevil problems, freeze the dry, shelled beans for four days. Then remove from the freezer and store in a dry place.

EATING BEANS

PREPARING:
Snap beans: Rinse and remove the stem and the tip, if desired. Snap the beans into segments, or cut them with a knife, or cook them whole.

Green shell beans: Shell the beans out of the pod like peas.

Dried beans: Shell out of the dry pods. Rinse the beans and pick out any debris just before using them.

FLAVORING: Snap beans and green shell beans go well with basil, dill, fennel, marjoram, mint, mustard seed, nutmeg, oregano, savory, tarragon, thyme, garlic, parsley, salt and pepper, butter, sauteed mushrooms, pimento, onion, Worcestershire sauce, horseradish, cashews, red sweet peppers, bacon.

Dry beans go well with marjoram, oregano, sage, savory, tarragon, thyme, diced pimento, onions, tomato sauce.

COOKING SNAP BEANS AND GREEN SHELL BEANS: Methods include steaming, boiling, grilling, baking, stir-frying. Snap beans can also be tossed with olive oil and roasted on cookie sheets in the oven till lightly browned.

Never cook green beans with lemon juice or they'll lose their bright color.

COOKING DRIED BEANS: Dry beans are usually soaked before cooking. Often, the soaking water is drained and then the beans are cooked in fresh water—this will help eliminate digestive difficulties. Dry beans bulk up during cooking because they absorb water, a little more than doubling in size.

- Overnight soaking. Cover the beans with cold water. Drain the next morning, then add more water and simmer for 2 hours.
- Quick soaking. Cover the beans with water and bring to a boil. After 2 minutes, remove the beans from the stove, cover them, and allow them to stand for 1 hour. Drain and add more water and simmer for 2 hours.
- Crock-Pot. First, place the beans in a saucepan and cover with water. Bring to a boil, then reduce heat to a simmer. After 10 minutes, drain off the water. Place the beans in a Crock-Pot with more boiling water and cook on low all day.
- Microwave with overnight soak. Cover the beans with cold water. Drain the next morning, then add more water and

cook at full power until the beans are boiling, about 10 minutes. Reduce power to 50 percent and cook the beans another 20 minutes or until tender.

- Microwave. Cover the beans with water and microwave on full power for 10 minutes. Cover the beans with a lid or plastic wrap and let them stand for 1 hour. Drain. Cover the beans with boiling water and microwave on full power for 10 minutes. Reduce power to 50 percent and cook the beans another 20 minutes or until tender.

NOTE: Be sure to add more water if the beans get dry during soaking or cooking.

NOTE: Green shell beans can be used in dry bean recipes without the lengthy soaking time. They keep the same bulk when cooked. To use, multiply the amount called for in dry bean recipes by two and a half.

Serving Ideas—Snap and Green Shell Beans

Steam or boil beans, drain, and stir in a pat or two of butter. Sprinkle with your favorite seasoning, above, or:

- add Worcestershire sauce and a sprinkle of minced onion
- add slivered or sliced almonds, perhaps with a few drops of soy sauce
- dress with Hollandaise, cream, mushroom, or cheese sauce

Chill cooked green beans and:

- serve with Italian or French dressing
- toss into chicken or tuna salads

Snap Beans with Almond Butter Sauce

1. Steam or boil beans until tender-crisp.
2. While the beans are cooking, melt ¼ cup butter and add ¼ cup slivered or sliced almonds. (Multiply recipe as necessary.)

3. Drain the beans and pour the butter sauce over them. Mix together and serve.

Options: You can add ¼ teaspoon nutmeg and/or ¼ teaspoon black pepper, if desired.

Snap Beans with Soy Sauce and Sesame Seeds

Cook green beans until crisp-tender. Toss with 1 tablespoon melted butter and 1 tablespoon soy sauce and sprinkle with 2 tablespoons sesame seeds. (Multiply as needed.)

Snap Beans with Red Peppers and Cashew Butter Sauce

1. Steam or boil beans until tender-crisp.
2. While the beans are cooking, melt ¼ cup butter in a small skillet and add ½ cup sweet red pepper cut into julienne strips and ½ cup cashews. Stir on low heat until the peppers are tender and the cashews are lightly browned. (Multiply these ingredients, as necessary.)
3. Drain the beans and pour the peppers and cashews over them. Mix together and serve. If desired, squeeze a little lemon juice over the beans just before serving them.

Italian Green Bean Salad

1. Use tender, young green beans. Remove stems, but do not snap the beans.
2. Place the beans in salted water and heat to boiling. Cook, uncovered, only until just barely tender-crisp. Remove from heat and drain.
3. Assemble the dressing by blending together: (multiply recipe, as needed)
   > ⅓ cup olive oil
   > 2 tablespoons wine vinegar
   > 1 clove garlic, minced
   > 1 teaspoon salt
   > ½ teaspoon prepared Dijon mustard
   > dash of pepper

4. Pour the dressing over the green cooled beans and toss together. Chill in the refrigerator about 2 hours.

5. Serve green beans on a bed of lettuce garnished with black olives, fresh onion rings, and tomato wedges.

Fresh Lima Beans and Celery

1. Heat ¾ cup water in a saucepan to dissolve 2 cubes chicken bouillon or 2 teaspoons chicken bouillon granules. Add:

> 1 cup diced celery
> 1 teaspoon minced onion

2. Cook, covered, until the celery is just tender. Stir in:

> 2 to 3 tablespoons butter
> 1/4 teaspoon dry mustard powder
> Salt and pepper as desired

3. Stir in 2 cups fresh green shelled limas and cook until limas are just tender. Serve.

Dried Lima Butter Beans

Really delicious!

1. Place 2 pounds dried lima beans (or navy beans or other white beans) in a kettle. Cover the beans with water. Bring the beans and water to a boil. Boil for 2 minutes, cover the pan, and take it off the burner. Let the beans soak in this water overnight.

2. In the morning, pour off the water and cover the beans with fresh water plus 5 or 6 chicken bouillon cubes. Simmer the beans, covered, on low about 4 hours, adding additional water, if needed.

3. Unless the water level is high, there is no need to drain the beans. Stir in 1 stick of butter (8 tablespoons) and heat until it's melted. Serve in bowls.

Dried Kidney Beans with Rice

1. Boil 3 cups of water in a saucepan and add 1 cup of dried red kidney beans. After 2 minutes, remove the beans from the heat and let stand 1 hour, covered.
2. Bring the beans to a boil again, then reduce heat and simmer on low for about 1½ hours until beans are tender. (More heat than that needed for a simmer risks splitting the beans.)
3. Fry 5 or 6 strips of bacon until crisp. Drain on a paper towel. Crumble.
4. After the beans have simmered, add:

> the crumbled bacon
> 1 onion, chopped
> 1 sweet green pepper, chopped
> 1 cup uncooked rice

5. Heat to boiling and reduce heat to a simmer. Cover and simmer 15 minutes without opening or stirring.
6. Remove from heat, fluff with a fork, and serve hot.

Dried Great Northern Beans with Tomato Sauce

1. Place 1 pound dried Great Northern beans in a large saucepan and cover the beans with water. Bring to a full boil; boil for 2 minutes. Shut off the heat, cover, and let stand for 1 hour. Then bring the beans to a simmer for 1½ hours.
2. Chop 2 large red or white onions and 2 or 3 cloves of garlic. Cook them in a large skillet in a little olive oil until the onions are tender.
3. Skin and chop meaty tomatoes to make about 4 cups. Stir the tomatoes in with the onions and add:

> 1 sweet pepper, chopped (it can be red,
>   yellow, or green)
> ¼ cup fresh parsley, chopped
> 1 teaspoon black pepper
> ½ teaspoon thyme
> ½ teaspoon oregano

4. Cook the tomato mixture on medium for about 5 minutes, stirring often.

5. Drain the beans and pour over the tomato sauce. Stir together and serve, garnished with parsley, if desired.

Dried Navy Beans with Ham

The amounts in this recipe aren't important (except for the baking soda). Experiment and make it to suit your own taste.

1. Cover navy beans with water and bring to a full boil. Leaving the lid on, remove from the heat and let stand for 1 hour.

2. Add ⅛ teaspoon baking soda and return the beans to the stove. Simmer until tender, about 20 minutes.

3. Saute chopped onion in a little butter until onions are tender.

4. Dice ham into quarter-inch cubes

5. Add the onion and the ham to the beans. Transfer the beans to a Crock-Pot and cook for several hours. Serve.

BEETS IN THE GARDEN

One Labor Day, The Farmer went to a tractor-pull contest while I stayed home to harvest beets for the freezer. To my surprise, I discovered that I'd grown a red beet that was the size of a basketball, weighing eleven pounds! What was my secret? Pig manure. That year, I had had The Farmer spread it on my garden in the fall and again in late winter. At planting time, I tilled it under and put in the garden. The end of the beet row was a little low, so the manure concentrated there. I ended up cooking my huge beet, and found that every bit of it was tender and delicious, so I froze it. That one beet provided the vegetable for many winter meals!

Beets are easy to grow. They produce a double crop because you can eat not only the beet roots, but also the tender tops, which are delicious. If your family dislikes store-bought red beets, try homegrown, which are much better tasting, or switch to my favorite, the golden beets, because they have a milder beet flavor.

LOCATION: Since the roots benefit from tilling, you probably will want to grow them in your vegetable garden, although the colorful tops do fit into a flower bed well.

GROWING RANGE: Everywhere.

SOIL REQUIREMENTS: Beets will grow in almost any soil, but it should be well tilled. Like all root crops, beets prefer moist, well-drained, loose soil, which allows the roots to grow larger and have smoother shapes. It also makes it easier to harvest the crop. Tilling in two inches of compost before planting is a good idea, especially if you have heavy soil or clay.

MOISTURE: Beets have a high water content and need moisture but hate soggy soil; if you have frequent rain, you might consider using raised beds or adding sand to your soil for drainage. Otherwise, water if you don't get an inch of rain each week.

LIGHT: Full sun is best but beets will tolerate partial shade.

PLANTING SEASON: Beets are a cool-season crop that can be planted in very early to midspring, and again in midsummer, ten weeks before the first frost date for fall harvest of tender young beets. Beets can tolerate light frosts in the spring and in the fall. Beets are heat tolerant, but extremely hot weather can make the beets and their greens tough and the roots can get woody.

HOW TO PLANT:
- Till the soil to prepare a loose seed bed.
- Since beet seeds are slow to germinate, you can soak the seed for twelve hours or more prior to planting to hasten the

process. This is especially useful when planting beets in midsummer, so that they will develop before frost.

- Plant the seed one-half to one inch deep and three or four inches apart. Or, plant the seed twice as thick and harvest every other plant as the season progresses, eating the culled plants as greens or baby beets.
- Water the seeds daily until the plants are up, not only to aid in germination, but also to help prevent the soil from crusting and preventing plant emergence.

ONGOING CARE:

- **Watering,** if rainfall is inadequate. If the weather gets dry and you're not watering the beets, they might go to seed and then be useless for eating.
- **Hand weeding** within the beet row because a tool could damage the delicate roots. This is necessary only once or twice in early summer and then the beets will be mostly weed-free.
- **Tilling** to keep the soil loose and aerated and the weeds down between the rows.

VARIETIES INCLUDE:

- **Ruby Queen**, which are deep red, have shorter tops, and are especially good for pickling. 52 days.
- **Golden Beets**, our favorite, have orange-yellow roots instead of the usual red. They can be allowed to grow large without losing tenderness or flavor. 50 days.
- **Detroit Dark Red**, which is an early beet that is good for most areas and stores well. 59 days.

YIELD: One beet per seed. The yield is high for a plant that takes up such a small space.

HARVESTING: You can begin to harvest beets when they are quite small, or they can be allowed to mature fully until the first severe frost. The small beets can easily be pulled by grabbing the tops; mature beets might need the assistance of a hand trowel. Be very careful not to bruise the beets or break or damage the roots or the tops where they are attached to the roots, which will cause bleeding and a loss of color and flavor.

Don't discard the tops when harvesting the young beets. The tender leaves can be cooked like chard and actually have more nutrients than spinach. The tops of mature beets are tough and bitter tasting.

You can break off a few leaves for cooking without harming the beet root, which is left in the ground.

The taste is improved if the beets mature in cool weather, like in late fall. If you live in a hot climate, you should attempt to harvest the beets when they are under three inches.

Beets in the Kitchen

STORING BEETS: Store the unwashed beets in a cool moist place (like a root cellar) until you are ready to use them. Or, gently knock off any dirt, wrap the beets in plastic, and store them in the refrigerator, where they will keep for many weeks. If you live in an area with mild winters, the beets can be left in the garden and dug when needed.

FREEZING BEETS:
- Cut off tops, leaving two inches, and leave entire taproot. Wash gently in cold water.
- Cook beets until tender (see "Cooking," below). Cool. Slide skins off and trim off tops and roots. Slice or dice, or leave whole, as desired.
- Pack into freezer bags or containers. Seal, label and date, and freeze.

FREEZING BEET TOPS:
- Cut off tops before cooking beets, leaving two inches on the root. Discard tough or damaged leaves. Wash in cold water.
- Blanch for two minutes. Cool and drain.
- Pack into freezer bags or containers, seal, label and date, and freeze.

EATING BEETS

PREPARING: Wash the dirt off the roots and tops using cold water. Both the tops and the roots can be eaten (see above). Leave the taproots, peels, and two inches of the tops on the beets when cooking.

FLAVORINGS: Beets go well with allspice, basil, bay leaves, caraway seed, cloves, dill, ginger, mustard seed, poppy seed, sage, savory, tarragon, thyme, mint, mustard, nutmeg, parsley, butter, salt and pepper, lemon or orange juice or zest, horseradish, yogurt, sour cream.

91

COOKING: Methods include boiling, baking, steaming.

NOTE: Cook beets whole until they are tender when pricked with a paring knife. Do not peel the beets or cut off the taproots, and be sure to leave at least two inches of the tops on, or else the beets will bleed and loose not only their color, but also their flavor. After cooking, place the beets in cool water until you can handle them. The skins will slide off easily. If you remove the skins quickly, while the beets are still warm, you can serve the beets without reheating them.

- To boil the beets, carefully rinse off any dirt without damaging the roots or tops, and cover them with water.
- To roast the beets in the oven or on the grill, wrap the beets in aluminum foil, without damaging the roots or tops.
- To steam the beets, put them in a steamer without removing the tap roots and be sure to leave on at least two inches of the tops.

Baby beets don't need to be peeled, which would be tedious. Just wash and eat them whole.

NOTE: Beet juice will stain clothing, which is why I wear old black garments when I'm doing a large batch. If you find stains on your kitchen counters, you can remove them with a little bleach or else rub them with the peel of a juiced lemon. Incidently, beets will also stain your urine pink or red—but it is harmless.

Cooked Beet Greens

If the tops are still fresh and tender, they can be boiled or steamed or wilted in butter like spinach or other greens. They have a wonderful, delicate flavor.

Fresh Beet Salad

We enjoyed this wonderful, but simple, salad on a cruise to Tahiti!
Chop fresh clean beets into matchsticks. Toss with oil-and-vinegar dressing and serve on a bed of lettuce.

Cooked Beet Salad

Cook beets and cool (see "Cooking," above). Remove skins, tops, and bottoms. Cut into cubes. Toss with thinly sliced celery and chopped sweet onions. Chill and serve.

Beets with Sour Cream

1. Cook beets till tender and cool. Remove the skin, tops and taproots. Cut into ¼-inch slices.
2. For the dressing, mix together the following for every pound of beets:

> ⅓ cup sour cream
> 1 tablespoon minced onion
> ½ teaspoon prepared horseradish
> salt and pepper to taste

3. Toss the dressing with the beets. Serve garnished with snipped chives, or toasted walnuts, if desired.

Baked Beets

Wrap each beet in aluminum foil and bake until tender, perhaps 40 minutes at 350 degrees F. Remove the foil and cut off the tops and bottoms; the skins will slide off easily. Slice and serve with butter, salt, and pepper. (NOTE: I prefer to boil the beets, unless I have the oven going anyway.)

Fresh Beets with Onion Butter Sauce

1. Boil whole beets (with the tops and taproots still on) till tender.
2. While beets are cooking, melt ¼ cup butter and add ¼ cup chopped onion, ½ teaspoon salt, and ⅛ teaspoon pepper. (If necessary, multiply the sauce recipe.)
3. Remove beet skins, tops, and roots. Cut the beets into slices or wedges.
4. Pour the butter sauce over the beets and mix it together.
5. Serve garnished with parsley, if desired.

Pickled Beets

An old Swedish dish!

1. Cover and cook 5 or 6 medium beets immersed in water with 1 tablespoon of vinegar and 1 teaspoon salt until tender, about 40 minutes. Drain and cool. Remove skins, tops, and taproots. Slice the beets.

2. To make dressing, mix the following in a small saucepan:

> 1/2 cup vinegar
> 1/3 cup sugar
> 1/3 cup water
> 1 teaspoon salt
> 1/4 teaspoon ground cloves
> 1/4 teaspoon ground cinnamon
> 1/8 teaspoon allspice
> 1/8 teaspoon pepper

3. Bring the dressing to a boil and simmer for 2 minutes.

4. Slice one onion and add to the beets. (Optional.)

5. Pour the dressing over all and stir well. Cover and refrigerate.

BROCCOLI IN THE GARDEN

Broccoli is a cool-season crop in the same family as cabbage and cauliflower. The plant grows about two feet tall and wide. The parts we eat are the green buds and their stems, which are actually the plant's flower stalk.

After you've harvested one big head, don't remove the plant from your garden, because it will develop lots of side shoots. These will develop into smaller broccoli heads that are just as delicious to eat, and the quantity of these small heads can yield several times the quantity of the original large head.

LOCATION: To avoid insect and disease problems, don't plant broccoli where any members of the cabbage family have grown for the previous three years: cabbage, cauliflower, Brussels sprouts, broccoli, kale, or kohlrabi.

In hot climates, position the broccoli near taller plants, like corn or pole beans, that will shade the broccoli from the afternoon sun.

GROWING RANGE: Broccoli can be grown everywhere, so long as you choose the appropriate varieties and get them started early enough so that the plants avoid too much time maturing during excessively hot weather.

SOIL REQUIREMENTS: Any of the cabbage family grows well on a wide range of soil types. Fertile, deep, well-drained loams are the very best as broccoli is a heavy feeder. If your soil isn't well drained, you can add sand or use raised beds. Fertilize well with well-rotted manure, compost or a purchased fertilizer, tilled into the soil.

MOISTURE: Regular watering is important if you don't get an inch to an inch and a half of rain per week. If the plants get dry for a period, they often develop a bitter taste, especially if it's hot and dry.

LIGHT: Full sun to light shade. Providing partial shade, such as covering the plant with shade cloth, will be beneficial during extreme heat.

PLANTING SEASON: A cool weather crop, broccoli is tolerant of frost and produces less when maturing in hot weather. Therefore, plant the seeds or seedlings outdoors for your season's first crop as soon as you can in very early spring.

In mid- to late June, you can direct-plant seeds in the garden to start another crop for fall harvest. This late broccoli can grow into late fall or even early winter because it is able to withstand some frost and a little snow and it will produce longer and have better yields if the crop is growing in cooler weather. Also, light frost makes the broccoli taste sweeter. Mature plants can withstand temperature dips into the twenties. If the weather is too cold, however, running below 50 degrees by day, the broccoli heads will be smaller and tend to go to seed prematurely.

If you live in an area with mild winters, you can plant another broccoli crop in late summer or early fall for harvest through the winter.

Varieties are available with longer or shorter maturity dates. Select those that work best with your planting times and growing season.

HOW TO PLANT: You can direct-seed broccoli in the garden up to two months before your last frost date, providing the soil temperature is at least 40 degrees F, day temperatures are often in the 60 degree F range, and night temperatures usually stay above freezing. These conditions don't reliably occur in many areas, so most people are better off starting with broccoli seedlings that are purchased from

a nursery or homegrown for their spring planting, and direct-seed their midsummer planting.

To grow your own seedlings:

- Start six weeks prior to transplant time in the garden, or six to ten weeks prior to the average frost-free date for your area.
- Plant the seeds half an inch deep in peat pots.
- Keep the peat pots evenly moist but not soggy. The seeds will germinate in about one week.
- Keep the indoor temperature cool, not more than 70 degrees F, to prevent the plant from becoming leggy.
- Give the seedlings full sun; if necessary, place them outdoors in a cold frame, especially if indoor temperatures exceed 70 degrees F.
- Prepare the outdoor planting area by tilling well. Mix in well-rotted manure, if you have it.
- Start hardening off the seedlings one week before transplanting in the garden.
- Transplant the seedlings outdoors about four weeks prior to the last frost date for your area.

If you're having an early spring, you can transplant them as much as 6 weeks before the last frost date, but monitor the weather for a severe frost warning.

If you're having a late spring, the seedlings can be planted outside up to two weeks past the frost date. However, this means you should adjust the indoor seed planting time, because the seedlings don't do as well if they are more than six inches tall or more than six weeks old at transplant.

- Plant the seedlings one or two inches deeper than they were growing indoors, or up to the base of the first leaves. Space the plants two feet apart.
- Cover the seedlings before a hard frost, until they are established and can withstand the temperature drop.
- If you have cutworms, place a collar around the young plants. Collars can be cut from paper towel or toilet paper rolls and then slit and slid around the plant stem. Or, use large cans with the tops and bottoms removed. These will also give some frost protection.

To start broccoli outdoors from seed:

- The soil temperature must be at least 40 degrees F for germination.
- Make sure the soil is well tilled.
- Plant the seed a quarter- to a half-inch deep, placing two or three seeds every two feet, to ensure germination. If planting for a fall crop, spacing the plants closer together, eighteen inches or so, helps them withstand cold weather.
- Keep the soil moist, but not soggy. Water daily until the seeds are germinated, if the soil shows signs of drying.
- After the seedlings are up and growing well, thin the seedlings down to one plant every eighteen inches to two feet by snipping off the weakest seedlings. Don't pull the culled plants because you'll risk damaging the remaining plant.

ONGOING CARE:

- **Tilling,** to keep the soil loose and aerated, which broccoli love, and to keep the weeds down, but don't till deeply or you'll damage the shallow roots.
- **Watering** regularly, which will keep the broccoli tender.
- **Hand weeding** close to the plants, as necessary.
- **Preventing** worm damage. Like the other members of the cabbage family, broccoli is subject to green caterpillars from eggs laid by small white butterflies. You can cover the heads with pantyhose before the butterflies appear, or spray or

dust the plants. If necessary, you can soak the broccoli in salted water to get rid of the worms prior to eating it.

VARIETIES INCLUDE:

- **Mariner Hybrid**, the one used in studies indicating that broccoli has anticancer properties. It grows heads seven or eight inches across and also produces many side shoots. Mature in 67 days.
- **Bonanza Hybrid**, ready in only 55 days, is great for freezing.
- **Green Comet** is ready in 40 days and takes summer heat better than the others, but it doesn't have side shoots after the head is harvested.
- **Packman** matures in 57 days, tastes great, and has many productive side shoots.
- **Small Miracle** broccoli plants grow only one foot tall and can be spaced only eight inches apart. It's ready in 55 days and is supposed to do well when direct-sowed in the garden.

NOTE: Be sure to select varieties that can mature before your weather turns hot, for best results. Most broccoli plants mature about 60 or 70 days after transplant, or about 80 or 90 days after direct-seeding.

YIELD: six to nine pounds or more in a ten foot row (six plants).

HARVESTING: Broccoli is ready when the head is still firm, the flower clusters are close together and tight, and none of the buds have opened to show flowers. Harvest broccoli by cutting the stem about three or four inches below the head yet above the leaf clusters, as this is where new broccoli side shoots will form.

The side shoots mature quickly; after they begin to mature, check them daily.

If the broccoli head is no longer firm and the flower clusters aren't close together and tight, the broccoli can still be eaten. But it might be woody, it will taste stronger, and it will have more odor as it cooks— which is why it's far better to harvest it at the younger stage.

Broccoli in the Kitchen

STORING: Place it in a plastic bag in the refrigerator. Don't wash it until you're ready to use it.

FREEZING:
- Young, tender stalks with firm heads freeze best. Wash. Remove leaves and woody stems or peel and slice the stems.
- Separate the broccoli into bite-sized portions. Rinse in cold water. (If you have bugs or worms, you can soak the broccoli in salted water first to get rid of them.)
- Blanch three minutes. Cool and drain.
- Pack into freezer bags or containers. Seal, label and date, and freeze.

EATING BROCCOLI

PREPARING: The entire head plus the stem can be eaten. If the stem seems tough, just peel the lower portion. If it still seems tough, cut off slices of the lower stem until it seems tender. The head can be left whole or cut up, as desired. Wash in cold water. To remove insects, soak the head in salt water.

FLAVORING: Broccoli goes well with basil, caraway seed, curry, dill, garlic, mustard seed, savory, oregano, thyme, lemon juice and zest, garlic, almonds, cheeses, cream sauces, and Hollandaise sauce.

COOKING: Methods include boiling, steaming, baking, grilling, stir-frying.

Cook the broccoli only until it is crisp-tender or you'll lose valuable nutrients and ruin the crisp texture and fine flavor. If boiling the broccoli, lift the lid off the saucepan several times as it cooks, or place the lid on loosely, to allow gases to escape so that the broccoli retains its bright color.

Try cooked broccoli with:

- butter or olive oil and toasted almond slivers or slices
- butter and a twist of lemon and/or any of the seasonings listed above
- Hollandaise, cream, mushroom, or cheese sauces
- a slice of hot ham as a bed for the broccoli; top with cheese or cheese sauce

Broccoli Salad Ideas

- Chill cooked broccoli and serve it with oil and vinegar, Italian, Ranch, or French dressing.
- Toss chilled cooked broccoli into chicken or tuna salad.
- Combine chilled cooked broccoli with chopped onion, raisins, crumbled bacon, and mayonnaise.

Broccoli and Ham Skillet

A quick and easy summer supper dish!
Melt two tablespoons of butter in a skillet. Stir-fry sliced onion and cut-up broccoli until almost done. Add ham cut into 2 × ½ × ½-inch strips. Heat through. Serve hot.

Cream of Broccoli Soup

1. Melt 2 tablespoons of butter in a large pan and saute one diced onion, 2 or 3 chopped celery ribs, and a minced garlic clove until tender.
2. Cut one large head of broccoli into small chunks and add it to the pan with 6 cups of chicken broth. Bring to a boil, then reduce heat and simmer until the broccoli is soft, perhaps 15 minutes. At the same time, in a medium-sized skillet, simmer 2 cups of cream to thicken.
3. Using a cordless hand blender or a food processor, puree the broccoli until smooth.
4. Stir some of the broccoli into the cream, then pour the cream into the soup pan. Add salt and white pepper to taste. Serve garnished with fresh parsley, if desired. Or top with shredded cheese.

BRUSSELS SPROUTS IN THE GARDEN

Another member of the cabbage family, Brussels sprouts are grown on a one-and-a-half- to three-foot-tall plant with a thick stalk that resembles a tree trunk. Leaf stems radiate out from the stalk and tiny cabbages grow at the base of each, starting at the bottom of the plant. They give a good return for the small space they take up in the garden. The crop should not be harvested until cool weather—preferably not until after a light frost.

LOCATION: To prevent insect problems and disease, don't plant Brussels sprouts where any members of the cabbage family have grown for the previous three years: cabbage, cauliflower, Brussels sprouts, broccoli, kale, or kohlrabi.

To save space, you can grow short-season crops, like lettuce and radishes, between the plants until they reach full size.

In hot climates, locate Brussels sprouts near taller plants, like corn or pole beans, that will shade the Brussels sprouts from the afternoon sun.

GROWING RANGE: Zones 3 through 9. The hardiest of all the cabbage family, established Brussels sprouts plants can withstand temperatures in the twenties, but extreme dry heat in summer will cause the lower sprouts to be loose and fluffy rather than firm and solid—although they will fill out and firm up in the cooler fall weather.

SOIL REQUIREMENTS: Brussels sprouts grow well on a wide range of soil types, and they especially like heavy soils, but they don't like standing in water for very long. If your soil isn't well drained, you can add sand or use raised beds. Unlike other members of the cabbage family, the ground for Brussels sprouts should be only lightly fertilized; too much nitrogen makes the stalk taller and the sprouts fewer and farther apart.

MOISTURE: Brussels sprouts require even moisture; do not allow the plants to dry out, especially during hot weather.

LIGHT: Full sun, although a little shade is desirable in extremely hot conditions.

PLANTING SEASON: Brussels sprouts require a long growing season, ideally in cool temperatures, 70 degrees F and under. They tolerate frost well but don't like heat. Unless you live in the South, start with seedlings transplanted outside in very early spring. Or start from seedlings or from seeds planted in early July for a fall and winter harvest. Plant so that the Brussels sprouts can mature before or after summer heat, or grow varieties that are heat tolerant.

HOW TO PLANT:
To grow your own seedlings:

- Start six weeks prior to transplant time in the garden, or six to ten weeks prior to the average frost-free date for your area.
- Plant the seeds half an inch deep in peat pots.
- Keep the peat pots evenly moist but not soggy. The seeds will germinate in about one week.

- Keep the indoor temperature cool, not more than 70 degrees F, to prevent the plant from becoming leggy.
- Give the seedlings full sun; if necessary, place them outdoors in a cold frame, especially if indoor temperatures exceed 70 degrees F.
- Prepare the outdoor planting area by tilling it well. Mix in a little well-rotted manure, if you have it. If you use a commercial fertilizer, be careful not to apply too much.
- Start hardening off the seedlings one week before transplanting in the garden.
- Transplant the seedlings outdoors four weeks prior to the last frost date, when they are five to seven inches tall.

If you're having an early spring, you can transplant them as much as six weeks before the last frost date, but monitor the weather for severe frost warnings.

If you're having a late spring, the seedlings can be planted outside up to two weeks past the frost date. However, this means you should adjust the indoor seed planting time, because the seedlings don't do as well if they are more than six inches tall or much more than six weeks old at transplant.

- Plant the seedlings one or two inches deeper than they were growing indoors, or up to the base of the first leaves. Firm the soil around the roots. Space the plants two feet apart.
- Cover the seedlings before a hard frost, until they are established and can withstand the temperature drop.

- If you have cutworms, place a collar around the young plants. These can be cut from paper towel or toilet paper rolls and then slit and slid around the plant stem. Or, use large cans with the tops and bottoms removed. These will also give some frost protection.

To start Brussels sprouts outdoors from seed:

- The soil temperature must be at least 40 degrees F for germination.
- Make sure the soil is well tilled.
- Plant the seed half an inch deep, placing two or three seeds every two feet, to ensure germination.
- Keep the soil moist, but not soggy. Water daily until the seeds have germinated, if the soil shows signs of drying.
- After the seedlings are up and growing well, thin the seedlings down to one plant every two feet by snipping off the weakest seedling. Don't pull the culled plants because you'll risk damaging the remaining plant.

Ongoing care:

- **Tilling,** to keep the soil from crusting and the weeds down, but do not till deeply near the trunk or you'll harm the roots.
- **Watering,** to keep the soil evenly moist but not waterlogged.
- **Hand weeding,** near the stalks until the plants are established.
- **Removing** the leaves as they yellow, starting at the bottom of the stalk, either by cutting them or breaking them off, leaving about two inches of leaf stem in place. This seems to stimulate the growth of the sprouts. The plant will eventually look something like a palm tree.
- **Pinching** off the tip of the plant in late fall to encourage the sprouts to finish developing before severe winter sets in is recommended by some gardeners. This keeps the plant from spending its energy on new buds at the expense of the existing ones. Don't be too hasty to top it, however, because if your winter remains mild, the plant will continue to grow. Also, the small, immature buds, although tedious to harvest,

are quite delicious to eat—which is why I never top my plants.

VARIETIES INCLUDE:

- **Tasty Nuggets Hybrid**, which produces sweet-tasting sprouts. 78 days.
- **Jade Cross** has firm, crisp dark-green sprouts that are packed closely together. Popular because it yields early and heavily and it's heat tolerant and resists bolting. Mild and sweet. Sixty to one hundred sprouts per plant. 80 days.
- **Long Island Improved** sets up to one hundred firm sprouts over a long season on a compact plant. Flavorful and freezes well. 90 days.
- **Hybrid Bubbles** is widely adaptable to heat and drought and is disease resistant. Very productive, yielding one-inch sprouts. 90 days.

YIELD: Each plant produces between fifty to one hundred one- to two-inch Brussels sprouts, weighing about two or three pounds total.

HARVESTING: Try to wait until after the first frost for the harvest, because the flavor will be improved. Also, the plant can withstand frost and will continue growing, so don't remove it when harvesting. The Brussels sprouts should be firm and compact.

First, break off the leaf, then twist the one- to two-inch sprouts off the stalk, starting from the bottom up as they mature. The harvest can go on this way for six to eight weeks.

If harsh winter weather is on the way with temperatures staying in the teens, maybe with sleet or snow, I take in the plant, stalk and all. It makes harvest easier, especially if the conditions are miserable outside. Some gardeners dig the plant out of the ground, leaving some dirt on the roots, and plant it in a five-gallon gallon bucket of moist soil in their unheated garage to extend the growing and harvest season even longer.

The top leaves are edible and can be used like cabbage leaves, so be sure to harvest them when you are finished with the plant for winter.

Brussels Sprouts in the Kitchen

STORING: Place the Brussels sprouts in a plastic bag and refrigerate, without washing them until you're ready to use them. They will keep a long time, especially if stored in the vegetable crisper with the bag partially open.

FREEZING:
- Choose compact, firm heads, which freeze best.
- Remove coarse, loose outer leaves. Rinse and sort by size.
- Blanch small Brussels sprouts three minutes, medium sprouts four minutes, and large sprouts five minutes. Cool and drain.
- Pack into freezer containers or bags. Seal, label and date, and freeze.

EATING BRUSSELS SPROUTS

Brussels sprouts can be cooked and served by themselves, or they can be added to casseroles or salads.

PREPARING: Wash the sprouts in cold water. Peel off the outer leaves if they are tough or yellowed. Don't trim the stems of the Brussels sprouts too close or the leaves will fall apart during cooking. Insert the tip of your paring knife in the core of each sprout, then repeat to make a cross; this will help the core cook as rapidly as the leaves.

FLAVORING: Brussels sprouts go well with basil, caraway seed, celery seed, dill, mustard seed, oregano, sage, thyme, parsley, butter, salt and pepper, almonds, pecans, pimento, sour cream, cheeses, cream sauces, Dijon mustard, lemon, bacon, walnuts or other nuts, nutmeg. Mix them with mushrooms, ham, squash, celery, carrots, or tomatoes.

COOKING: Methods include steaming, boiling, stir-frying, grilling, baking.

If boiling, use more water than usual for vegetables, perhaps an inch.

Like all the cabbage family, do not cover tightly during cooking, or else remove the lid often to release the gases so that the Brussels sprouts retain their color.

Be sure not to overcook the Brussels sprouts; they should be tender-crisp for the best flavor, texture, and color. If boiling them, for example, only let them cook for three minutes.

Serving Ideas

Cooked Brussels sprouts can be served with:

- sour cream
- hot cream sauces
- cheese sauces
- tomato sauce
- raspberry sauce (See Raspberry Sauce recipe in *Fabulous Fruits and Berries*.)

Fresh or cooked Brussels sprouts are good tossed with a vinaigrette dressing and chilled.

Brussels Sprouts with Cheese

Cook Brussels sprouts in water and drain. Mix in melted butter and a little minced onion. Sprinkle with Gruyere or Parmesan cheese and serve.

Brussels Sprouts with Lemon Butter

Cook Brussels sprouts in water and drain. Melt butter and add fresh lemon juice. Drizzle over the Brussels sprouts, toss together, and serve with a dash of paprika.

Brussels Sprouts with Pecan Butter

1. Clean sprouts and cook them in 1 inch of boiling water or chicken broth. Cover loosely with a lid and cook just until tender-crisp.
2. Melt butter in a saucepan and add minced onion and chopped pecans in this proportion: per every ¼ cup butter add 2 tablespoons onion and ¼ cup chopped pecans.
3. Drain the Brussels sprouts, and pour the butter sauce over them.
4. If desired, garnish with pimento strips and fresh parsley. Serve.

Creamed Brussels Sprouts with Nutmeg and Almonds

1. Place Brussels sprouts in boiling water and reduce heat to simmer. Cook until tender.
2. Place cream in a small skillet and simmer until thickened.
3. Drain the Brussels sprouts and pour the cream over them. Top with nutmeg and slivered almonds or crisp bacon bits.

Brussels Sprouts with Sour Cream and Almonds

1. Cook Brussels sprouts in water until tender. Drain.
2. Combine sprouts with the following:

> ¾ cup sour cream
> ½ cup toasted slivered almonds
> ¼ cup chopped pimento
> salt and pepper, as desired

3. Place in the top of a double boiler over boiling water until heated through. Serve.

Brussels Sprouts in Beer

Place Brussels sprouts in a saucepan and cover with beer. Simmer until the sprouts are tender, adding more beer as necessary. Remove from the stove; stir in a pat or two of butter and salt and pepper as desired. Serve hot.

CABBAGE IN THE GARDEN

Cabbages can have smooth or crinkled leaves and the color can be pale whitish—or bluish-green or purple. All cabbages are edible and all can be used as ornamental plants. Last year I planted a ring of reddish-purple cabbage around my dwarf Alberta spruce and they looked lovely against the airy bright green tree foliage. In the garden, pale blue-green cabbage looks terrific behind rows of deep green onion tops. Purple cabbage is striking planted next to rows of bright green carrot fronds or the chartreuse frills of leaf lettuce, because of the contrast in color and texture. And not only are they beautiful, but they are easy to grow!

LOCATION: Cabbages can be grown in the garden, in flower beds, or in the landscape.

Cabbage likes cool weather and benefits from shade protection in the heat of the summer. You can locate the cabbages near taller plants, like corn or even canna flowers, which will shade them from the afternoon sun. I've found that cabbage grows well in the shade of our satellite dish, which has black metal mesh 9 feet in diameter. Or you can put black mesh shade cloth over hoops, available in garden centers and catalogues.

To prevent insect and disease problems, don't plant cabbage where any members of the cabbage family have grown for the previous three years: cabbage, cauliflower, Brussels sprouts, broccoli, kale, or kohlrabi. Cabbages benefit from growing where peas or beans were planted the previous year.

GROWING RANGE: Cabbage grows everywhere, so long as you choose the planting dates and varieties so that the plants can avoid too much time maturing during excessively hot weather. Established plants can withstand frost.

SOIL REQUIREMENTS: Fertile, deep, well-drained loam is the very best, as cabbage is a heavy feeder, but it will grow in sandy soil or even heavy clay so long as it drains moisture away. If your soil isn't well drained, you can add sand or use raised beds. Fertilize heavily with well-rotted manure or compost tilled into the soil, or use a purchased fertilizer.

MOISTURE: Regular watering is important, if you don't get one inch of rain per week. If the plants get too dry, they'll often develop a strong or bitter taste. It's best to keep cabbages evenly moist; if they get water after being too dry, the sudden influx of moisture can cause the heads to crack. (If this happens, harvest the cabbage right away before insects take up residence.) If possible, water at the ground level so that water doesn't pool on the lower leaves and cause disease.

LIGHT: Full sun except in hot weather.

PLANTING SEASON: Cabbages love cool weather, so start them from transplanted seedlings in very early spring. Or plant from seeds from midsummer to early fall in warmer areas for harvest in fall through winter. You can choose cabbage varieties that are ready early, midseason, or late, depending on your weather conditions.

HOW TO PLANT: If you don't have a long growing season that's cool and moist before the onset of summer heat, you'll need to transplant homegrown or nursery seedlings outdoors.

To grow your own seedlings:

- Start six weeks prior to transplant time in the garden, or six to ten weeks prior to the average last frost date for your area.
- Plant the seeds a quarter-inch deep in peat pots.
- Keep the peat pots evenly moist but not soggy. The seeds will germinate in about one week.
- Keep the indoor temperature cool, not more than 70 degrees F, to prevent the plant from becoming leggy.
- Give the seedlings full sun; if necessary, place them outdoors in a cold frame, especially if indoor temperatures exceed 70 degrees F.
- Prepare the outdoor planting area by tilling well. Mix in well-rotted manure, if you have it.
- Start hardening off the seedlings one week before transplanting into the garden.
- Transplant the seedlings outdoors about four weeks prior to the last frost date for your area, or when daytime temperatures are in the 50 degree F range.

If you're having an early spring, you can transplant them outside as much as six weeks before the last frost date, but monitor the weather for a severe frost warning.

If you're having a late spring, the seedlings can be planted up to two weeks past the frost date. However, this means you should adjust the indoor seed planting time, because the seedlings don't do as well if they are more than 6 inches tall or more than six weeks old at transplant.

- Plant the seedlings one or two inches deeper than they were growing indoors, or up to the base of the first leaves.
- Space the plants two feet apart. Or, plant them six inches apart and harvest every other one while young until the plants that remain to grow to maturity are two feet apart.
- Cover the seedlings before a hard frost, until they are established and can withstand the temperature drop.
- If you have cutworms, place a collar around the young plants. Collars can be cut from paper towel or toilet paper rolls and then slit and slid around the plant stem. Or, use large cans with the tops and bottoms removed. These will also give some frost protection.

To start cabbage outdoors from seed:

- The soil temperature must be at least 40 degrees F for germination.
- Make sure the soil is well tilled.
- Plant the seed a quarter- to a half-inch deep, placing two or three seeds every two feet, to ensure germination. If planting for a fall crop, spacing the plants closer together, eighteen inches or so, helps them withstand cold weather.
- Keep the soil moist, but not soggy. Water daily until the seeds are germinated, if the soil shows signs of drying.
- After the seedlings are up and growing well, thin the seedlings down to one plant every two feet by snipping off the weakest seedlings. Don't pull the culled plants because you'll risk damaging the remaining plant.

ONGOING CARE:
- **Tilling** can be done between the young plants; when the plants spread out it is only necessary in any paths you've left between the rows. Don't till under the plant leaves, as the roots are shallow.
- **Watering** should be done regularly, if rainfall is inadequate. It's very important that cabbages have a steady supply of moisture to keep them sweet and tender.

- **Slicing** the soil. If the cabbages have been through a dry spell (perhaps you've been on vacation or are worried about your farm well running dry) and a heavy rain is on the way, you risk the heads splitting open. You can forestall this by vertically inserting a corn knife or shovel in the soil about six inches from the base to make a slit on one side of the plant no more than six inches wide. This cuts some of the roots and slows down the uptake of water. Be aware that it will also slow down the growth of the cabbage.
- **Weeding** will be minimal to nonexistent, once the plants are established, because the spreading cabbage leaves leave no space for weeds to root.
- **Preventing** worm damage. Small white butterflies appear in summer and lay eggs on the cabbage. These hatch into green worms that feed on the leaves. Use row covers or a spray or powder to keep worms under control. Or try this: cover each cabbage head with a section of pantyhose leg, tying the nylon around the base, leaving the loose outer leaves uncovered (tie it with the hose or something stretchy or you could choke and kill the cabbage). The white butterflies will be unable to lay their eggs through the barrier and the pantyhose will expand along with the growth of the head.

VARIETIES INCLUDE:

- **Late Flat Dutch**, which gets large flattened heads up to thirty pounds at maturity. A good keeper. 105 days.
- **Premium Late Flat Dutch** is similar to Late Flat Dutch, but the heads get to twelve to fourteen pounds. 105 days.
- **Hybrid Stonehead** yields smaller heads of four to six pounds that resist splitting. 67 days.
- **Cabbage King Slaw** gets heads of about fifteen pounds that are sweeter flavored. 105 days.
- **Hybrid Golden Cross** are small plants that can be spaced closer together in the garden. Excellent for short, cool growing seasons. 40 days.
- **Ruby Perfection Hybrid**, my favorite, which has a deep reddish-purple leaf. Red cabbages are sweeter than the greens and are very eye-catching in the garden. 85 days.

YIELD: Each mature plant will give you one large head, and after the harvest, you might get several additional, smaller heads, depending on variety and weather conditions. In Alaska, where the summers are cool and the sun shines all day and nearly all night, we saw heads growing to eighty or ninety pounds!

HARVESTING: You can harvest the cabbage even when it's quite young, if you want to, but to get the most out of the plant, cabbages are usually harvested when the heads are large and firm.

Carefully cut the cabbage off just under the head, leaving the large, loose outer leaves and any tiny cabbages that are growing underneath the head, undisturbed on the plant. These smaller cabbages will grow, although not to the size of the original head, giving you an additional tasty crop.

If you notice that a head has split, harvest it immediately to keep it from rotting and to prevent insects from finding it. Either use it right away or refrigerate it.

Cabbage tastes sweeter after a light frost.

Cabbage in the Kitchen

STORING: Wrap the cabbage in plastic and store in the refrigerator without first washing it.

FREEZING: Cabbage stores so well when it's kept in a cool place that I choose not to freeze it to conserve my freezer space. But if you want to freeze cabbage, here's how:

- Solid heads with green leaves freeze best.
- Remove the tough outer leaves. Wash the head in cold water. Cut the head into wedges and remove the core or shred the cored cabbage.
- Blanch cabbage wedges three minutes, shredded cabbage one and a half minutes. Cool and drain.
- Pack into freezer bags or containers. Seal, label and date, and freeze.

EATING CABBAGE

Cabbage is delicious raw, served in wedges. Or it can be shredded and made into a salad or slaw. The leaves can be cooked whole or chopped or wedges cut with part of the core can be steamed. Cabbage can be added to soups, stews, and casseroles.

PREPARING: Remove the outer leaves only if they are damaged or tough, because these contain the most nutrients. Rinse the cabbage head in cool water and drain.

By cutting through the core the long way, halve the cabbage and then quarter it. If the quarters are too large, you can halve them, making eighths. Place the wedges on their sides to easily cut off the core.

To serve cabbage wedges that are steamed or boiled, do not remove the core, because the leaves will fall apart. But if serving cabbage wedges raw, remove the core.

If using only part of the head, you can peel off a few leaves and leave the rest intact, or you can cut out a wedge. Wrap the remaining cabbage in plastic and refrigerate.

For ease in chopping or shredding cabbage, use the thickest blade on the food processor or run it through the vegetable-slicer attachment on a stand mixer.

FLAVORING: Cabbage goes well with: basil, bay leaf, caraway seed, celery seed, dill, mint, mustard seed, nutmeg, oregano, rosemary, sage, savory, tarragon, thyme, parsley, onions, butter, sour cream, salt and pepper, cream and cheese sauces, mustard sauces, bacon.

Cabbage slaw can include apples, pineapples, onions, marshmallows, green peppers, carrots, raisins, cucumbers, mayonnaise, sour cream, oil and vinegar dressing.

COOKING: Methods include boiling, steaming, braising in butter, baking.

To prevent red cabbage from acquiring a bluish cast when it's cooked, just add 1 teaspoon of lemon juice or vinegar or apple cider vinegar to the cooking liquid.

Place the lid slightly ajar when cooking any of the cabbage family (cabbage, broccoli, cauliflower, Brussels sprouts, turnips). A tight seal can cause a disagreeable cooking odor and flavor. Run an exhaust fan, if possible.

Serving Ideas

- Raw shredded cabbage tossed with orange sections and crushed pineapple.
- Raw shredded cabbage tossed with diced cucumber and chopped celery.
- Cooked cabbage drizzled with melted butter and sprinkled with salt and pepper, as desired.

Red-and-Green Cole Slaw

1. Shred half of a green cabbage and half of a red cabbage and place in a bowl. (Or use all green cabbage.)
2. Add ⅓ cup finely chopped onions and ⅓ cup chopped sweet green pepper.
3. Blend together ½ cup mayonnaise, 2 teaspoons sugar, 1 teaspoon salt, 1 teaspoon lemon juice, 1 teaspoon cider vinegar, and ¼ teaspoon pepper. Pour over the cabbage mixture and stir well.
4. Cover and chill until serving time.

Cole Slaw with Boiled Dressing

A farm favorite for many years!

1. In a saucepan, combine:

> 1 cup white vinegar
> ½ cup salad oil
> 1 teaspoon celery seed
> 1 teaspoon salt
> 1 teaspoon prepared mustard
> ⅛ teaspoon pepper

2. Boil the mixture for 3 minutes. Cool. This will be the dressing.
3. In a large bowl, combine:

> 1 large head of cabbage, shredded
> 1 onion, chopped
> 1 carrot, shredded
> ⅓ of a sweet green pepper, chopped (NOTE: To save
>   time, I run the vegetables through my mixer's shred-
>   der using the coarse blade.)
> ½ cup sugar

4. Pour the cooled dressing over the cabbage mixture and stir well. Chill and serve.

Fried Cabbage

1. Fry half a dozen strips of quality bacon in a large skillet until crispy. Remove the bacon to paper towels. Pour off the excess grease, but do not scrape the pan.
2. Cut one head of cabbage into slices or chunks. Fry the cabbage in the bacon grease till tender-crisp.
3. Crumble the bacon on top of the cabbage and serve.

Cabbage and Apple Skillet

Stir-fry shredded or chopped cabbage in butter or apple juice with chopped or diced apples and a little sliced celery or onion. Leave the apple skins on for added color. For a variation, sprinkle on a little dry mustard powder and top with shredded cheddar cheese.

119

Easy Creamed Cabbage au Gratin

1. Steam fresh or frozen cabbage in quantity desired.
2. In a separate saucepan or small skillet, simmer heavy cream (perhaps 1 cup cream per 4–6 servings) until thickened. Sprinkle with salt and white pepper, or other flavoring, as desired.
3. Combine the cabbage and the thickened cream. Serve hot.
4. Or, top the cabbage with a little shredded cheddar cheese and lightly brown under the broiler or in the oven. Serve.

Easy Baked Cabbage au Gratin

1. Coarsely shred one small head of cabbage. (This can be done quickly and easily using a mixer with a shredder blade or a food processor.) Cook the cabbage until just tender by steaming it or boiling it in water. Drain well and turn out into a casserole dish.
2. Combine and pour over the cabbage:

> 2 eggs, beaten with a fork
> 1 cup milk
> 1/2 cup grated American cheese
> 2 tablespoons butter, melted
> salt and pepper as desired

3. Bake at 350 degrees F for about 30 minutes. Serve hot.

Mom's Easy Cabbage Casserole

Cut up one head of cabbage and steam or boil it. Drain and place the cabbage in a greased casserole dish. Spoon one can of cream of potato soup over the cabbage, directly from the can. Top with sliced or shredded cheese. Bake at 350 degrees F about 20 minutes until cheese is melted and lightly browned. Serve.

CARROTS IN THE GARDEN

Carrots come in many sizes and shapes, from six- to eight-inch-long slender varieties to shorter, thick and tapered or cylindrical roots to really short, round balls the diameter of quarters. Although we usually think of carrots as being orange, they can range from the true yellow of the Sweet Sunshines to the red-orange of Thumbelinas. Early ancestors to today's carrots were even purple!

Carrots are related to parsley (not surprising, considering their foliage) and to the wildflower Queen Anne's Lace (and will develop similar white flowers if they have long enough to grow). They are worth raising in the garden because homegrown carrots are much sweeter and more tender than anything you can buy.

LOCATION: Although carrots are traditionally raised in a vegetable garden, carrot tops are pretty and decorative when grown in beds with flowers. The smaller varieties, like Parmex and Thumbelina, can even be combined with flowers in window boxes or pots.

Crop rotation is a good practice to prevent disease and insects.

GROWING RANGE: Everywhere. They tolerate light frost as well as heat.

SOIL REQUIREMENTS: The ideal soil is light and friable, because heavy soil makes it harder for the carrots to grow and requires digging the carrots at harvest. If your soil is heavy, add peat and sand or plant varieties that are short and stocky. Deep, loose soil is best for the longer varieties. The soil should be free of rocks and hard clods, which cause misshapen carrots. Don't use a high-nitrogen fertilizer, as this causes poor flavor and sometimes makes the roots fork.

MOISTURE: Carrots need even moisture. The seeds won't germinate unless they are kept moist by daily watering. The water should be a gentle spray or mist so you don't wash out the tiny seeds.

The plants need a steady supply of moisture as they grow. Insufficient soil moisture can cause carrots to split, or fork into 2 or more roots. A dry spell followed by a soaking rain can cause mature carrots to crack.

LIGHT: Full sun.

PLANTING SEASON: In the North, up to three weeks before the final frost date in early spring, through late summer or eight to twelve weeks before the first fall frost, depending on your climate and the variety chosen.

In the South, carrots can be planted midwinter through spring and midsummer through fall.

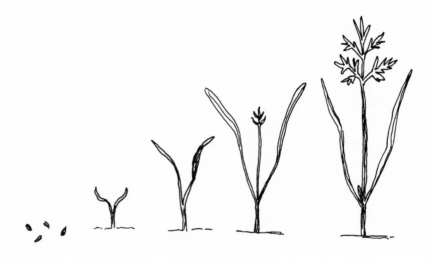

HOW TO PLANT: Carrots are direct-seeded in the garden, usually in rows. Germination is slow, taking one to three weeks.

- Start planting about three weeks before the last frost date, as soon as the ground can be worked and the soil temperature is above 45 degrees F.
- Till the soil deeply to loosen it, mixing in well-rotted manure or compost, if needed.
- Plant the seed a quarter- to a half-inch deep. Since the seed is so fine, sprinkle it in the row about 1 inch apart, and later thin it in stages so that the carrots maintain at least half an inch of space between them as they grow larger.
- The surface soil must be kept moist not only for germination, but also to keep the soil from crusting, preventing the delicate plants from emerging. A thin layer of peat moss, sawdust, or fine sand will help keep the moisture in. Or cover the seeds with black plastic until they sprout.
- Do another planting two or three weeks later to harvest mature carrots over a longer period.

ONGOING CARE:
- **Weeding,** because the young seedlings are unable to compete.
- **Tilling,** to keep weeds down between the rows and to keep the soil loose.
- **Watering,** if rainfall is insufficient throughout the growing season, will keep the carrots sweet and tender. Try to keep the carrots evenly moist because a sudden influx of water can cause older carrots to split, especially after a dry spell.
- **Thinning** the carrots until they are spaced three or four inches apart. Fill the remaining holes with soil. To thin, pull and eat every other carrot. There should never be less than half an inch of space between carrot roots.
- **Covering** the exposed carrot shoulders with soil. If sunlight gets to them, they will turn green and taste bitter. When tilling, you can throw a little dirt into the row, or use a hoe.

VARIETIES INCLUDE:

- **Parmex**, a baby carrot, very small and round and very sweet. They can be easily grown in containers. 50 days.
- **Thumbelina**, which are red-orange, round, and small. They can be harvested when they're the diameter of dimes, quarters, or half-dollars. Also can be grown in containers. They are sweet and tender and are not prone to splitting or cracking. 70 days.
- **Short and Sweet**, which grow about four to five inches long. They don't mind heavy or poor soil. 68 days.
- **Danvers Half Long** are cylindrical rather than tapered, and grow six to seven inches long. They are crisp and sweet. 75 days.
- **Tendersweet**, a long seven-inch carrot that is very sweet and has no core. 75 days.
- **Sweet Sunshine** is a six-and-a-half-inch true yellow carrot that is crisp, tender and juicy. Be sure you have loose, deep soil and steady moisture for this one. 72 days.
- **A#1 Hybrid** gets a whopping twelve inches long, is tender and juicy, and has a small core. 70 days.

YIELD: Carrots can produce up to one pound per foot of row for the longer varieties.

HARVESTING: Carrots can be harvested at any time; they don't have to be mature to be eaten—tender young carrots are delicious. If you start the harvest early, you can plant the carrots a little thicker and then pull every other carrot.

Pull the roots up by grasping their tops near the roots and gently twisting so you don't break off the carrots. If necessary, first loosen the soil with a shovel, being careful not to damage the roots.

Harvest the last of the crop before the first frost, ideally after a rain so that the roots will pull easier.

In warm climates, carrots can be harvested all winter. In colder climates, they can be harvested until the ground freezes. To delay freezing, cover the carrots with square hay bales or mulch.

Give the carrot tops to the hogs—they love them—or lay them in the carrot rows as mulch.

Carrots in the Kitchen

STORING: Carrots keep very well stored raw in the refrigerator crisper drawer. Or you can put them in plastic, but be sure to punch holes in the bag.

- Cut or twist off the tops.
- Don't peel the carrots until using them, if at all.
- Don't store carrots with apples, because apples emit a gas that causes carrots to rot.

FREEZING:
- Tender, young carrots without woody cores freeze the best.
- Wash and scrub the skins and peel, if desired. Slice, dice, or quarter carrots, or you can leave the small ones whole.
- Blanch cut carrots three minutes, whole carrots five minutes. Cool and drain.
- Pack into freezer bags or containers. Seal, label and date, and freeze.

EATING CARROTS

Carrots are wonderful eaten raw or cooked, alone or roasted with meats, or combined with meats or other vegetables in soups, salads, casseroles, and stews.

Because they contain a lot of natural sugar, I often use a little carrot in recipes instead of using refined sugar—for instance, to sweeten tomato sauce or soup—and it gives the dish a subtler flavor.

PREPARING: Scrub the carrots well in cold water and cut off the tops and tips, scrubbing the skins with a soft brush and leaving the skin on for maximum nutrition. Or peel, if desired, using a vegetable peeler. If the shoulders have turned green due to exposure to the sun, just cut them off.

Carrots can be left whole, sliced crosswise or lengthwise, diced, or shredded.

FLAVORING: Carrots go well with: allspice, bay leaves, caraway seed, cinnamon, chives, cloves, curry, ginger, dill, fennel, ginger, mace, marjoram, mint, mustard, nutmeg, oregano, parsley, rosemary, lemon, thyme, parsley, butter, salt and pepper, onions, raisins, cream and cheese sauces.

COOKING: Methods include boiling, steaming, stir-frying, baking, grilling. When serving carrots as a vegetable side dish, don't cook them to mush, which not only ruins the texture and taste, but destroys nutrients.

Homegrown carrots are wonderful raw or cooked. Try steaming them and serve them topped with butter and maybe chopped parsley.

Serving Ideas

- Splash a little cinnamon schnapps over buttered, cooked carrots.
- Pour a little orange juice over the cooked carrots and sprinkle them with curry powder.
- Cream cooked carrots with peas and new potatoes.
- Stir-fry carrot slices with broccoli, cauliflower, onions, etc.
- Season cooked carrots with butter and curry powder and top with toasted chopped cashews.
- Toss together shredded carrots, diced apples, and raisins.
- Try shredded carrots, chopped celery, and diced cucumber.

Carrots with Lemon Cream Sauce

1. Boil or steam sliced carrots till tender-crisp.
2. While the carrots are cooking, simmer 1 cup of heavy cream in a small skillet or saucepan until somewhat thickened. Stir in 3 tablespoons grated cheddar cheese and ⅛ teaspoon white pepper. Add 1 tablespoon lemon juice. (Multiply the sauce recipe, if necessary.)
3. Drain carrots and serve with the sauce poured over them. Garnish with parsley, if desired.

Baked Carrots

1. Clean and cut up eight carrots into strips or cubes. Steam or boil in a little water until tender; drain. Place the carrots in an ovenproof dish.
2. Combine and pour over the carrots:

> ½ cup sour cream or mayonnaise
> ¼ cup water
> 2 tablespoons finely minced onion
> 2 tablespoons prepared horseradish
> salt and pepper, as desired

3. Drizzle a little melted butter over the carrots and lightly sprinkle with paprika.
4. Bake at 375 degrees F for about 30 minutes, or convection bake at 400 degrees F for 10 to 15 minutes, and serve.

CAULIFLOWER
IN THE GARDEN

Mark Twain wrote, "Cauliflower is nothing but cabbage with a college education." He meant that it grows higher and has a more refined flavor, but he also might have been referring to the greater knowledge it takes to raise cauliflower well.

Although cauliflower is in the same family as cabbage, it is not quite as easy to grow. The main reason? Cauliflower prefers weather in the cool 60 degree F range but will tolerate temperatures up to 75 degrees F. Few of us have these conditions long enough for cauliflower to come to full maturity. Yet with just a little extra effort, I managed to have fabulous cauliflower this summer despite record-high heat and humidity. You can, too!

HERE'S HOW:

- Select short-season varieties.
- Transplant seedlings into the garden as early in the spring as is possible. Cauliflower can withstand light frosts of short duration. If necessary, provide protection against prolonged heavy frost by covering the plants with old sweatshirts or blankets, or use inexpensive row covers, or create a cold frame.

- Provide cauliflower with shade protection during the heat of the day. Plant it next to something tall, like corn, or provide it with a shade-cloth-covered frame.

Cauliflower is a bit of a challenge to grow, but if you provide the right conditions, you'll be rewarded with taste treats that are unsurpassed by store-bought varieties.

LOCATION: To prevent insect and disease problems, don't plant cauliflower where any members of the cabbage family have grown for the previous three years: cabbage, cauliflower, Brussels sprouts, broccoli, kale, or kohlrabi. Cauliflower benefits from growing where peas or beans were planted the previous year.

GROWING RANGE: Everywhere, but time planting to avoid extreme heat and cold. Cauliflower is the least cold-hardy of the cabbage family and tolerates light frost best in the fall when the plant is mature.

SOIL REQUIREMENTS: Cauliflower is a heavy feeder, like cabbage, and requires a generous amount of well-rotted manure or fertilizer. It likes rich, loose, well-drained soil with lots of humus.

MOISTURE: Cauliflower needs a consistent level of moisture from germination through harvest. Otherwise, cauliflower heads remain small and develop a bitter taste. And if the weather is also hot, the head might bolt. Water if you don't get one inch of rain per week.

LIGHT: Full sun except in hot weather.

PLANTING SEASON: Time your planting so that the cauliflower will mature during cool weather.

- Transplant seedlings in very early spring so that the cauliflower is mature before the heat of midsummer.
- Plant seeds in early to mid summer, about twelve weeks before the first frost date, for harvest in the fall. This is the easiest way to have successful cauliflower.

- If you have mild winters, you can plant seed in late summer for a winter harvest or late winter for a spring harvest.

HOW TO PLANT:

To grow your own seedlings:

- Start six weeks prior to transplant time in the garden, or six to ten weeks prior to the average last frost date for your area.
- Plant the seeds half an inch deep in peat pots.
- Keep the peat pots evenly moist but not soggy. The seeds will germinate in about one week.
- Keep the indoor temperature cool, not more than 70 degrees F, to prevent the plant from becoming leggy.
- Give the seedlings full sun; if necessary, place them outdoors in a cold frame, especially if indoor temperatures exceed 70 degrees F.
- Prepare the outdoor planting area by tilling it well. Mix in a lot of well-rotted manure, if you have it. If you use a commercial fertilizer, be careful not to use too much.
- Start hardening off the seedlings one week before transplanting in the garden.
- Check the seedlings for a tiny bud in the center of the top growth. This will become the cauliflower head. If you don't see this bud, discard the seedling because you won't have a crop.
- Transplant the seedlings outdoors four weeks prior to the last frost date when they have at least three true leaves in addition to the two original sprouting leaves.

If you're having an early spring, you can transplant them as much as six weeks before the last frost date, but monitor the weather for severe frost warnings.

If you're having a late spring, the seedlings can be planted outside up to two weeks past the frost date. However, this means you should adjust the indoor seed planting time, because the cauliflower won't produce as well if they are much more than six weeks old at transplant.

- Plant the seedlings one or two inches deeper than they were growing indoors, or up to the base of the first leaves. Firm the soil around the roots. Space the plants two feet apart.
- Cover the seedlings before a hard frost, until they are established and can withstand the temperature drop.
- If you have cutworms, place a collar around the young plants. Collars can be cut from paper towel or toilet paper rolls and then slit and slid around the plant stem. Or, use large cans with the tops and bottoms removed. These will also give some frost protection.

To start cauliflower outdoors from seed:

- The soil temperature must be at least 40 degrees F for germination, closer to 60 degrees F is better.
- Make sure the soil is well tilled.
- Plant the seed half an inch deep, placing two or three seeds every two feet, to ensure germination.
- Keep the soil moist, but not soggy. Water daily until the seeds have germinated, if the soil shows signs of drying.
- After the seedlings are up and growing well, thin the seedlings down to one plant every two feet by snipping off the weakest seedlings. Don't pull the culled plants because you'll risk damaging the remaining plant.

ONGOING CARE:
- **Tilling** to keep the soil friable and the weeds down. The roots are shallow, so don't till deeply.

131

- **Watering** regularly—this is very important. It's best done at ground level—overhead watering can cause rotting after tying the leaves for blanching.
- **Weeding** by hand next to the plants.
- **Preventing** worm damage. Cauliflower is subject to the same green worms that attack cabbage, but these are very easily controlled. Use row covers or a spray or powder to control the pests.
- **Blanching** white cauliflower heads to keep them creamy-colored and tender. This is done by clipping the green leaves near the top of the plants together above the head with a clothespin or a twist-tie. Some gardeners just bend the plant leaves over the head, even tucking them underneath the head on the opposite side. The idea is to keep the sun off the head yet allow air circulation to the head. Blanching is done as the white begins to form and the head is about two or three inches across. A week or ten days later, you can harvest the head. Be sure to blanch when the head and leaves are dry so that you don't seal in moisture that can cause rotting or disease. Also, uncover the heads after a rain to allow them to dry out.

NOTE: Having said all this, I must add that I never blanch hybrid cauliflower varieties and have great success. Most of the time my heads stay a nice creamy white, and only occasionally have they started changing color at harvest time. Blanching is more necessary on the older varieties. At worst, unblanched cauliflower will develop a greenish or purplish cast and its flavor won't be as mild and sweet, but its nutrition will be increased. You can also purchase self-blanching varieties, whose leaves cover the head (see the illustration on page 132).

VARIETIES INCLUDE:
NOTE: Only the white headed varieties might need blanching.

- **Farmer's Extra-Early** produces in only 40 days and is extremely heat resistant.
- **First White Hybrid**, maturing in only 50 days.
- **Hybrid Snow King** can withstand heat and produces large, tender, mild-flavored eight-inch heads in 60 days. Recommended in the South.
- **Snow Crown Hybrid** yields two-pound heads, matures early, and develops even in adverse conditions in 60 days. Recommended for the home gardener.
- **Snowball Self-Blanching** develops six- to eight-inch heads and is said to be self-blanching because the leaves curl over the head. They don't require tying to blanch unless the weather is very hot. 72 days.
- **Chartreuse** produce bright green heads that taste better than white-headed cauliflower, but it takes 115 days after transplanting the seedlings.
- **Purple Head** and **Violet Queen** also take a long, cool growing season of 110 days. The purple heads turn green when cooked.

YIELD: Perhaps six heads in a ten-foot row, depending on variety.

HARVESTING: Don't wait until the flower clusters become loose and open (although these are still edible). Cauliflower is ready when it is firm, the florets are tight and close together, and the individual florets have not separated or grown above the head.

Harvest by cutting the head off the stalk. Unlike broccoli, which develops side shoots after the main head is removed, cauliflower produces only the one head. You might as well pull the plant after it's harvested.

If harsh winter weather is on the way, some gardeners dig the immature plants out of the ground, leaving some dirt on the roots, and plant them in five-gallon buckets of moist soil in their unheated garage. The cauliflowers will mature for harvest.

Cauliflower in the Kitchen

STORING: Wrap it in plastic and store it in the refrigerator. Eat it or freeze it fairly soon, as it will get black mildew spots—although these can be shaved off.

FREEZING:
- Select compact heads, which freeze best.
- Cut or break the head into uniform pieces, about one inch in size. Soak in salt water, if necessary, to remove insects. Rinse and drain.
- Blanch cauliflower three minutes. Cool and drain.
- Pack into freezer bags or containers. Seal, label and date, and freeze.

EATING CAULIFLOWER

Cauliflower can be eaten raw, added to salads or relish plates with a dip. Cooked, it makes wonderful soups, casseroles, and stir-fries.

PREPARING: Wash in cold water. Trim off or shave any speckling or bruising on the head. Divide into flowerettes, cut into wedges or bite-sized chunks, chop, or cook whole.

FLAVORING: Cauliflower goes well with caraway seed, celery salt, chives, curry, dill, ginger, mace, nutmeg, savory, thyme, tarragon, parsley, butter, salt and pepper, lemon, cheeses, cream and cheese sauces, salad dressings, and vegetable dips.

COOKING: Methods include steaming, boiling, stir-frying, baking, grilling. Be careful not to overcook cauliflower, as it turns mushy.

NOTE: If boiling the cauliflower, you can add 1 teaspoon of lemon juice to the water to prevent the nice creamy white color from yellowing.

Serving Ideas

- Fresh cauliflower, broken into bite-sized florets, tossed with chopped green pepper, celery, and pimento. Use a vinaigrette or other dressing of choice.
- Fresh cauliflower, chopped carrots, celery, and radishes tossed with prepared Ranch dressing (or dressing of choice).
- Fresh cauliflower, frozen peas, crumbled bacon, shredded cheddar cheese, and prepared buttermilk dressing (or dressing of choice).

Cauliflower with Cheese Sauce

1. Boil or steam cauliflower till tender-crisp.
2. While cooking the cauliflower, simmer 1 cup of heavy cream in a small skillet or saucepan until somewhat thickened. Stir in ¼ cup shredded cheddar cheese and ⅛ teaspoon white pepper. (Multiply the sauce recipe, if necessary.)
3. Serve the drained cauliflower with the sauce poured over it. Garnish with parsley or diced sweet red pepper, if desired.

Cauliflower Frosted with Cheese and Almonds

This is so easy, and looks fancy!

1. Leave the cauliflower whole but cut the leaves and the woody stalk off the head so that it will sit head-up.
2. Cook the whole head of cauliflower in a steamer until tender-crisp. Or, heat water in a saucepan large enough to hold the entire head. Place the cauliflower in the boiling water and reduce the heat to low.
3. Place the cauliflower head in an ovenproof serving dish. Mix together ½ cup sour cream or mayonnaise and 2 teaspoons prepared mustard. Spread over the cauliflower.
4. Sprinkle ¾ cup shredded cheddar or American cheese over the mayonnaise mixture.
5. Stud the cauliflower head with ½ cup slivered almonds, if desired.
6. Bake the cauliflower in a preheated oven at 375 degrees F for about 10 minutes, or until cheese melts. Slice and serve.

Cauliflower Soup

The Farmer loves this soup!

1. Melt 2 tablespoons of butter in a large pan and saute 1 diced onion, 2 or 3 chopped celery ribs, and a minced garlic clove until tender.
2. Cut one large head of cauliflower into chunks and add it to the pan with 6 cups of chicken broth. Bring to a boil, then reduce the heat to a simmer and cook until the cauliflower is soft, perhaps 15 minutes. At the same time, in a medium-sized skillet, simmer 2 cups of cream to thicken.
3. Using a cordless hand blender or a food processor, puree the cauliflower until smooth.
4. Stir some of the cauliflower into the cream then pour the cream into the soup pan. Salt and pepper the soup to taste. Serve garnished with fresh parsley, if desired.

CORN IN THE GARDEN

One of two major crops in our area, corn is grown in vast fields that surround our house. Originally called maize and related to grass, corn was cultivated by the native Americans for centuries. For a long time, many Europeans considered it to be only "pig food," and a family friend who emigrated from Denmark before World War I would never even taste it. Maize was much shorter than corn, and the seeds were borne in a small ball at the top of the plant.

Now our corn has large ears midway up the side of the plant and tassels at the top. The tassels produce an abundance of pollen, which falls down onto the silks, which look like pale yellow hair hanging from the tips of the green shucks covering the undeveloped ear. Each silk is in reality a hollow tube that leads to a single kernel. Pollen travels up this tube to fertilize the kernel. When an ear is missing kernels, it's because something happened to prevent pollination, so those kernels could not develop.

Corn pollen is carried by gravity and the wind, not by bees. If we have a nice gentle rain when the tassels start to release pollen, The Farmer is very happy, because the downpour helps bring the pollen to the ears, ensuring a good crop.

To create hybrids, rows of one type of corn are grown next to a different type. All of the tassels must be hand-removed from the one "female" type so that the silks will receive pollen from the other "male" type—a hot, labor-intensive job that must be done in short order, usually by high school kids who work in crews.

Although we've eaten our field corn, it doesn't taste as good as sweet corn from the garden. Field corn is raised for commercial purposes and for livestock feed, and is high in starch. The Farmer selects his seed from a number of hybrids; some are bred to mature early, others withstand drought or disease or short growing seasons, some have a high amount of lysine, etc. In contrast, sweet corn is bred to be high in sugar content, so that it tastes great to humans. (And raccoons and deer!) Don't underestimate the importance of field corn in your life; it feeds the livestock that give you meat, and it is made into the oils, starches, and corn syrups—to name only a few products—that are found in virtually every processed food and drink. And there are thousands of nonfood uses for corn products, too!

Popcorn has a hard starch in its kernels that explodes when heated, which is different from sweet corn or field corn. The plant is shorter, only four to five feet tall, and the kernels are small and rounded on smaller ears. Sweet corn is usually six or seven feet tall with ears about eight inches long, and field corn is much taller and has longer ears. The popcorn-growing capitol of the world is only a few miles from where we live; companies there supply most of the popcorn that is available in grocery stores.

Besides field corn, sweet corn, and popcorn, you can grow special hybrid baby corn with tiny ears for Oriental recipes, Indian corn with multicolored kernels, and ornamental corn that is raised for its colorful striped foliage. (I planted the latter this year in my walled-in courtyard "secret garden." I chose a short variety, only four or five feet tall, that would have no ears, because I wanted the prominent red-white-and-green striped foliage. But the corn grew to eleven feet, there were no red stripes, only two leaves had faint white stripes, and most stalks developed ears six to eight feet off the ground! Iowa is definitely the "Tall Corn State"!)

There is nothing that can match the goodness of stepping outside your back door to collect the first sweet corn of the season fresh from your own garden, stripping down the crisp green husks, and plunging the golden ears into a boiling kettle, to be eaten off the cobs a few minutes later, slathered with butter. Homegrown corn is a real treat—it's not to be missed!

LOCATION: Try to plant corn in the garden where peas and beans grew the previous year. Never plant corn where corn grew the previous year.

It's recommended that you plant popcorn away from sweet corn and separate the varieties of each by at least 400 feet to discourage cross-pollination, although this won't work if you live in farm country because field pollen can be carried a mile or more on the wind. The best solution might be to time the planting so that different types or varieties are not pollinating at the same time.

If you need to conserve space, consider planting vine crops, like pumpkins or cucumbers, next to the corn, allowing them to spread between the corn plants, or plant pole beans in the rows to grow up the corn stalks. Unless they're being used for support, the corn plants can be cut down after their ears are harvested, if desired. But you might want to leave the stalks to dry to tie together into corn shucks for Halloween and Thanksgiving.

GROWING RANGE: Corn grows everywhere from South and Central America to Canada. Corn is a warm-weather crop and should not be exposed to frost.

SOIL REQUIREMENTS: Corn loves loose, rich, deep, well-drained loamy soil that will still retain moisture, but it will do well in most soils, with amendments. Use lots of well-rotted manure, compost, or a nitrogen fertilizer, as corn is a heavy feeder.

MOISTURE: Must be consistent and plentiful, ideally an inch of rain a week—more in hot climates or sandy soil. Sweet corn needs more moisture to germinate than other types of corn.

LIGHT: Corn needs full sun.

PLANTING SEASON: Most corn can be planted midspring, as soon as the soil can be worked and the ground temperature is above

The Farmer in his tractor

50 degrees F, but sweet corn requires warmer soil, of at least 60 or 65 degrees F, and 75 degrees F is better. Once the growing point is above the soil, sweet corn can be damaged by frost, so don't plant it before the last frost date.

HOW TO PLANT: Sow the seeds directly in the garden.

- To prepare the seed bed, till the soil thoroughly and deeply.
- Make furrows six inches deep and place the corn in the furrow, spacing the seeds six inches apart in rows two and a half to three feet apart.
- Place one fish head over each kernel—just kidding, but this is how the native Americans fertilized their corn long ago!
- Cover the seed with one inch of soil and firm it.
- Water in the furrow, and as the corn plant grows tall enough, gradually fill in the furrow. This way the corn will develop extra roots higher up the stalks, which will better anchor it against wind, and supply the plant with greater quantities of water and nutrients.

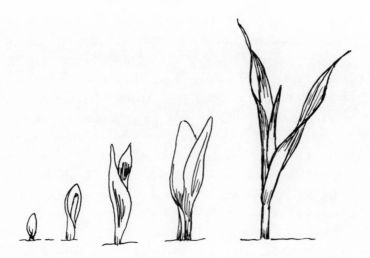

Other pointers:

- Plant blocks of short rows. Pollination is essential and hard to accomplish when corn is planted in a single, long row. Instead, plant at least four shorter rows side by side in a block formation so that the pollen can shower down onto the silks in abundance.
- Plant different varieties with the same maturity dates at least ten days apart to prevent cross-pollination.
- For a continuous harvest, plant the corn in two-week intervals or plant corn with differing maturity dates.

ONGOING CARE:
- **Watering,** in the furrow until it's filled in with soil, then water in the row or, during pollination, use an overhead sprinkler. For good ear development, moisture must be plentiful from the tasseling until harvest.
- **Tilling** between the rows and throwing dirt into the furrows as the corn plants grow, eventually mounding dirt at the base of the plants. Stop tilling about a month after the corn germinates, when the plant becomes large enough that the leaves might be damaged by the tiller. By that time, there will be few weeds and the soil should have become loose and aerated.

- **Thinning** the corn to twelve inches apart if your soil is not rich, fertile, deep loam or if there is risk of insufficient moisture or fertilizer.
- **Discouraging** wild animals, especially raccoon and deer. The biggest threat to the crop is raccoons, who especially love sweet corn. They can smell when it's ripe and will know that it's ready before you do! Many methods have been used by farmers to keep the raccoons away from the corn, including electric fences, ultrasound machines, sprays, whirligigs, live traps, etc. A farm dog will chase them away, although raccoons can be vicious and attack and harm even a large dog. *My very-best-ever solution:* Tie plastic grocery bags to electric fence posts and position them at the ends of every corn row so that the bags hang about three feet off the ground. It works so well, that the only ears I lost this year were eaten by deer the day before I got the bags up (see the illustration on page 44).
- **Pollinating:** If you don't have room to plant your sweet corn in blocks to ensure fertilization, you can hand-pollinate the ears by shaking pollen out of the tassels onto a creased sheet of paper, then tapping the pollen onto the new corn silks while they are soft and yellow. Do this every day for a week.

NOTE: Corn is vulnerable to strong winds, which can knock it down during bad storms. In fact, a large patch of The Farmer's field corn and part of my sweet corn is lying down as of this writing. When this happens, the corn sometimes will rise up on its own; if it's too bad, you might have to gently assist it, or in worst cases, stake it up. Of course, The Farmer doesn't support the wind-damaged corn in his large fields—it would be an impossible task!

SWEET CORN VARIETIES INCLUDE: NOTE: There are hundreds of varieties, so be sure to check on which are most appropriate for your area. Also, the harvest date can vary greatly with your growing conditions.

- **Hybrid Kandy Korn,** a favorite of mine because it has such a sweet "corn" flavor that tastes great fresh and frozen. Can be harvested for at least fourteen days past maturity and still be tender and sweet. 91 days.

- **Indian Summer** has eight-inch ears with an unusual mixture of white, red, yellow, and purple kernels. 79 days.
- **Ruby Queen,** which has eight-inch ears with all red kernels on a seven-foot stalk. It must grown next to Breeder's Bicolor (or a similar hybrid) for pollination. Pretty and delicious. 74 days.
- **Breeder's Bicolor** grow six feet and has white and yellow kernels on eight-inch ears. 73 days.
- **Hybrid Silver Queen** has eight- to nine-inch ears with all-white kernels on eight-foot stalks. 88 days.
- **Hybrid Mini Sweet** produces about forty tiny ears of corn per five-foot-tall plant. These are eaten cob and all, often in stir-fries or pasta dishes. Sometimes they're pickled. Ears start forming when the plant is only twenty inches tall. Harvest spans one month and it begins from the bottom up when the ears are two to three inches long.

POPCORN VARIETIES INCLUDE:

- **Hybrid Gourmet Gold**, which dries quickly and pops well. Also good for caramel corn. Mature in 105 days.
- **Japanese Yellow Hull-less** has no hulls to stick to your teeth. Ready in 110 days.
- **Strawberry Popcorn** has cute, two-inch ears that are dark red and have a rounded shape resembling a strawberry. The short, four-foot stalks produce several ears. Although decorative, the kernels pop just like regular popcorn. 105 days.

YIELD: one or two ears per corn plant, depending on hybrid.

HARVESTING SWEET CORN: Just twist and snap the ear down to break it off of the cornstalk.

Sweet corn is bred to taste sweet, as the name implies, but the sweet flavor can be lost if it's picked too old or left in the sun too long after harvest, because the natural sugar converts into starch. Sweet corn that is harvested too young has small immature kernels that are not yet sweet. Overripe sweet corn is tough and starchy. Sweet corn that is shriveled or has dents in the outer kernels is definitely too old. Mature corn is too hard for human consumption without some sort of processing. The Farmer prefers corn that is on the young side, and I prefer corn that's plump and well ripened, so I cook some of each for our different palates!

One method of estimating the date when the sweet corn ears will be ready to eat is to note the date that the ears start showing silks. About three weeks later, the first ears can be harvested, earlier if the weather is warm. Watch the corn closely, because some varieties are at their best for less than a week.

Tips for determining if sweet corn is ready for harvest:

- The outer silks turn from soft pale yellow to a dry brown.
- The tips of the ears will change from being sharply pointed to rounded and full.
- The ear should feel fat inside the shucks, making them tight to the tips.
- The kernels should be plump and rounded, with no spacing between the rows. To check for this, peel the shucks back a little on the ear to examine them before harvest. If the ear is not yet ripe enough, just replace the shucks and allow the ear to age a few more days before picking it.
- The kernels should be a rich golden yellow (although there are hybrids that are all white or a mixture of white and yellow at maturity and others that are all red or have multicolored kernels that include shades of brown).
- The kernels should be full of milk. If you press your thumbnail into a kernel, a whitish liquid should spurt out. If it's watery, the ear is underripe.
- Don't give up after checking only one ear, because the ears don't reach the peak of ripeness all at the same time.

NOTE: Be sure to take your ears into the house as soon as you can after they're harvested for peak flavor, because they'll start converting sugar to starch immediately. How fast this happens depends on the corn variety. Either eat it, chill it, or freeze it right away.

HARVESTING POPCORN: Pick the popcorn ears off the stalks in fall when the kernels are hard and the stalks and the shucks are paper-dry. If late fall weather stays wet and rainy for a long time, you might want to harvest the ears a little early and lay them out to dry in a single layer in your garage or some warm, low-humidity area. Keep drying it until a sample pops well, then put it in storage.

NOTE: One summer the weather got so hot the popcorn popped right off the stalks in the fields; the cows and pigs thought it was a snow blizzard, so they lay down and froze to death—just kidding! This is a very old tall tale from the early settlers who raised their corn using work horses instead of tractors.

Today our field corn is harvested by machines after the plants have died and turned a light yellow-beige. The ears are hard, dry, and dented, and usually start to hang down from the sides of the plants. The Farmer harvests our fields with a combine, a huge machine that cuts the plants off at the ground and shells the kernels off the cob, depositing the grain in a big hopper and blowing everything else on the ground to become humus. The hopper is emptied at the end of each round into large grain wagons; the wagons are then hauled into town so that the grain can be sold. This is much easier than the old method of harvesting corn, which our fathers and grandfathers had to do by hand, walking through the fields. They wore special gloves with a little metal hook on the palm so that they could break an ear off the stalk, use the hook to pull the shucks off the ear, and toss the ear into a horse-drawn wagon, all in one smooth motion. Handpicking corn was back-breaking work done under pressure because the crop had to be harvested after maturity but before winter set in. It was stored in corn cribs until it was needed, and it still had to be shelled from the cob. The Farmer is grateful that times have changed!

Sweet Corn in the Kitchen

STORING: Sweet corn keeps well if quickly chilled and refrigerated. The ears can be stored in their husks, but I usually refrigerate them in plastic bags after husking.

FREEZING:

- Freeze only mature sweet corn that's not too young (or the milk will freeze sour) or too old (where the corn has dented or turned starchy). It's better to be a little too mature than too young. Certain hybrids freeze better than others; often the extra-sweet types are best.
- Remove husks and silks, and cut off the tips if necessary. (See how below, under "Preparing.")

To freeze corn on the cob:

- Blanch ears that are two inches in diameter for eight minutes, larger ears for ten minutes. Cool and drain.
- Wrap each ear in freezer plastic. Pack ears in large freezer bags.
- Seal, label and date, and freeze.

NOTE: I rarely freeze corn on the cob because it takes up too much freezer space. However, you might want to freeze enough for a family holiday, say, Thanksgiving. To eat frozen corn on the cob, thaw the ears for two hours in their freezer wrapping and then cook them in boiling water for ten minutes, covered with a lid.

To freeze corn kernels, blanching method:

- Blanch the ears five or six minutes, according to size. Cool and drain.

- Cut corn off the cob, taking care not to cut so close as to get any of the cob. This is best done with a small cutting board in a cake pan. If the pan or cutting board shifts, place a clean, damp dishcloth under them. Use a long knife or a special corn-cutting tool with the knife shaped like a ring. After you've cut the corn off each ear, scrape the dull edge of the knife down the ear to collect any milk left on the cob.
- Pack premeasured amounts in freezer bags or containers.
- Seal, label and date, and freeze.

To freeze corn kernels, baking method:

- Cut the kernels off the fresh corn cobs to make about twenty cups. Place the kernels in a large ovenproof pan. (I use a large meat roaster.)
- Top with 1 pound of real butter, cut up.
- Pour over 1 pint of half-and-half
- Bake at 325 degrees F for 1 hour, stirring occasionally. Don't allow the corn to brown.
- Remove the corn from the oven. Stir well. Set the pan in ice water for fifteen minutes.
- Pack the corn into freezer bags or containers. Seal, label and date, and freeze.

EATING SWEET CORN

What is the proper way to eat sweet corn?

Some folks eat lengthwise, three or four rows at a time, following the rows from one end of the ear to the other. Others eat round and round, rotating the ear in a continuous motion from one end to the other.

"City" folks like to use the little handles you insert in each end of the ear, probably because it keeps the butter off their fingers. This doesn't bother real farmfolk, who just keep a napkin handy between eating corn ears to wipe fingers and greasy chins. Farmfolk will concede one advantage to using the handles—it keeps the hot ear from burning your fingers!

August in Iowa means grilled hamburgers topped with homemade pickle slices, a bright-red slab of beefsteak tomato, a thick slice of sweet onion, and rich lettuce leaves, alongside a golden yellow ear of steaming sweet corn—all homegrown. What could be better! Top off the meal with one of my pies from *The Farmer's Wife Guide to Fabulous Fruits and Berries*.

PREPARING: To husk sweet corn, divide the silks and husks at the tip, taking about half in each hand. Hold the ear firmly with one hand, and yank half the husks and silks straight down with the other hand. Repeat with the remaining husks. If some of the shucks didn't rip off, bend them to the base of the ear, and snap them off with the stem end.

The secret to good shucking is to get a good grip on the silks as well as the husks at the top of the ear. If you do this right, you won't have any stray silks to deal with. It takes a little practice. If you're not successful at first, don't worry, you can remove any remaining silks by rubbing a damp washcloth from the tip to the base of the ear, or you can use one of the soft brushes designed for this purpose.

After the corn is husked, farmfolks usually break off the tips of any undeveloped corn—this allows more ears to fit into the pan. Use a paring knife to cut out any bad areas, say where a kernel is darker than the rest, or any area that might have been damaged by bruising or bugs.

FLAVORING: Parsley, pepper, celery seed, chives, chili powder, coriander, curry powder, marjoram, nutmeg, rosemary, sage, savory, tarragon, bacon, onion, salt, celery salt, onion salt, garlic salt, butter, and diced sweet red pepper, which adds flavor and a color accent.

DO NOT follow anyone's advice to add sugar to sweet corn—this ruins the natural flavor!

COOKING: Methods include grilling, boiling, steaming, frying, baking.

What to do with the leftover cooked ears of sweet corn? Refrigerate them and when you have enough for a meal, cut the kernels off the cob and fry them in a little butter. It's great! Or add the kernels to soups, casseroles, or salads.

Roasting Ears

"Roasting ears" is a farmwife term for corn that is simmered in water in a large kettle. This is our all-time favorite method of preparing corn!

I recommend using a large meat-roasting pan because it is oblong and the ears fit in better with little wasted space. Use your largest burner, or have the pan straddle two burners. Fill the roaster just over half full of water and bring the water to a full boil before adding the ears. The ears should be immersed in the water, or be at least half under water. Cover with a lid and bring to a boil again before reducing the heat to a good simmer. Once or twice, remove the lid and use tongs to rotate the ears so that all the kernels have a turn in the water. The corn is ready to serve when it's tender (try pricking a kernel with your paring knife) and when the color has deepened to a rich yellow, perhaps 6 or 7 minutes. Serve with lots of real butter and pass the salt!

Grilled Sweet Corn with the Shucks

Great time-saver when preparing corn for a crowd!

Trim off any dark green "tails" or leaf tips that protrude outward from the husks as these can catch fire. Turn down the shucks but don't tear them from the cob. Remove all the silks and return the shucks upright, smoothing them back around the ear. Place the ears on the preheated grill, turning occasionally, for about 25 minutes or until done. The husks will be dry and browned. The kernels will be steamed inside the husk and there will be no kettle to clean! Serve with salt and butter.

Grilled Sweet Corn on the Cob in Aluminum Foil

The corn is cooked in butter, and there is no cleanup!

Shuck the ears and remove the silks. Lay each ear on a piece of aluminum foil, sprinkle it with salt and pepper if desired, add a generous pat of butter and seal the foil around the corn. Place on the preheated grill, turning occasionally, for about 20 minutes or until done.

Baked Sweet Corn on the Ear

Follow either of the directions for grilled sweet corn, above. Bake at 350 degrees F for 20 or 25 minutes.

Chive Butter

Soften 1 stick of butter, add 1½ tablespoons of finely snipped chives or onion, ¼ teaspoon salt, and ⅛ teaspoon pepper. Spread on corn.

Corn and Cream Cheese

A favorite!

1. Using about 6 or 7 leftover cooked roasting ears, cut the corn off the cob or use frozen corn kernels to equal 3½ to 4 cups. Place the corn in a saucepan and add:

> ¼ cup cream or milk
> 3 ounces of cream cheese
> 1 tablespoon butter
> Salt and pepper, as desired

2. Cook over low heat, stirring constantly, until heated through and the cheese and butter have melted. Do not allow to boil. Serve.

Baked Corn Pudding

Easy and delicious!

1. Cut corn off the cob to make 2½ cups (or use frozen). Place it in a 6-quart casserole dish that has been coated with vegetable spray.
2. Add:

> 3 eggs, beaten with a fork
> 1½ cups heavy cream or half-and-half
> Salt and pepper, as desired
> ¼ cup melted butter

3. Stir ingredients together. Bake at 350 degrees F for 45 minutes or until browned and a knife inserted comes out clean. Serve hot.

Colorful Corn Soup

A very old farm recipe with a new twist!

1. Cut the kernels off of 6 ears of sweet corn to make 3 cups. Be sure to scrape the cobs with a knife to get all the corn milk. Place the corn in a kettle and add 2 cups of water. Simmer until tender.
2. Add ½ of a sweet red pepper, diced, and 6 or 8 thinly sliced green onions, including the tops.
3. Mix 6 tablespoons melted butter with 3 tablespoons of flour. Stir into the corn.
4. Gradually stir in 1 quart of milk. Bring to a boil, reduce heat to medium-low, and simmer the soup for 5 minutes.
5. In a cup, beat the yolks of 2 eggs. Spoon some of the hot soup mixture into the eggs, then slowly pour the egg mixture into the soup and stir well. Salt to taste. Serve.

Corn and Pepper Salad

A good recipe for leftover corn on the cob!

1. Combine:

> 2 to 3 cups cooked corn (cut corn off 5 or 6 cooked ears)
> ½ cup diced sweet green pepper
> ¼ cup diced sweet red pepper
> 1 or 2 jalapeño peppers, diced (optional)
> 1 cup cherry tomatoes, cut in half
> ½ onion, chopped
> ¼ teaspoon salt

2. Top with the dressing recipe for Italian Green Bean Salad, page XXX.
3. Chill at least 2 hours before serving.

Popcorn in the Kitchen

Popcorn was given to us by the native Americans, who poked a stick into the end of the ear and roasted it over the fire until the kernels popped. Another method was to heat a clay pot filled with sand on the fire until it was very hot, then pull it out of the fire and stir kernels of popcorn into the sand. The popping action caused the kernels to jump out of the sand, ready to eat. We now have easier methods to pop corn; see "Cooking" below.

STORING: Shell the corn off the cob and store it in a sealed glass jar or plastic bag at room temperature. Small, inexpensive gadgets for easily stripping the corn from the cob are available.

FREEZING: Place the shelled kernels in a freezer container or bag. Some people think frozen popcorn will pop better.

EATING POPCORN

Popular notion has it that popcorn is not fattening if you leave off the butter and don't pop it in oil. This is not at all true, as popcorn is still a carbohydrate that your insulin converts to body fat. So go ahead and enjoy your homegrown popcorn from time to time—and don't hesitate to use the butter!

PREPARING: The popcorn needs to be well dried in the fall sun. Once dry, prevent the corn from taking on moisture on humid days or from rain by picking it and storing it in sealed containers.

FLAVORING: Season popped corn with grated cheddar or Parmesan cheese, curry powder, salt, garlic salt, onion salt, dried onion soup mix simmered in ½ cup melted butter, rum flavoring, ginger.

COOKING: Methods include using a popcorn popper, the stove, or the microwave.

- **For the popcorn popper,** follow the manufacturer's directions. Some pop the corn with no oil at all, if that is your preference.
- **On the stove,** pour out ¼ cup oil to coat the bottom of a covered pan. Place the pan on a burner on high heat. When 2 kernels tossed into the pan pop readily, it's hot enough. Add about ½ cup popcorn kernels and cover the pan, reducing the heat to medium. Shake the pan as the corn pops. When the popping action slows down, remove the pan from the heat or you risk burnt popcorn.
- **For the microwave,** there are contraptions for popping the shelled corn. Or try popping the corn on the cob and save yourself the trouble of shelling it first. Husk well-dried corn and place the cob in a paper bag. Microwave on high for 3 minutes or until the popping action slows down.

NOTE: For every ¼ to ⅓ cup of kernels, you get about 1 quart of popped corn.

NOTE: If the popcorn no longer pops well, try adding about 2 tablespoons of water per one pound of kernels in a lidded jar. Shake well. Repeat this if the kernels still don't pop well.

Serving Ideas

Popcorn can be a topper for tomato soup, cheese soup, or beer-and-cheese soup.

Elaine's Easy Caramel Popcorn

1. Pop 2 batches of popcorn (15 cups of popped corn or about ⅔ cup of kernels). For cleaning ease, place the popped corn in a brown paper grocery bag with the top edges rolled down halfway. Or, place the popped corn in two large cake pans or other ovenproof containers coated with vegetable spray.

2. Place in a medium saucepan:

> ¼ cup light corn syrup
> ½ cup dark brown sugar, packed
> ½ teaspoon salt (optional)
> I stick butter (½ cup)

3. Bring to a boil and reduce heat to a good simmer. Cook for 4 minutes, stirring once or twice.
4. Remove the syrup mixture from the heat and add ¼ teaspoon baking soda and 1 teaspoon vanilla. The mixture will bubble up.
5. Pour the syrup mixture over the popped popcorn and stir well. Place the popcorn in a preheated 350 degree F oven for 5 or 10 minutes and serve. (Do not allow paper bag to touch heating elements.)

Easy Peanut Butter Popcorn

1. Place 6 cups of popped corn in a large pan. Stir in 1 cup salted dry-roasted peanuts.
2. In a saucepan, mix together ½ cup sugar, ½ cup lightcorn syrup, and ½ cup peanut butter. Bring to a boil.
3. Pour the syrup mixture over the popped corn and blend well. Serve.

Easy Popcorn Balls

1. In a saucepan, combine:

> 2 cups sugar
> I cup light corn syrup
> I cup water
> 3 tablespoons butter

2. Cook on medium heat until the liquid is at the soft crack stage, or it measures 260 degrees F on a candy thermometer.
3. Pour the mixture over 8 cups of popped corn. Mix thoroughly. With buttered hands, shape into balls. Serve.

Easy Cinnamon Popcorn

Melt 1 stick of butter and stir in ½ cup sugar and 1 tablespoon cinnamon. Mix it well into 12 cups of popped corn. Serve.

Colored Popcorn

Combine 1 cup sugar and 1 cup light corn syrup in a saucepan. Bring the mixture to a boil. Stir in one 3 ounce box of gelatin, any flavor or color. Pour over 6 to 8 cups of popped popcorn and mix well. If you use less popped corn, it can be shaped into wreathes, Valentine hearts, etc. Or use more popped corn for a loose corn snack. Combine several colors and flavors for a fun treat.

Popcorn Snack Mix

1. Spread 1 gallon (16 cups) of popped corn in a shallow baking pan.
2. Combine in a saucepan and heat until blended together:

> 1 cup golden raisins
> ½ cup crunchy peanut butter
> ½ cup honey (TIP: Coat the measuring cup with vegetable spray first.)
> 1 cup nuts

3. Pour the mixture over the popped corn. Mix together well.
1. Bake at 350 degrees F for 10 or 15 minutes, stirring twice. Serve.

Mom's Easy Popcorn Bars

These can be flavored with chocolate, butterscotch or peanut butter chips!
1. Place 10 cups of popped corn and 1 cup salted Spanish peanuts in a large bowl. Mix together.
2. Using a double boiler, melt ⅓ cup butter and 4 cups miniature marshmallows. Add one 6-ounce package of chocolate chips, butterscotch chips, or peanut butter chips and stir until melted and well blended.
3. Pour the marshmallow mixture over the popped corn and nuts. Mix well.
4. Turn out the popcorn into a 9 × 13-inch cake pan coated with vegetable spray. Press it evenly in the pan. Chill.
5. To serve, cut the popcorn into bars.

CUCUMBERS
IN THE GARDEN

Cucumbers are fast and easy to grow, and so productive! Like their cousins, the zucchini, they tend to produce more fruit than the average gardener can begin to use!

One summer, my small one-hill vining cucumber patch was enormously productive. I canned 65 quarts of pickles, a friend canned 35 quarts, and several families were constantly supplied with more cucumbers than they could eat—all born on my vines. Finally, I'd had enough, so I decided to tear out the patch. Imagine my astonishment when I discovered that all those cukes had come from one single plant. It must be some kind of record—credit the pig manure!

Cucumbers have quite a history. The Victorians considered bent cucumbers improper, so they placed the developing fruit in glass tubes to force them to grow straight.

Cucumber blossoms are either male or female. The males live only one or two days, then wither and drop off the vine. The female blossoms live three days and can be identified by the bulge behind the flower that becomes the cucumber; they must be fertilized by bees on the first day for the best fruit.

Vines with all female blossoms produce the most harvest, but they need a male for a pollinator; nurseries usually include one in your seed packet.

Seedless hybrids come from self-fertile all-female plants, so they do not need a pollinator. Choose these especially if you live in a high-rise apartment or if the bees in your area have been destroyed by pesticides. These varieties also work well if you're growing the cucumbers under fabric row covers to keep them warm or to protect them from insects, or in greenhouses.

TYPES OF CUCUMBERS:

- **Picklers** produce smaller, crisper cucumbers that have a matte skin covered with little bumps.
- **Slicers** are larger, usually five to eight inches long; have shiny, smooth skins; and are used for eating, both raw and cooked.
- **Dual purpose** varieties can be used for pickles when they are small and for eating when they are larger.

Some cucumbers are better for making pickles (called picklers), others are better for eating fresh (called slicers). Most slicers are long and smooth; picklers are bumpy and blocky in shape and are bred to stay crisper when processed into pickles. It is best to select the type for your chosen use, but there are varieties that will perform both functions if your space is limited. Any cuke can be pickled if used when it's very small.

Picklers and slicers are available on two types of plants:

- **Bush,** which take up only three feet of space, yet produce full-sized cucumbers.
- **Vine,** which can sprawl to cover an area eight or ten feet in diameter.

Most cucumbers are vines, although there are compact vines and even bush forms that take up one third the space of regular vines.

The "burpless" cuke hybrids were developed for people who like cucumbers but find the cukes don't agree with their digestion. These are best as slicers.

Cukes can't cross with other vine plants like melons or squash.

LOCATION: Plant cukes in a new location every year, preferably one where any kind of squash, pumpkins, or melons haven't been grown for two or three years.

Since cucumbers must be planted so late, they could be inter-cropped with cauliflower. By the time the cauliflower heads are harvested and the plants removed, the cucumber vines are ready to inhabit their area.

To conserve space, cucumber vines can be planted to grow on a trel-lis, up three tall poles tied together to make a tripod or teepee, along a rustic fence or up a chain-link fence, or even over your dog's house.

The bush types grow well in containers, as do the vine types if you provide some sort of support.

GROWING RANGE: Everywhere. Cucumbers love hot, dry weath-er so long as their roots get plenty of moisture. They can't tolerate even a slight frost, and they don't like long periods of cool, damp weather.

SOIL REQUIREMENTS: Cucumbers like moist soil with lots of humus, but they hate to be in standing water, so the soil needs to be well drained. They will tolerate most soils if you mix in compost and well-rotted manure or fertilizer and the soil supplies enough moisture to the roots.

MOISTURE: Must be plentiful. Don't allow the roots to go dry; water regularly if you don't get sufficient rain. Cucumbers are mostly water and so they must have a steady supply at their roots to grow well; without it they become bitter.

LIGHT: Cucumbers like at least eight hours of full sun; they can be grown in partial sun, but the yield will be reduced.

PLANTING SEASON: Don't plant cucumbers too early. Wait until after the last frost date and the soil is warmed to at least 60 or, better yet, 70 degrees F, and the night temperature is at least 50 degrees F. To hasten the warming of the soil, lay down black or clear plastic on the bare ground.

If you live in a warm climate, you might want to start your first planting in early spring, a second planting in early summer, and a third planting in early fall, to extend the growing season.

HOW TO PLANT: Cucumbers are best grown from seeds planted outside. Some people start seedlings four weeks before transplant time, but if the seeds are planted outside in warm soil, they'll grow quickly and do better than seedlings, because cucumbers dislike being transplanted.

Growing the vines on a support is a good idea. Not only does it conserve garden space, but it keeps the plants and the cucumbers off the ground. Humidity and moisture encourage diseases and pests, and fences or trellises allow air circulation, preventing the conditions that cause problems. Vines on a support produce more cucumbers, and they'll grow longer. Plus, the cucumbers can be harvested easily!

Either way, with or without support:

- First, thoroughly till the soil for the cucumber patch. Mix in compost and well-rotted manure or fertilizer.
- If you want vine cucumbers to grow on supports, have the supports in place prior to planting.
- Consider burying a perforated plastic milk jug (gallon-size) in the ground near the cucumbers before planting them. Leave two inches of the jug above the soil to make it easy to fill with water.

Planting methods for direct-seeding vine types:

- In rows: Plant the seeds one inch deep and eight to ten inches apart in rows at least six feet apart.

- In hills: Plant three or four seeds in a cluster and space the clusters at least four or five feet apart. Later, thin these down to two or three seedlings per hill, depending on how rich and moist your soil is.

To direct-seed the bush types:

- Plant three or four seeds one inch deep in hills spaced three to four feet apart, depending on variety.

To start from seedlings:

- Start about four weeks before transplant time.
- Use peat pots to minimize root damage at transplant.
- Plant the seeds half an inch deep, two per pot, later snipping off one.
- Keep the seeds evenly moist and warm (above 70 degrees F) and give them full sun.
- Harden the seedlings off one week before transplant.
- Transplant the peat pots into warm ground after the last frost date.
- Protect the seedlings if there is any chance of frost.

ONGOING CARE:

- **Mulching** to keep moisture in the soil and to keep the vines and the cucumbers off of damp soil. Do this after the plants are established, so that the soil is warmed by the sun during germination.
- **Hand weeding** among the plants, if necessary, being careful not to disturb the cucumbers' root system, which is close to the surface. As the plants become established, few weeds will appear and weeding becomes unnecessary.
- **Tilling** around the vines until they spread to cover the entire bed.
- **Watering** at the roots to keep the plant dry, if possible; otherwise, water in the morning so that the plants dry quickly in the sun and won't sit wet overnight. The vines might wilt

160

a little during the heat of the day; keep them well watered.

- **Training** the vines. On the ground, direct the vines in a clockwise spiral to conserve space. If using supports, the vines might need to be tied here and there with something soft, like strips of old pantyhose; when they are about one-third grown, the cucumbers will cling to their support with tendrils that coil, like peas, and will climb six to eight feet.
- **Stepping** carefully when tending the vines, so that the vines, and especially the vine tips, aren't harmed.
- **Staying out** of the cucumbers when the foliage is wet, to avoid transmitting disease.
- **Picking** the cucumbers when they are ready and before they reach maturity. If just one cucumber turns yellow (except for the yellow Lemon variety), the entire plant will stop producing flowers. Keeping up the harvest also discourages insects and disease.
- **Pinching off** the vine tips about two weeks before frost, to send the plant's energy into maturing the existing cucumbers rather than developing new ones.

VARIETIES INCLUDE: NOTE: Some cucumbers bear female flowers only; to have fruit, you'll need to plant another variety close by. Seed companies generally include the male seeds in the packets of otherwise female cucumbers—be sure to plant these specially marked seeds. Only one or two male plants are necessary.

Picklers

- **Hybrid Little Leaf,** a great pickler. The vines are compact and have small, two-inch leaves that make it easy to spot the cucumbers. Produces heavily over a long season, often twenty to thirty 3- to 5-inch cucumbers despite high heat, drought, or cool temperatures. Does not need a pollinator and is disease resistant. 62 days.
- **Hybrid Bush Pickle,** which spread just two and a half to three feet and starts producing four-inch picklers early in the season. The cucumbers have a cool, mild flavor and the

vines are disease resistant. Grows well in containers; the vines can trail or be trellised. Harvest in 45 days.

- **Pickalot Hybrid** is a compact, all-female pickler that gets to four feet. It's ready in 54 days and bears all summer. Disease resistant. The cucumbers are best picked at five and a half inches but are good at any size.

Slicers

- **Bush Champion,** a slicer that, as its name implies, is a compact bush. The cucumbers are large, up to eight inches, and the plants produce vigorously. Harvest in 55 days.
- **Salad Bush Hybrid,** a slicer that has compact vines only twetny-four inches long. Disease resistant, and it grows well in containers and in hanging baskets. Produces a high yield of tender, crisp, dark-green eight-inch cucumbers with smooth skins over a long season. Harvest in 57 days.
- **Sugar Crunch Hybrid,** a slicer with small four-inch cucumbers that are crisp, crunchy, and sweet. Produces in 57 days and yields up to sixty or seventy cucumbers on each compact vine.
- **Hybrid Burpless**, which is billed as the mildest cucumber on the market. Harvest when the fruits are nine to ten inches, but they're still good when larger. The cucumbers are sweet and mild, and the vines are best grown on a support. Takes heat and humidity and produces heavily, up to thirty pounds per plant. 60 days.
- **Lemon,** which produces roundish yellow-skinned cucumbers in 65 days. The fruits are eye-catching when the vines are trained to trellises. The crunchy, extra-sweet slices are attractive in salads. Use them in recipes the same as you would regular slicers.
- **Palace King Hybrid**, an Oriental type of cucumber, grows very long, twelve inches and over, yet stays a slender two inches in diameter. The fruits grow straightest when the vines are trained to a support. 62 days.

Dual Purpose

- **Double Feature Hybrid,** both a slicer and a pickler with high yields. For pickles, harvest fruits when they're under four and a half inches long; for eating, harvest fruits when they're under seven inches in length. The cuke slices have an unusual squarish shape. 50 to 57 days.

HARVESTING: The cucumbers should be firm, well shaped, and bright or dark green, but not yellow. Grasp and twist the cucumber; give it a quick snap and the stem will break. If you can't get the knack of doing this without harming the plants, just cut the cucumbers off the stems.

For pickles, the cucumbers need to be harvested young, green, and small. They should be less than an inch and a half in diameter.

For eating, cucumbers can be harvested when they are bigger, perhaps six or seven inches, even up to twelve inches, depending on the variety planted. Beyond that, give them to the hogs!

Harvest daily, because cucumbers can get too large overnight!

If even a light frost is looming, quickly harvest all the remaining cucumbers, as they will be ruined if left on the vines.

YIELD: Depends on variety. I always get far more than the expected ten fruits per plant on slicing varieties and twenty fruits per plant on picklers.

Cucumbers in the Kitchen

STORING: Refrigerate cucumbers in the crisper drawer. Use them fairly quickly; since they are mostly water, they'll dehydrate and start to shrivel.

FREEZING: Cucumbers don't freeze well; they turn to mush because they are mostly water. The exception is Mom's Very Easy Frozen Pickles recipe, below.

EATING CUCUMBERS

Pickler cucumber varieties are made into all types of pickles. Slicers go well in all kinds of fresh salads, especially in combination with lettuce, tomatoes, peppers, radishes, and any kind of dressing. Sliced cucumbers can be added to sandwiches and made into dip. Many people don't realize that this type can also be cooked.

PREPARING: Wash in cold water. Usually cucumbers are not peeled, which is good because most of the nutrients are found in the skin. Cucumbers can be sliced crosswise or lengthwise, cubed, diced, or even shredded.

FLAVORING: Cucumbers go well with allspice, basil, chives, dill, mint, mustard, tarragon, thyme, bacon, lemon, onion.

COOKING: Methods include frying and steaming.

Serving Ideas

- Thickly cut cucumber slices can be fried 3 or 4 minutes in butter or olive oil.
- Steamed cucumber slices can be served with dilly sour cream.
- Raw cucumber slices can be served with pineapple cubes.
- Raw cucumber cubes can be tossed with shredded cabbage and slivered celery.

Cold Cucumber Soup

Excellent, and so easy!

1. Place in a food processor:

> 1 large cucumber, peeled and seeded (NOTE: Seed a
> cucumber by cutting it in half the long way and
> scraping out the seeds with a spoon.)
> 1 large shallot or about 2 tablespoons minced onion
> 1 cup cottage cheese
> 1/2 cup half-and-half
> 1/4 cup sour cream
> 1/3 cup fresh mint leaves

2. Blend together until smooth and pureed.
3. Chill. Serve in small bowls, laying additional mint leaves on top of the soup, if desired as a garnish.

Hot Cucumber Soup

Wonderful! Even people who don't like cucumbers will enjoy this soup!

1. Cut cucumbers in half the long way. Use a teaspoon to scrape out the seeds. Chop to make 3 cups. Chop 3 ribs celery. (I use a food processor for this.)
2. In a saucepan, melt 1/4 cup butter. Stir in the cucumber and the celery and cook until the cucumbers are very tender.
3. Add 2 cups water and 2 chicken bouillon cubes or 2 teaspoons chicken bouillon granules. Bring to a boil, reduce heat, and simmer on medium about 10 minutes or till celery is soft.
4. Puree the soup with the cordless blender or use a food processor.
5. Combine 2 egg yolks and 1/4 cup heavy cream in a cup and beat well with a fork. Drizzle into the hot cucumber mixture, stirring constantly. Cook and stir until the soup is smooth. Salt to taste. Serve with a dusting of paprika.

Mom's Easy Cucumbers in Mayonnaise

A multigenerational farm recipe!

1. To make dressing, combine:

> 1/2 cup mayonnaise
> 1/4 cup milk
> 1/4 cup sugar
> pinch of celery seed
> pinch of dill seed
> dash of salt, as desired

2. Slice 3 cucumbers, stir in the dressing, and mix well. Refrigerate until chilled. Serve.

Easy Cucumbers in Sour Cream

Excellent! Highly recommended for people who don't like cucumbers with the traditional sugary dressing.

1. Thinly slice one large (6- or 7-inch long) cucumber into a bowl.
2. To make dressing, combine:

> 1/2 cup sour cream
> 1 1/2 tablespoons cider vinegar
> 1 tablespoon snipped chives or minced green onion or
>   shallots
> 3/4 teaspoon salt (or to taste)
> 1/8 teaspoon pepper

3. Pour dressing over the cucumber slices and toss. Chill before serving.

Very Easy Refrigerator Pickles

1. In a large, non-reactive container (I use a quart jar with lid), combine:

> 1 cup sugar
> 1/2 cup vinegar
> 1/2 cup onion, quartered and sliced (optional)
> 1/2 sweet green pepper, chopped (optional)
> 1 1/2 teaspoons pickling salt or plain salt, non–iodized
> 1 teaspoon celery seed (optional)

2. Clean and slice, but do not peel, cucumbers to make 3½ to 4 cups.
3. Put the cucumbers into the liquid solution in the jar, shaking occasionally to coat the cucumbers well. Fill the jar to the top, pressing the cucumbers in so that they are crowded. The cucumbers will shrink in the solution.
4. Store in the refrigerator. These will keep for months. They will be ready to eat the next day.

NOTE: Double this recipe if you are using a half-gallon jar.

NOTE: To easily can other kinds of pickles, buy Mrs. Wage's Pickling Spice Packets. They come in several flavors, including dill, sweet, and kosher. Each packet will season 10 to 12 quarts of pickles. Available from mail-order catalogues, see "Sources."

Mom's Very Easy Frozen Pickles

1. Thinly slice cucumbers to make 2 quarts (8 cups). Mix in 2 tablespoons pickling salt (it's coarser than regular salt and doesn't have iodine). Add 1 chopped onion, if desired. Let this mixture stand 2 hours, then drain.
2. Mix together 1½ cups sugar and ½ cup vinegar. Pour over the cucumbers.
3. Store in the refrigerator or freeze.

EGGPLANT IN
THE GARDEN

Related to tomatoes, peppers, potatoes, and even the deadly weed nightshade, this rather odd vegetable originated in India, where it was grown and eaten for over four thousand years before it got around to the rest of the world. In the Americas, eggplant was first introduced by Thomas Jefferson. The eggplant is a perennial in tropical climates, but it is grown as an annual everywhere else. Naturally, the plant prefers a warm growing season.

Eggplants are a decorative plant, with fruits that range from deep purple to pale lilac shades, from stripes in magenta and ivory to green and white, and there are varieties of perfectly oval, all-white fruits that resemble eggs. Unlike other vegetables, there is little difference in taste between the varieties—eggplant tastes like eggplant. So you can select the types that will do well in your growing area, or that will look pretty in your garden, without regard to flavor.

LOCATION: Don't grow eggplant where tomatoes, peppers, or potatoes have grown for the past three years or where strawberries grew the previous year. Don't plant in a low area where cold air will accumulate.

Although eggplant is usually found in vegetable gardens, the attractive lavender flowers and colorful fruit on plants one to three feet tall could be incorporated into flower beds or landscaping.

Eggplant is also a good container plant, requiring no staking. Grow eggplant in five-gallon dark-colored or black pots to keep the roots warm.

Like tomatoes, eggplants grow well in greenhouses.

GROWING RANGE: Eggplants thrive wherever they can have long, hot summers; they love high heat and humidity and they don't do well in extended cool, damp weather.

SOIL REQUIREMENTS: Sandy, moist, and warm soil is preferable but eggplant tolerates a wide range of soils. Add plenty of compost and well-rotted manure or the same commercial fertilizer as for tomatoes.

MOISTURE: Eggplant needs moderate moisture. Water if you don't get one inch of rain weekly.

LIGHT: Full sun.

PLANTING SEASON: Eggplant is a warm-weather plant that loves hot temperatures and warm soil. It is intolerant of extended weather below 50 degrees F and cannot stand the slightest frost. If the plant is blooming in weather below 60 degrees F, it won't set fruit. However, don't get discouraged. With a few simple techniques, you can grow eggplant even in short-season climates.

HOW TO PLANT: Eggplants can be direct-seeded only in areas with long, hot growing seasons. In less-than-ideal climates, compensate by selecting short-season varieties, transplanting seedlings, warming the soil with black plastic, and/or using row covers.

Growing your own seedlings:

- Start eight to ten weeks prior to transplant time.
- Soak the seed in water overnight.
- Plant the seeds a quarter-inch deep.

- Keep the soil moist and warm, between 80 and 90 degrees F, at least for eight or ten days or until the seedlings sprout leaves. This can be done by using bottom heat.
- Give the seedlings full sun.

Transplanting the seedlings:

- Wait until well after all danger of frost, two or even three weeks past the last frost date for your area, when the day temperatures are in the 70s and the night temperatures are usually above 50 degrees F.
- Till the ground thoroughly to loosen the soil. Mix in well-rotted manure, compost, or commercial fertilizer.
- Laying down black plastic about one week before transplant will warm the soil, and leaving it in place for a while will help get the seedlings off to a good start. In cool climates, the black plastic can be used as a mulch, and you can plant the seedlings in it through slits.
- Harden off the plants one week prior to transplanting.
- Space the plants two and a half to three feet apart in rows two and a half to three feet apart.
- Use cutworm collars, if cutworms are a problem in your area; they should extend one and a half inches into the soil and one and a half inches above the soil.
- Place a one-gallon plastic milk jug with the bottom cut out over each plant as a mini-greenhouse for two weeks after transplanting the seedlings outdoors.

ONGOING CARE:

- **Mulching** (with organic material) isn't necessary, because the roots like to be warm. If you decide to mulch to retain moisture, using black plastic is the best choice. For other mulches, wait until the soil is very warm and the plants are established.
- **Covering** the eggplants with a special fabric designed to increase the warmth to the plants is beneficial if your summer is cool. It will also keep out insect pests.
- **Weeding,** as needed.
- **Tilling,** to allow moisture to penetrate into the soil and for aeration, especially if your soil is heavy.
- **Watering,** as necessary, so that the plants get at least one inch of water weekly; more in dry or very hot areas. Be sure the water gets to the roots if using a black plastic mulch. Adequate moisture is especially critical when the fruit is developing.

- **Staking** the plants if the heavy fruits are too much of a burden for the stalk.
- **Covering** the plants when temperatures dip will prolong the harvest.

VARIETIES INCLUDE:

- **Black Beauty**, the traditional shiny black oblong pear-shaped fruit with pale cream-colored flesh; this is the one you most often see in the store. Tolerates drought. The fruit weighs up to three pounds. 73-85 days.
- **Hybrid Ghostbuster**, which is probably the type that got the plant named eggplant, because with its white skin and oval shape it really looks like a large egg. It's a little sweeter tasting than the black variety, and can be eaten or used as an ornamental. 72 days.

- **Eggplant Millionaire Hybrid**, an Oriental type that has slender fruits up to twelve inches in length that have great flavor and are ready to harvest in 55 days. Excellent for short growing seasons.
- **Eggplant Purple Rain Hybrid** has six-inch oval fruits that are an unusual wine-purple color with creamy white streaks on short eighteen-inch plants. It's almost seedless and it's sweet-flavored. 66 days.
- **Ichiban Hybrid**, an Oriental-type eggplant with long, slender purplish-black fruits one and a half inches wide and ten inches long on tall plants thirty to thirty-six inches in height. A prolific producer. 56 days.

NOTE: Eggplants are self-fertile, so you can grow only one plant of any variety, if desired.

YIELD: Each of the larger varieties usually produces two or three fruits per plant, although four to eight fruits are possible in areas with long, hot summers; the smaller varieties yield more. The Oriental varieties, with longer, thinner fruit, have high yields, sometimes up to forty-five eggplant per plant.

HARVESTING: Remove the fruit from the plant by cutting the stem, leaving the cap and part of the stem on the fruit.

The eggplants' harvest should begin when the fruits are full sized, starting when they're three to five inches long for the best-tasting, most tender results. The flesh should be firm, but not hard. The skin should be glossy, but even so, don't allow the fruit to get too large, because the quality won't be as good.

The eggplant is definitely overripe if the skin is dull, the fruit feels soft, and the seeds inside have turned brown. Overripe eggplants will be tough and bitter, so give them to the hogs!

Eggplant in the Kitchen

STORING EGGPLANT: Eggplant will dehydrate, so refrigerate it wrapped in plastic. It will keep about two weeks.

FREEZING EGGPLANT: Eggplant is not the best freezer, but if you want to try, here's how:

- Select eggplants that are not overmature; they should not be larger than six to nine inches.
- Wash, peel, and cut the eggplant into ⅓-inch slices.
- Blanch four minutes in one gallon of water with ½ cup of lemon juice.
- Cool and drain.
- If you intend to later fry the eggplant, place two pieces of waxed paper or freezer paper between the slices.
- Pack in freezer bags or containers. Seal, label and date, and freeze.

EATING EGGPLANT

Eggplant isn't eaten raw; it must be cooked, usually with strong flavoring, to make it palatable. The flesh is like a sponge; it really soaks up liquids and oils, so when frying it's best to use a nonstick pan or you'll find yourself adding lots of oil, which the eggplant will absorb, becoming heavy or greasy.

PREPARING: Wash the eggplant, cut off the stem, then slice or dice it according to the recipe. If the eggplant is nearly too mature, the skins might be tough and need to be removed. Otherwise, except for purees, leave the skin on, because it contains the largest share of the nutrients.

FLAVORING: Eggplant goes well with basil, curry powder, marjoram, oregano, Italian spice blend, garlic, parsley, Parmesan and mozzarella cheeses, sweet peppers, hot peppers, tomatoes.

COOKING: Methods include grilling, frying, baking, and broiling. Eggplant can be steamed or boiled, but it will taste bland unless combined with something else, like tomatoes and sweet peppers.

Baked or Roasted Eggplant

Just prick the skin here and there and bake the whole fruit at 375 degrees F for 30 minutes. Cool and discard the skin. The flesh can be pureed. If you add plain yogurt, olive oil, and lemon juice, the puree can be served as an appetizer with olives, sweet peppers, and crackers or pita bread.

Fried Eggplant

Very quick and so good!
1. Clean one medium eggplant, 7 or 8 inches long. Cut crosswise into ¼-inch slices.
2. Heat ¼ cup olive oil in a large skillet on medium-high heat.
3. Place 1 cup ground crumbs in a pie tin and add pepper to taste. (Make crumbs by placing pork rinds, soda crackers, or stale bread in a food processor.)
4. Place 1 egg in a second pie tin and whisk until yolk and white are blended.
5. Dip eggplant slices in the egg and then in the crumbs and fry in the heated skillet about 3 minutes, or until the crumbs are browned. Turn slices and fry another 3 minutes until other side is browned. Remove to a paper towel on a serving plate. Serve hot with a dollop of sour cream or plain yogurt, if desired.

Grilled Eggplant

1. Wash eggplant; do not peel it. Cut it lengthwise into 8 wedges.
2. Combine:

1/3 cup olive oil
2 tablespoons tarragon white wine vinegar
I clove garlic, minced
1/4 teaspoon oregano
dash of salt

3. Generously brush the olive oil mixture over the eggplant wedges.
4. Grill the eggplant until tender, turning each piece once. Serve.

Eggplant Dip:

Great with raw vegetables!

1. Wash a fresh eggplant. Prick the skin 4 or 5 times with a paring knife. Bake at 400 degrees F for about 40 minutes. Cool. Remove the skin. Place the eggplant in a food processor.
2. Add:

I onion, skinned and quartered
I clove garlic, skinned
1/4 cup lemon juice
2 tablespoons olive oil
I 1/2 teaspoons salt

3. Puree the mixture in the food processor until smooth. Serve chilled.

Eggplant Salad

1. Wash and peel one medium eggplant and cut it into ¾-inch cubes. Place the cubes in a saucepan with 1 cup water and ½ teaspoon salt. Bring to a boil, reduce heat to a simmer, and cover the saucepan with a lid. Cook about 10 minutes. Drain and cool.
2. Make the dressing by combining:

2 tablespoons white wine vinegar
I clove garlic, minced
1/2 teaspoon dried oregano
1/2 teaspoon salt
1/4 teaspoon pepper

3. Pour the dressing over the eggplant and stir in one chopped tomato and ¼ cup fresh minced parsley and chill for several hours.
4. Right before serving, stir in ¼ cup olive oil.

Baked Eggplant and Tomato Casserole

I usually double this dish for my family!

1. Cut 1 eggplant into chunks. Place it in salted water, cover, and simmer until tender.
2. Drain and mash the eggplant. Stir in:

> 2 tablespoons butter
> 2 large eggs, beaten with a fork
> 1 tablespoon minced onion
> 1/2 teaspoon dried oregano
> 1/4 teaspoon black pepper
> 1/2 cup shredded cheddar or cheddar cheese blend

3. Coat a 1-quart casserole with vegetable spray. Turn the eggplant mixture into the casserole dish. Top with sliced tomatoes and 1/2 cup of shredded cheddar cheese.
4. Bake at 350 degrees F until lightly browned. Serve.

KALE IN THE GARDEN

Kale is another member of the cabbage family, and the plant develops rather stiff, ruffled green or bluish-green leaves but no head. There are also lovely ornamental kales, the "flowering" varieties called "the peacocks of kale," which have eye-catching red, white, or pink centers bordered with green. All kale is edible, but the traditional green kales have the sweetest flavor and are favored for eating. Flowering kale is used primarily as a garnish.

As one of our hardiest vegetables (and one of our most nutritious), kale can be harvested even during winter months, and this highly nutritious plant is exceptionally easy to grow.

LOCATION: To prevent insect and disease problems, don't plant kale where any members of the cabbage family have grown for the previous three years: cabbage, cauliflower, Brussels sprouts, broccoli, kale, or kohlrabi.

Kale can be planted in the garden near taller crops that provide shade during the heat of the day. Kale can also be used as a foliage plant in your landscaping or flower beds, particularly if they are partially shaded.

If your winters are severe, give some thought to a location that might provide the plants with some shelter and be easily accessible for harvest even under snow.

GROWING RANGE: Kale can be grown everywhere, zones 1 to 11. Although it can withstand a lot of heat, it should be grown during the cooler part of the year, because high temperatures make the kale tough and bitter-tasting, especially if the soil is also dry. Kale is one crop that can tolerate a severe frost and weather into the teens (lower if it's under a blanket of snow or mulch), and it can be harvested even during winter.

SOIL REQUIREMENTS: Fertile soil full of humus is ideal, but kale is adaptable even to poor soil so long as it won't be in standing water. Amend your soil by mixing in compost and well-rotted manure.

MOISTURE: Kale likes damp weather. Be sure to keep the seeds moist during germination and the plants watered throughout the entire growing season. Kale withstands drought, but it adversely affects the eating quality.

LIGHT: In hot climates, kale is best grown in semishade; otherwise give it full sun.

PLANTING SEASON: Kale prefers to grow during cool weather, even into winter. Kale can be started in early spring for harvest before the heat of summer.

The best planting time is around midsummer, when the hot weather is beginning to abate, six or more weeks before the first frost. If you want to do only one planting, make it this one because the kale will produce a better crop for a long period.

HOW TO PLANT: You can start seedlings in peat pots six weeks before transplant time, but why bother when the plants are so easily grown direct-seeded in the garden?

About four to six weeks before the last frost date and when soil temperature is at least 40 degrees F, plant seeds half an inch deep and six inches apart in rows two and a half feet apart. Even moisture improves germination.

Later, thin the planting down to one seed every twelve inches.

The prime planting time is in midsummer, or up until six weeks

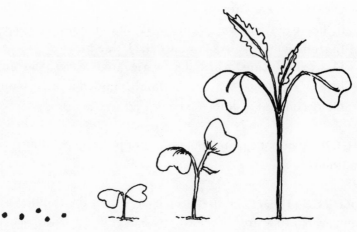

prior to the first frost date. This will allow the plants to have a good start in preparation for winter, and leaves from these plants can be harvested prior to fall.

ONGOING CARE:

- **Tilling** to keep the soil loose and the weeds down.
- **Watering** as needed, during dry weather.
- **Thinning** the row by removing every other plant before their leaves touch. (Eat the thinned plants.)
- **Removing** yellowed leaves and discarding them.
- **Preparing** for severe winter weather: Cover the base of the plant with soil up to the bottom leaves and mulch over the plants after several frosts, if you don't have a protective layer of snow.
- **Pulling back** the mulch in very early spring, to allow new growth if the plants survived winter. Harvest any new growth, then discard the spent plants and start over.

VARIETIES INCLUDE:

- **Dwarf Vates Blue Curled**, which forms compact twelve-inch-tall plants that are an attractive bluish-green. 55 days.
- **Dwarf Blue Curled Scotch**, which has tightly curled blue-green leaves on compact twelve-inch-tall plants that taste mildly pungent. Withstands winter with little protection. 55 days.

- **Dwarf Green Curled** gets fifteen inches tall and thirty inches wide, and has white ribs and yellow-green leaves. Extremely hardy in cold weather. 50 days.
- **Flowering Kale**, which has variegated leaves and grows twelve to fifteen inches tall. Mainly planted as an ornamental although it is edible. 55 days.

YIELD: About one pound of greens per plant, depending on growing conditions.

HARVESTING: The first crop comes from the thinned immature plants, when they are three or four weeks old.

Start eating the lower leaves about eight weeks after the planting date. To harvest, just break or cut off the leaf and its stem.

Frost improves the flavor of kale, making it taste sweeter. For this reason, some gardeners wait until after the first frost to begin the harvest.

For eating kale raw, pick only the young, tender leaves toward the top and center (but don't harm the growing tip). For cooking kale, use the larger outer leaves. Leave on the plant any leaves that have become old, tough, and woody.

In winter, do not harvest more than two or three leaves from each plant at one time. If your winters aren't too harsh, you can continue harvesting green leaves all season. If the plants survive until spring, you can harvest new top growth.

Kale in the Kitchen

STORING KALE: Place the unwashed leaves in plastic bags in the refrigerator. They should be stored dry, and any moisture on the leaves should be blotted.

FREEZING KALE:
- Select tender young leaves without a tough stem.
- Blanch for two minutes.
- Cool and drain. Chop, if desired. (This conserves space.)
- Package in freezer bags, squeezing out all possible air.
- Seal, label and date, and freeze.

EATING KALE

I enjoy eating raw kale, although The Farmer thinks it's too tough to chew, which is why kale is usually cooked in liquid. Undercooked, kale is tough and leathery—but we can't complain, because these qualities enable the kale to survive cold weather. To compensate, kale needs to be well cooked and then it will be tender and delicious. Kale has a rich cabbage flavor that should not be bitter; in fact, kale tastes a bit sweet after a frost.

Kale is used like spinach or Swiss chard (though it stays firm), and it's great in soups, stews, and casseroles. Raw, it's a colorful garnish, or it can be used in salads. Be sure to select only the tender younger leaves for eating raw.

PREPARING: Wash the leaves thoroughly. Fold the leaf in half and cut off the tough stem or lay the leaf flat on the cutting board and make one cut along the steam on each side. After the stems are removed, the leaves are chopped before they are eaten.

FLAVORINGS: curry powder, parsley, butter, olive oil, lemon juice, salt and pepper, bacon, sausage. Kale has been traditionally mixed with mashed potatoes or beans for hearty "peasant" fare.

COOKING: Methods include boiling, steaming, and stir-frying. Be sure to cook it sufficiently to soften the leaves, or they can be tough and chewy. Blanching the kale before cooking it releases the best flavor. After blanching, kale can be substituted in any recipe for spinach or Swiss chard.

To blanch the kale, put the leaves in salted, boiling water for four or five minutes.

Serving Ideas

- Finely chopped fresh kale can be tossed in a vinegar-and-oil dressing and added to a salad.
- Chopped and boiled or steamed kale can be served with melted butter.
- Blanch the kale, then saute it in butter or olive oil. Add diced ham, if desired.

Kale with Bacon and Potatoes

1. Wash and chop the kale. Peel and dice an equal amount of potatoes.
2. Fry several pieces of bacon in a skillet. When crisp, remove the bacon to a paper towel. Pour off excess grease, but do not scrape the pan.
3. Add the kale and the potatoes to the skillet and stir-fry until tender. Toss in the crumbled bacon and serve hot.

Creamed Kale

Remove the tough stems and coarsely chop the kale. Steam it or cook it in a little water. Drain. Meanwhile, simmer cream in a saucepan or skillet until somewhat thickened (use one cup of cream per 4 to 6 servings). Mix the cream and the kale and top with shredded cheddar cheese. Lightly brown the cheese under the broiler, if desired. Can garnish with hard-boiled egg slices, if desired.

Kale and Mashed Potatoes

The Farmer loves this! Multiply the recipe for a family.

1. Clean, quarter, and boil 1 pound of white potatoes till tender.

2. Cut off the stems of fresh kale and chop the leaves finely to make 1½ cups, packed. Place the kale in boiling water and cook until tender.

3. Drain the potatoes and add 2 tablespoons butter and 2 tablespoons milk. Mash together.

4. Drain the kale and add it to the mashed potatoes. Stir together and salt and pepper to taste.

5. Serve hot, topped with a pat of butter, like regular mashed potatoes.

Kale and Potato Soup

1. Separate the stems from the kale leaves.

2. Finely chop the leaves to make 2 cups, tightly packed, and mince the stems to make 1½ cups.

3. Heat 2 tablespoons of olive oil in a large saucepan. Add and cook together:

> 2 cloves garlic, minced
> 1 cup chopped onion
> 1 ½ cups minced stems from the kale leaves.

4. Stir in:

> 1 cup diced potato
> 3 cups chicken stock (or substitute 3 cups water plus 3
>   bouillon cubes)
> ½ teaspoon ground coriander
> 1 bay leaf
> dash of mace

5. Bring the mixture to a boil, then reduce the heat and simmer for 20 minutes.

6. Fish out the bay leaf. Use the hand blender to puree the mixture in the pan or use a food processor.

7. In a large skillet, heat 2 tablespoons of olive oil. Add:

> 4 ounces of chorizo sausage or other seasoned
>   sausage, diced

8. After the sausage is heated and lightly browned, stir in the 2 cups of chopped kale leaves. Stir constantly. When the kale has softened, after 1 or 2 minutes, remove the skillet from the heat.

9. Pour the sausage and kale into the pureed mixture and heat through. Salt, as desired, and serve hot.

KOHLRABI IN THE GARDEN

Although kohlrabi is actually in the cabbage family, it looks a bit like a turnip. Unlike the turnip, which grows in the ground, the kohlrabi stem swells and resembles a pale-green bulb growing an inch or two above the ground, with the leaves rising out of this "bulb."

If you've never tried kohlrabi, you're in for a treat. Its white flesh is crisp like a turnip, but it is much milder, rather like cauliflower, although it's not as sweet. It can be eaten raw or cooked and is very easy to grow.

LOCATION: Kohlrabi is usually planted in rows in the garden. Avoid planting it where any member of the cabbage family grew the previous year: cabbage, Brussels sprouts, kale, cauliflower, broccoli, kohlrabi, or radishes.

GROWING RANGE: Everywhere. Although it likes cool weather, kohlrabi can tolerate heat and some frost.

SOIL REQUIREMENTS: Like many other members of the cabbage family, kohlrabi prefers light rich soil, but it tolerates most soils so long as they hold moisture and have drainage.

MOISTURE: Regular watering is important, if you don't get one inch of rain per week. If the plants get dry for a period, they often develop a strong or bitter taste. If they get rain after being too dry, the sudden influx of moisture can cause the kohlrabi to crack.

LIGHT: Full sun, but kohlrabi tolerates some shade.

PLANTING SEASON: Direct-seed in the garden as soon as the soil can be worked in early spring, four to six weeks prior to the last frost date. Succession-plant seeds at two-week intervals for a continuous crop, or plant a second crop in midsummer for fall harvest.

HOW TO PLANT: Sow the seeds half an inch deep and space them four to six inches apart. The ground should be well tilled before planting.

Although kohlrabi is usually direct-seeded in the garden, I sometimes start a few seedlings indoors to get an early harvest. I transplant them when they are four or five weeks old into the kohlrabi row when I'm planting the seeds.

ONGOING CARE:
- **Watering,** to keep the soil evenly moist. Otherwise kohlrabi will get woody, especially in hot weather.
- **Weeding,** by hand within the rows and close to the rows to protect the shallow roots.
- **Tilling** to keep the soil light and friable.

VARIETIES INCLUDE:

- **Early Purple Vienna,** which has purple skin and whitish green flesh. Very tender and mild-flavored. 60 days.
- **Early White Vienna** has pale green skin and creamy white flesh. Very tender and mild- flavored. Excellent for freezing. 55 days.
- **Hybrid Grand Duke** is ready in only 48 days. The pale green bulbs are mild and slightly sweet, and the texture remains crisp even when the bulbs get large.
- **Kohlrabi Kossak Hybrid** develops bulbs that are eight to ten inches in diameter in 70 days. Since they are so much larger than other varieties, space the plants twelve inches apart.

YIELD: One bulb per plant, twenty bulbs per ten-foot row.

HARVESTING: You can begin the kohlrabi harvest when the bulb is the size of a golf ball, although usually I wait until it's two or three inches in diameter. If you allow kohlrabi to grow past this size, and the weather gets hot, you risk having the vegetable turn woody and hard to chew. With a sudden influx of rain, the larger kohlrabi might split. If the weather stays cool, I've been able to have wonderful kohlrabi four inches in diameter, but normally you can expect kohlrabi this size to be spongy.

The stem is very tough, so I recommend pulling the plant out of the ground and then cutting off the root portion, rather than trying to cut the standing plant, unless you're harvesting young bulbs.

Trim off the outermost leaves, which are the largest and toughest, and leave them in the garden row. The rest of the leaves, as well as the bulbous part of the stem, can be eaten.

Harvest every other plant to allow the remaining kohlrabi more space to grow.

Kohlrabi in the Kitchen

STORING: Kohlrabi keeps well in the refrigerator for a long time, in plastic bags or in the crisper drawer. Eat the leaves first, as they tend to wilt. Although kohlrabi is in the cabbage family, the leaves are much milder and sweeter than cooked cabbage.

FREEZING KOHLRABI:
- Choose tender young stems, which are best for freezing.
- Trim top and bottom, peel and wash. Cut into slices, dices, or, if small, you can freeze the whole kohlrabi.
- Blanch slices two minutes or whole kohlrabi three minutes. Cool and drain.
- Pack in freezer bags or containers. Seal, label and date, and freeze.

FREEZING KOHLRABI LEAVES:
- Follow directions below for preparing kohlrabi leaves, but cut off the stems if they seem tough.
- Blanch two minutes. Cool and drain.
- Pack in freezer bags or containers. Seal, label and date, and freeze.

EATING KOHLRABI LEAVES

Cut the leaves and stems off the bulbous kohlrabi, perhaps discarding the lowest leaves if they are tough. Rinse the leaves in cold water and inspect them. Cook them whole or cut them up. Steam or boil in a little water till bright green and tender. Drain and stir in a pat of butter. Lightly salt, if desired.

EATING KOHLRABI

PREPARING: Peel the kohlrabi, taking just the thinnest amount of skin. Then cut it into strips, dice, or other desired shapes.

COOKING: Kohlrabi can be steamed or boiled in a little water. Since it's a rather dense vegetable, boiling is my recommendation. Dot with butter and lightly salt, if desired.

FLAVORING: Parsley, butter, garlic, ginger, chili, mustard seed, salt and pepper, onion, Parmesan and other cheeses.

Raw Kohlrabi

Serve the strips on a relish plate, to be eaten as finger food. Great as is, or provide a dip. Kohlrabi is delicious on all kinds of vegetable salads.

Kohlrabi Hash Browns

Kohlrabi can be shredded and fried in a little butter or oil. Serve with salt and pepper, as desired. This is a good use for kohlrabi that isn't quite as young and tender.

Creamed Kohlrabi

Excellent!

1. Wash, peel and cut the kohlrabi into $\frac{1}{2}$-inch cubes to make 5 cups.
2. Cover and cook the diced kohlrabi in water until tender. Drain.
3. Stir the following into the kohlrabi:

> 2 tablespoons butter
> 1 tablespoon lemon juice
> dash of tabasco
> 1 $\frac{1}{2}$ tablespoons dry dill weed
> $\frac{3}{4}$ teaspoon salt
> $\frac{1}{8}$ teaspoon pepper
> 1 cup heavy cream

4. Bring the uncovered kohlrabi mixture to a boil, then reduce the heat to a simmer. Remove it from the heat when the cream has thickened somewhat.
5. Pour the kohlrabi into an ovenproof pan and sprinkle on 2 or 3 tablespoons grated Parmesan cheese and $\frac{1}{3}$ or $\frac{1}{2}$ cup shredded Swiss cheese.

6. Place the kohlrabi under the broiler just until the cheeses lightly brown.
7. Serve hot.

NOTE: To save effort, cook the kohlrabi in a pan that will go from the stove to the oven.

Kohlrabi Soup

The Farmer loves this one!

1. In a large saucepan, heat a little olive oil and stir in 1 clove minced garlic and 1 cup coarsely chopped onion. Cook until the onion is golden. Add a sprig of fresh parsley and ¼ teaspoon dried basil (both optional).
2. Reserve the leaves from 2 or 3 kohlrabi (also optional). Dice or julienne the kohlrabi to make 2½ or 3 cups. Dice or julienne 2 carrots.
3. Add the kohlrabi and the carrots to the saucepan, reserving the kohlrabi leaves. Pour in 4 cups chicken broth (or use water and 4 chicken bouillon cubes). Bring to a boil and simmer for 10 minutes or until the kohlrabi is tender.
4. Quarter the kohlrabi leaves and stir into the soup (optional). Simmer it an additional 3 minutes. Salt as desired. Serve.

Easy Kohlrabi and Cheese

1. Peel, slice, and cook 6 kohlrabi in a small amount of boiling water till tender. Drain.
2. In another pan, melt 2 tablespoons butter and stir in 1 cup sour cream, ¼ cup milk, and 1 cup shredded American or cheddar cheese. Heat through until cheese melts and stir until smooth.
3. Combine the kohlrabi and the cheese sauce. Sprinkle with chopped green onion, if desired. Serve.

LETTUCE IN THE GARDEN

What a diet staple, and it's so fast and easy to grow! Lettuce varieties number in the hundreds, or maybe even the thousands. The leaves come not only in different shapes, but also in many different colors and textures, from pale yellow-green to red-violet to dark purplish green. There is nothing you can buy that compares in taste—and nutritional value—to homegrown lettuce.

TYPES OF LETTUCE:

- **Leaf lettuce** doesn't develop a head, and loose leaves are harvested. It gives the quickest harvest, usually in forty to fifty days, and it can tolerate some heat. The leaves can be smooth or frilly, and can be light green, dark green, red, or brown in color. Highly recommended for the home garden because it's quick and easy to grow, and also because it has a lot of nutrition.
- **Butterhead lettuce** forms a loose, soft head that is smooth and buttery and with rounded leaves that are darker green toward the outside and pale yellow or whitish green on the inside. It requires fertile soil and a steady temperature in the cool 60-degree-F range without much fluctuation. It's the best-tasting lettuce, but it's also more fragile and perishable than other types of head lettuce, which is why it's not common in stores.

190

- **Romaine,** sometimes called cos lettuce, is a tall upright plant with smooth, dark green outer leaves loosely over-lapped around the developing lighter-colored inner leaves. The long leaves are held erect by rigid midribs that are crunchy and juicy. Romaine tastes best when it matures during cool weather.
- **Crisphead** varieties form a dense head, like the familiar whitish green iceburg lettuce you can buy in any grocery store. It takes the longest growth period of all lettuces, usually sixty to eighty days before it's ready to harvest. Not recommended for the home gardener.

LOCATION: Plant lettuce where it wasn't growing the year before. I always plant light-green leaf lettuce next to a row of green onions for the contrast in color and texture (and also because they're both planted in early spring).

The traditional Farmer's Wife plants lettuce in rows in her vegetable garden, but it looks great growing in flower beds, too. The leaf type grows well in window boxes or in containers on a balcony or deck, and I've even grown it successfully through winter in pots in my living room.

Many gardeners with limited space interplant lettuce with other, slower-growing crops because the lettuce is up and eaten and gone before the other plants need the space.

GROWING RANGE: Everywhere. Lettuce prefers to grow in temperatures in the 60 degree F range. Romaine and crisphead types need a long, cool growing season; leaf lettuce takes the shortest season, and butterhead types are in between. If you live in a hot, dry climate, grow the lettuce in the cooler winter months or give it partial shade and grow heat-resistant varieties. Otherwise, lettuce is great in the spring or fall.

SOIL REQUIREMENTS: Lettuce grows in any soil that stays moist but is also well-drained so that water doesn't pool. Work in lots of well-rotted manure or compost. Don't use too much commercial fertilizer, if any; a better choice would be fish emulsion. Excess nitrogen can make lettuce taste bitter, even when it's grown in cool weather and had adequate moisture.

MOISTURE: The roots of lettuce are not large, and the plants need a constant, steady supply of moisture for the best taste and tender leaves. Water weekly if you haven't received at least one inch of rain. Early-morning watering reduces the chance for disease. Direct the water to the roots rather than the tops.

LIGHT: Lettuce likes full sun but can tolerate partial shade because it keeps the plant cooler in warm climates.

PLANTING SEASON: Early spring, so that the crop can mature and be harvested before the heat of summer. Start a second crop in midsummer for a fall harvest. Lettuce can survive a light frost, but it dies in a hard frost. Hot weather causes it to bolt and taste bitter, especially if it's also dry.

HOW TO PLANT: Leaf lettuce can be direct-seeded everywhere, and butterhead can be direct-seeded in most areas, but if your cool growing season is short, you can try starting romaine and crisphead types from seedlings.

To have a continuous supply of lettuce, plant a third of a row in succession every two weeks starting in early spring. Start a second row in mid- to late summer, also planting a third of the row in succession

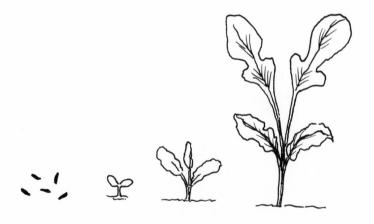

every two weeks to stretch out the harvest season. NOTE: Lettuce seed does not germinate well in hot soil; provide some shade or else plant the lettuce near taller plants.

Although it's risky, I start the first planting of lettuce as soon as the ground can be worked and the soil is above freezing, as much as eight weeks before the last frost date. Sometimes you'll lose this crop to frost, but the seed is inexpensive, and when you do get a crop it's wonderful! To play it safe, you might want to wait until four weeks before the last frost, or even two weeks before the last frost. You can use row covers for protection against heavy frost in early spring, and again in late fall, if desired.

Direct-seeding leaf lettuce in the garden:

- A five-foot row is sufficient for a small family, for each planting.
- Plant in early spring, as soon as the soil reaches 35 degrees F.
- Plant the seeds a quarter-inch deep and about one inch apart.
- Space the rows thirty inches apart, although you can make them as narrow as fourteen inches if your space is really limited.
- Keep the row evenly moist, using a fine mist to prevent washing out the fine seeds. If necessary, cover the row with black plastic or a quarter-inch layer of peat moss to preserve moisture.
- If desired, do additional plantings every two weeks, until eight weeks before hot weather.

To grow lettuce seedlings indoors:

- Plant the seeds three to six weeks before transplant time, a quarter-inch deep in peat pots.
- Give them bright light, but not hot temperatures.
- Harden the seedlings outdoors for one week before transplant time.
- Transplant the seedlings into the garden when they are at least three inches tall, from six weeks before the last frost date to three weeks after the last frost date in your area, when night temperatures stay above 25 degrees F.
- Cover the transplants if a heavy frost is on the way.

- Space head lettuce twelve to sixteen inches apart each way or in rows two and a half feet apart.

ONGOING CARE:

- **Thinning** the lettuce by pulling up every other plant and eating the thinnings. Do this several times until the remaining plants are three to six inches apart. (Although some experts recommend spacing leaf lettuce nine inches apart, most gardeners have it four to six inches apart. Since lettuce roots are small and my soil is fertile, I space mine about three inches apart with great success.)
- **Tilling** to keep weeds down and the soil loose and able to accept moisture. Set the blades to shallow depth and take care near the lettuce row.
- **Harvesting** the lettuce regularly, to encourage new growth and to keep the plants from going to seed.
- **Covering** the plants with a black mesh shade screen during the hottest days of summer to keep the plants from bolting.
- **Covering** the plants with plastic tunnels will extend the growing season into the winter, and the lettuce can survive to 10 degrees F without using a heater.

VARIETIES INCLUDE:

Leaf lettuce

- **Black-Seeded Simpson**, a farmer's wife's favorite! Large, light green, frilly leaves are sweet, crisp, and tender on plants nine inches tall and wide. It can tolerate some summer heat and drought and keeps well in the refrigerator. Harvest in about 45 days.
- **Simpson Elite** is similar to the Black-Seeded Simpson but can be harvested a month longer without tasting bitter. 48 days.
- **Salad Bowl** is sweet and tender, heat resistant, and slow to bolt. The bright green leaves taste great, although I don't like to clean this variety because the leaves have deep lobes. 45 days.

- **Red Sails** has slightly ruffled bronze-red leaves and is slow to bolt. 40 days.
- **Royal Red** has intense red leaves that are attractive in salads and in flower beds. 50 days.
- **Green Ice** has bright-green, fringed, ruffled leaves that are sweet and crisp. Slow to bolt. 45 days.
- **Prizehead** has light green leaves edged in red ruffles. 45 days.

Butterhead

- Bibb, one of my very favorites because it is so sweet. It forms small heads that remain soft, but it takes 75 days, which means you must get them planted in very early spring to harvest before the heat of summer. I sometimes harvest them before maturity to beat the heat.
- Buttercrunch, which has sweet, buttery leaves that are somewhat heat resistant, is ready in 65 days. The outer leaf is bright green; the heart of the small, loose head is pale yellow. A favorite!
- Sweet Red has leaves that are burgundy red on the outer edges, which fades to green and then to creamy green near the center. 54 days.

Romaine

- Parris Island gets ten inches tall and has dark leaves with mild flavor. 75 days.
- Paris White Cos is also ten inches tall. 70 days.
- Giant Caesar gets a tall sixteen inches and has the texture of a butterhead. 70 days.
- Little Caesar gets eleven to twelve inches tall in 70 days.

Crisphead

- Ithaca, which has glossy, frilly leaves and forms five-inch medium-green heads. Fairly heat tolerant and recommended for warmer climates. 75 to 85 days.

195

- Burgundy Ice, which has burgundy outer leaves with crisp light green inner leaves. Forms a small- to medium-sized head. 77 days.
- Summertime is a compact variety that produces a crisp ice-burg-type head that stays sweet even in hot weather. 70 to 75 days. If you want to try head lettuce, this is the one.

YIELD: Varies widely depending on type, variety, and growing conditions.

HARVESTING:
- Leaf lettuce: the harvest can be started any time. You can either break off the outer leaves or you can cut off a length of the lettuce row about one and a half inches above the ground—I recommend the latter. Either way, the plants will grow new leaves in fairly short order. Leaf lettuce benefits from regular harvest, which encourages tender new growth and discourages the plant from bolting (going to seed). If the plant grows leaves along a tall stalk, it is getting ready to bloom and the leaves will taste bitter—discard these plants.
- Head lettuce: Cut it off at the ground. The root will die.

Lettuce in the Kitchen

STORING LETTUCE:
- Loose-leaf lettuce stores well in the crisper drawer of the refrigerator for at least three or four days—longer if it's cleaned and wrapped as described.
- Head lettuce keeps best if the leaves are left attached to the core until needed. See below.
- Store torn leaves in the refrigerator covered with a damp cloth or paper toweling.

FREEZING LETTUCE: Not recommended.

EATING LETTUCE

Lettuce is added to many sandwiches, and it's the basis for numerous salads. But it can also be served wilted, or made into soups, or just shredded and floated on top of soups as a garnish. Or make appetizers by stuffing and rolling up lettuce leaves with mixtures of cream cheese, chopped onion, diced vegetables, herbs, and even nuts.

PREPARATION:

Cleaning leaf lettuce by hand

Like generations of farmwives before me, I pour cold water into my kitchen sink and dump in a big armload of freshly cut lettuce leaves. After a hasty swish and inspection of each leaf, the leaves are laid out on a large terry towel beside the sink. They can be allowed to partially air dry, or gently pat the tops with another terry towel. Mound the clean leaves on a large cotton or linen tea towel, wrap them up, and place them in a large plastic bag in the vegetable drawer in the refrigerator. Do not close the plastic bag.

A few hours later, the lettuce will come out of the refrigerator nice and crisp. This method is preferred if you're feeding a large group or when you want enough lettuce for several days' use, say, when a heavy rain is coming and you know you won't be able to get into the garden for a few days. It will store well for a week, sometimes longer, depending on the variety you planted.

Cleaning leaf lettuce with a salad spinner

To prepare enough for up to three or four salads, inspect the leaves, removing any bad spots. Place the leaves inside the spinner. Fill the spinner with water, swish with your hands, drain, and spin dry. Or, if you have one of the newer designs that rinses and swishes in one operation, follow the instructions with your unit. Pull the string or push the knob to make the basket go round, thus spinning away the moisture. Works great!

Head lettuce is prepared the same as leaf lettuce. First remove the tougher outermost leaves. Peel off the number of leaves needed, rinse, and dry. Wrap a barely damp paper towel around the rest of the head and place in a plastic bag in the refrigerator.

Cut or tear?

If you are eating the lettuce right away, it's okay to cut it up with a knife. But if you refrigerate it for later use, knife cuts will turn brown unless you use one of the specially designed plastic knives. Otherwise, tear the lettuce by hand and it can be stored without turning brown.

You can tear up lettuce prior to a dinner party, place it in a bowl, and refrigerate it covered with a damp—but not dripping—cloth. Farmwives always use cotton tea towels for this purpose, but several paper towels will work also.

When to add the dressing?

- To keep the lettuce leaves from becoming soggy, add the dressing just before serving.
- When using oil and vinegar or oil and fresh lemon juice for a dressing, toss the leaves with the oil first, then sprinkle with the vinegar or lemon juice.

FLAVORING: Lettuce goes well with many seasonings, including basil, chives, dill, tarragon, parsley.

COOKING: With a few exceptions (see below), lettuce is not cooked.

Cream of Lettuce Soup

Quick and easy!
1. Melt 2 tablespoons of butter in a large saucepan and stir in ½ cup chopped onion. Cook until the onion is tender.
2. Stir in 4 cups of torn-up leaf lettuce that is firmly packed. Reduce heat to low and cover the lettuce with a lid for 3 or 4 minutes, until it's wilted.
3. Add 1 tablespoon instant chicken bouillon, 1 cup of milk, and 1 cup of cream. Raise the heat to medium and simmer together, stirring constantly, until milk is somewhat thickened. Turn off the burner, but leave the pan on it.
4. Add ¼ teaspoon salt and ¹⁄₁₆ teaspoon pepper, or to taste.
5. Using a cordless blender right in the saucepan, blend the soup until it is smooth or use a food processor.
6. Serve the soup hot. If desired, garnish with additional shredded lettuce, parsley, or mint leaves.

Lettuce Stir-Fry

In a large skillet, stir-fry a little minced garlic and the same amount of minced gingerroot. Quickly add torn lettuce, stirring constantly, removing the pan from the heat as soon as the lettuce is wilted. To serve, sprinkle soy sauce and sesame seeds on top.

OKRA IN THE GARDEN

It's easy to see that okra is related to hibiscus and hollyhocks when you look at their lovely pale yellow flowers with red centers. The flowers develop into erect seedpods, and these are the part that is eaten while they are still green and immature. Dwarf plants get about two feet tall, standard sized plants get four to seven feet tall, and some varieties in the South grow to ten or twelve feet tall. The more compact plants are stiffly upright with a lovely canopy of dark green leaves. A warm-weather crop, this vegetable has been traditionally grown in the South where many other vegetables fizzle out during the hot summers.

LOCATION: Don't plant okra where it grew the previous year.

Okra can be added to the landscaping; in hot climates, the taller varieties can serve as a hedge. The foliage on the shorter, compact okra varieties would make a stunning addition to a flower bed; unfortunately, the lovely flowers are hidden.

GROWING RANGE: Zones 4 to 11, or where okra can have at least ten weeks of warm weather. Okra doesn't like cool, damp, cloudy climates, and it is very susceptible to frost damage.

SOIL REQUIREMENTS: Most soils will work so long as they are well drained. Till in a lot of well-rotted manure or compost before planting, or use a fish emulsion every three weeks or another commercial fertilizer after a few seedpods have formed. Avoid using too much nitrogen or you'll get more leaves and fewer flowers.

MOISTURE: Okra likes to be somewhat dry. Water if there is insufficient rain. Too much moisture favors leaf development over pod development.

LIGHT: Full sun.

PLANTING SEASON: In the South, okra can be planted in early spring and again in midsummer. In the North, it needs to be started indoors and transplanted after all risk of frost is over.

HOW TO PLANT:
To direct-seed outdoors:

- Start when the temperature is at least 60 degrees F by day and 50 degrees F at night.
- Till the soil well and mix in lots of well-rotted manure.
- If desired, heat the soil with black plastic before and after planting.
- Soak the seeds overnight or else lightly sand them with sandpaper or an emery board.
- Plant the seeds a half-inch to an inch inch deep, spacing the seeds one foot apart in rows two and a half to four feet apart, depending on the size of the variety chosen.
- Thin seedlings to two or three feet apart, if growing a taller variety.

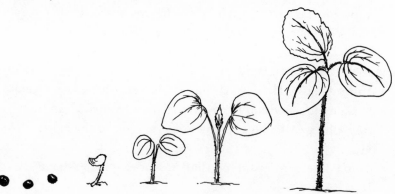

To start your own seedlings:

- Plant the seeds indoors four weeks before the last frost date.
- Keep the pots warm, 80 degrees F is ideal, and away from cold drafts.
- Harden the seedlings off one week before transplanting time.
- Transplant the seedlings after all danger of frost is past.
- Space plants fifteen to eighteen inches apart in two-and-a-half- to three-foot rows.

ONGOING CARE: NOTE: Whenever you are working around okra plants, you might want to wear long sleeves and gloves. Some people have a reaction to the prickly hairs on the leaves that's like rubbing against spun fiberglass. To avoid this, plant Clemson Spineless, which doesn't have the hairs.

- **Mulching** is not necessary.
- **Tilling** to keep the soil loose, with the blades on the shallow setting.
- **Watering** as needed when the soil becomes dry, but do not overwater.
- **Weeding** as needed.
- **Harvesting** the okra regularly, to get them before they're too large and to stimulate the plant to keep producing till frost.
- **Cutting** the plants back about one-third or even more in midsummer will control the height and stimulate a second crop—do this only if you live in the South and have a very long growing season. Water well after pruning.

VARIETIES INCLUDE:
- **Annie Oakley II**, a dwarf that produces a high yield of tender, spineless pods on three- to four-foot plants. It can tolerate cooler weather, making it a good choice for the North. 48 days.
- **Dwarf Lee** is a bush type that produces spineless pods. 53 days.

- **Clemson Spineless** grows into a five-foot bush with smooth pods and is less likely to cause skin reactions. Good for both short seasons and areas with hot summers. The first harvest starts in about 55 days.
- **Clemson Spineless 80** grows to four feet tall and is extremely productive. The pods are straight and spineless. 56 days.
- **Baby Bubba Hybrid** grows only two to three feet tall and is suitable for containers or flower beds. Very productive. 53 days.
- **Cajun Delight** produces an abundance of tender dark green pods that are less fibrous. 49 days.
- **Dwarf Green Long Pod** has seven- to eight-inch dark green pods on plants that only get two and a half to three feet tall. 50 days.

YIELD: Perhaps one pound or more per plant, depending on the variety and the length of the growing season.

HARVESTING: The harvest begins when the plants are about two months old and the pods are about two to three inches long. Okra pods grow vertically with the stem at the base; to harvest, bend the pod outward, away from the plant, and cut it off at the stem with nippers. Take great care not to knock off other blossoms. Check the plants daily as the okra pods quickly grow too large and too fibrous to eat.

Okra in the Kitchen

STORING OKRA: Place the pods in a perforated plastic bag in the refrigerator without washing them first. Use within a day or two or freeze until you need them as the okra will get tough in storage.

FREEZING OKRA:

- Select tender, young pods, which freeze best.
- Wash and cut off the stem end, taking care not to cut into the seed cavity.
- Blanch three minutes if pods are under four inches in length, five minutes if pods are longer. Cool and drain.
- Pack in freezer bags or containers. Seal, label and date, and freeze.

NOTE: The pods are frozen whole, but they can be sliced while frozen to be added to soups and stews, as needed.

EATING OKRA

Sliced okra is often added to soups, stews, and tomato sauces not only for the added flavor, but also because the liquid inside okra is a natural thickening agent.

Very young okra (two inches long or less) is delicious eaten raw, perhaps with a light sprinkle of salt.

PREPARING: Rinse okra in cool water. Although it's not necessary, you can cut off the stem end, taking care not to cut into the seed cavity so the juices won't leak out and water won't get inside during cooking. The stems are edible if left on.

If the pods are fuzzy, they can be scrubbed with a brush or scraped with a knife.

Okra can be cooked whole or cut crosswise into slices.

FLAVORING: Chili powder, curry powder, garlic, mustard, oregano, bacon, onion, pimiento, butter, and lemon juice.

COOKING: Methods include steaming, boiling, frying.

Serving Ideas

- Fry okra for 1 or 2 minutes in a hot skillet with a little olive oil and a minced garlic clove plus a chopped hot pepper, if desired.

- Add okra slices to omelettes and quiches along with tomatoes.
- Deep-fry the whole okra after they've been boiled about eight minutes and dried with a paper towel.

Grilled Okra

Thread okra crosswise onto two skewers and brush them lightly with olive oil. Place the okra over medium heat, turning once, until the exterior darkens and blisters. Serve hot.

Boiled Okra

Simmer okra in a covered saucepan until tender. Drain and season with butter and salt and pepper, if desired.

Okra Salad

Just marinate the boiled okra, above, in a prepared vinaigrette dressing or use the dressing in the Italian Green Bean Salad recipe on page 83.

Okra with Lemon Butter

Delicious!
1. Clean whole okra, selecting pods under 3 or 4 inches in length. Place them in a large skillet with ¼ inch of water. Bring the water barely to a boil, then reduce the heat to a simmer. Add the juice of half a lemon to the water. Cook until the okra is tender. Do not overcook.
2. Melt butter and squeeze in the juice from the other half lemon. Stir together and drizzle the butter over the drained okra. Serve with salt and pepper, if desired.

Okra with Chili Sauce Dip

This dip is also great with grilled okra.
1. Boil okra in salted water until tender. Serve warm, cool, or chilled.

2. To make sauce, combine:

> 1/2 cup mayonnaise
> 2 tablespoons prepared chili sauce or catsup or Unketchup
> 1 tablespoon Worcestershire sauce
> one or two dashes of hot pepper sauce

3. Serve okra on an appetizer plate with the bowl of sauce for dipping.

Fried Breaded Okra

The Farmer's favorite!

1. Leave the okra whole or cut the okra in half lengthwise.
2. Heat 1/4 cup of butter or olive oil in a skillet on medium high heat.
3. Place ground crumbs in a pie tin and add pepper to taste. (Make crumbs by placing pork rinds or soda crackers or stale bread in a food processor.)
4. Place 1 egg in a bowl and whisk until yolk and white are blended.
5. Carefully dip the okra in the egg and then in the crumbs and fry in the heated skillet about 5 minutes, or until the crumbs are browned on all sides. Serve hot immediately. (Discard any unused egg.)

Okra and Tomatoes

1. Saute one chopped onion in 2 tablespoons olive oil in a skillet till golden brown.
2. Add 1 1/2 cups chopped tomatoes and 1/2 teaspoon cumin. Bring to a boil.
3. Add 3 or 4 cups of okra slices and salt, if desired.
4. Simmer for 20 minutes or until okra is tender. Serve.

Okra with Corn and Tomatoes

1. Cook 2 cups of sliced okra in 1/2 cup butter on medium heat in a large skillet until tender, 6 or 7 minutes.
2. Cut the kernels off of 6 ears of sweet corn. Add the corn to the okra and cook another 10 minutes.
3. Stir in 3 diced tomatoes and cook another 2 minutes. Serve.

ONIONS IN THE GARDEN

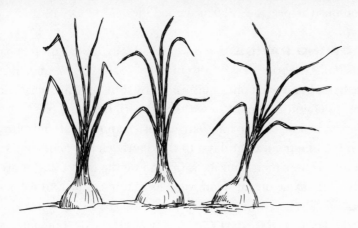

A nice row of onions looks so perky and cheerful in the garden, and I love the contrast of the tall, spiky, dark green tops next to a row of rounded, ruffly chartreuse leaf lettuce. Onions emerge from the ground as quickly as radishes, but soon surpass them in height, and they are the first new garden crop visible from a distance. They can be harvested early and I run to the garden for fresh onions for nearly every meal from late spring through fall. For this reason, you might consider planting them near the kitchen.

But onions don't have to be planted in rows. How about growing an oval or kidney-shaped onion bed in your landscaping along with California poppies? Just scatter the poppy seed on top of the soil after you've set out the onions, for a lovely splash of color. The poppies decorate the onions as they are maturing, and remain after they're harvested, so that there is no gap in the bed.

This relative of the lily has been in use for centuries around the world to season all sorts of dishes. And onions are very easy to grow— every gardener should have some!

LOCATION: Onions are traditionally grown in rows in the vegetable garden, but they can be incorporated into landscaping or flower beds. If garden space is at a premium, mix onions in with other crops, because they take little space, and if used as green onions, they are harvested in a few weeks' time. Onions are sometimes interplanted with other crops to repel insects.

Rotating the onions rows so that they don't grow where you planted onions the previous year is a good idea.

GROWING RANGE: Everywhere. Ideally, onions prefer to grow in cool, moist weather, especially in their early stages, and like hotter weather when developing mature bulbs. But they are very adaptable to other conditions and can withstand both heat and frost.

In the North, choose long-day varieties appropriate for our fifteen- or sixteen-hour summer days. In the South, choose short-day varieties suitable for fourteen-hour days. Or choose the newer day-neutral varieties. Get advice on this from your local nursery or Extension office.

SOIL REQUIREMENTS: Any well-drained—but not dry—soil. Add well-rotted manure, and if your soil is heavy, work in compost. If your soil might be too soggy, mix in sand or used raised beds. Till thoroughly so the soil is fine and loose.

Using commercial fertilizer with too much nitrogen results in lots of top growth at the expense of bulb size and thicker necks on mature onions, which won't keep as long into winter.

MOISTURE: The secret to great onions is that they have a continuous supply of moisture, because they are made mostly of water. Dry conditions slow down the growth of the bulb and makes the onion strong-flavored and less tender. Onions don't like to be in soggy soil or standing water.

LIGHT: Full sun.

PLANTING SEASON: Onions can be planted outside in the spring as soon as the soil can be worked, and they are able to withstand light frost. In warm climates, fall planting produces a winter harvest. Either way, starting the onions in cooler weather is desirable. Onions like to grow their tops in cool weather, and their bulbs in warm weather.

HOW TO PLANT ONIONS: Onions can be started from seed, from sets, or from plants. Starting from seeds takes the longest growing time, and these onions can be susceptible to disease. Starting onions from plants results in the largest bulbs. But I recommend that you start from sets, which is the quickest, easiest—and most popular—way to grow onions, and they rarely get disease. The best sets are actually the smaller ones, a half-inch or so in diameter. Our local store sells red, yellow, and white onion sets by the pound; you scoop the quantity desired out of bins or barrels into paper sacks.

NOTE: Although I prefer wide spacing between rows, if you have limited space, you can make the rows closer or wider, or do mass-planted rows or beds, spacing the onions six inches in all directions. Don't make the beds so deep that you can't easily reach to the center; one or two feet is a nice width for wide row planting; four or five feet should be the maximum for beds.

Prepare the seed bed by tilling it thoroughly and deeply and mixing in well-rotted manure or compost.

If you want a continuous supply of green onions, succession-plant the sets every two weeks.

Seed grows into onion plants. Direct-seed the onion seed outside, or start the seeds indoors to grow your own plants for transplanting outdoors in early spring. Be patient, it can take two or three weeks for germination.

- Outside: Plant the seed a quarter- to a half-inch deep and-half an inch apart in two-and-a-half-foot rows, four to six weeks before the last frost date or when the soil temperature is at least 45 degrees F. In warm climates, sow the seed

209

in the fall for winter harvest. Most seeds direct-sown out-doors will require 90 to 130 days, some as much as 170 days, before harvest.

- Or start the seedlings indoors eight or ten weeks before transplant time. Using flower pots or trays, scatter the seeds thickly, then cover them with a quarter-inch of soil. Keep the soil evenly moist to aid germination. The tops will look like grass. If the tops grow too tall, trim them back to four inches and eat the trimmings—this won't harm the plant.
- Harden off the plants by exposing them to cold, but above-freezing, night temperatures for a week.
- Transplant the seedlings outside by following the directions for onion plants below.

Sets are tiny dormant onion bulbs that will grow roots and tops after they are planted.

If you want both green and mature onions, sort the bulbs by size into large and small. Use the large bulbs for growing green onions and plant the smaller bulbs (yes, the smaller bulbs—this is not a typo) for growing mature onions. The reason is that the larger bulbs are more likely to go to seed when growing mature onions.

NOTE: Most gardeners plant white onion sets when growing them for green onions.

- Start planting the sets from six weeks before the last frost date to two weeks after.
- For green onions, plant the bulbs two to three inches deep and one to two inches apart with the root end down. (The deeper planting produces more white edible stems.)
- For large mature onions (sometimes called dry onions or storage onions), push the bulbs into the well-tilled soil so that the root end is down and the bulb is barely covered in the soil. Space the bulbs four inches apart or much closer if you plan to harvest them continuously and thin them in the process.
- Use a misting setting to water the bulbs well after planting them, so you don't disturb the bulbs.

Plants have roots and tops and are transplanted into your garden. They will produce the largest mature onions.

- Transplant the onions outdoors from six weeks before to two weeks after the last frost date.
- The soil should be well tilled, loose, and free of clumps— loose soil is essential.
- Place the plants in a shallow container of water for a few hours before planting.
- For green onions, place the plants two or three inches deep and one half to one inch apart. If you like, punch planting holes with a dibble, although this is unnecessary if the soil has been well tilled.
- For large mature onions, push the plants into the ground, root-end down, so that the bulb portion is just covered. Space the plants four to five inches apart to get the largest bulb.
- Firm the soil with your hands, so that the plants don't topple.
- Water the plants with the mist setting until they are established so that you don't wash them out of the soil. Don't allow the plants to dry out.

HOW TO PLANT SHALLOTS: Shallots are small, rather like green onions, but they form in bunches, like cloves. The flavor is mild and delicious, and they are often used as seasoning in gourmet recipes. They are expensive to buy, yet easy to grow. Although they are a different species of the onion family, they are grown similar to onions.

Shallots grow bulblets in clusters; these should be separated and planted individually. You can start your shallots by using those purchased for eating from your grocery store or by buying them from a nursery or seed catalogue.

- Shallots should be planted as early as the soil can be worked in the spring. Or in warm climates, they can be fall-planted for winter harvest.
- The soil should be well tilled and loose.

- Press each shallot clove with the root ends down so that they are barely in the ground.
- Space the bulbs three to five inches apart in rows two and a half feet apart or closer if you want to conserve space. Be sure to plant them separate from your onions so that you don't confuse the two.
- The planted shallot will grow into a cluster with eight or twelve bulblets.
- Ongoing care, harvest, and storage is the same as for onions, although shallots mature earlier than onions. Shallots can be eaten at any point in their growth. Their tops can be cut at soil level and eaten, and this will actually stimulate bulb production.
- You can save some of your harvest, particularly the smaller bulbs, to plant in the next season.

ONGOING CARE:

- **Watering,** to keep the bulbs evenly moist. Quit watering in the fall when the tops have died down.
- **Thinning** and eating the onions by pulling every other one. They can grow close together but should not be touching each other.
- **Tilling** to keep the soil loose and the weeds down between the rows. Set the tiller blade to the shallow depth.
- **Weeding,** as necessary.
- **Removing** seed heads, if the tops should bloom, to direct the plant's energy into forming the bulb. It would be well to select that onion for eating.

VARIETIES INCLUDE:

- **Red Hamburger** is a big sweet red onion that has a short day length of twelve hours and is appropriate for the South. 75 to 95 days.
- **White Bermuda** is extra early and mild and is a short day type. 185 days.
- **Yellow Granex** is a short day variety that is grown and sold as "Vidalia." It develops thick, flattened bulbs that are very mild and sweet. 182 days.

- **Texas Grano** is a short day, extra-large yellow sweet onion that is heat and drought tolerant and it stores well. 168 days.
- **Hybrid Southern Belle** is a sweet and mild short day variety that is slow to bolt. 130 days.
- **Hybrid Candy** is a day-neutral sweet onion that grows well everywhere. The bulbs get large and store well. 85 days.
- **Super Star Hybrid** is a day-neutral white onion that is mild and sweet and very large; it grows everywhere. 105 days.
- **Sweet Sandwich** needs longer day lengths of thirteen to sixteen hours and is better grown in the North. When mature, these onions store well. 105 days.
- **Walla Walla** is a large, round, sweet, white onion with flattened bulbs. A short-keeper. Best in the North. 90-115 days.
- **Hybrid First Edition** is a brown long-day onion that stores exceptionally well. 105 days.
- **White Sweet Spanish** is mild and sweet with medium-to-large bulbs. It grows best in the North and West. 110 days.
- **Yellow Sweet Spanish** is a long-day variety that produces extra-large bulbs that store well. 110 days.

NOTE: Check with your local nursery or Extension office for recommendations for your area. Day length and other considerations might affect the varieties recommended.

YIELD: Around seven pounds of mature onions per ten-foot row, depending on your growing conditions.

HARVESTING: Shallots can be harvested green and eaten with the tops, or mature; treat them the same as onions.

Green onions are harvested very young, starting when they are only six inches tall, and are usually eaten with the tender tops. As the season progresses, they will grow into medium-sized onions that can be harvested at any time or at the mature stage.

Mature onions and shallots are harvested when the tops fall over and the bulb has ripened.

To ripen: If the tops are yellowing but haven't fallen over on their own, you can bend them over (but don't break them off) to hasten the ripening process before winter sets in; then leave them in the ground for a couple weeks to develop a tougher skin for storage. The bulbs should be half exposed in the row; if not, pull away some of the soil. Properly ripened onions store better and longer and so do onions that ripen closer to winter.

To cure: The bulbs should be spread out thinly to dry for two or three weeks before storage. Some gardeners dry them in the sun, but you risk sun scald and you've also got to monitor the weather so that they don't get wet or frozen. I find it's better to put them inside in a cool, dark, and dry place. You can cut the tops off, leaving at least 1 inch on the bulb, if desired, or you can leave them on (my preference). After the onions are dry, you can rub off the dirt and the loose papery skin. If desired, make an onion braid. Properly cured onions keep longer in storage.

To make an onion braid, tie twine or cord into a circle. Twist the bottom up to form a double loop and thread the tops of one onion through both loops as the bottom anchor. Then wrap the onion tops twice around the cord and slide it down. When it's time to use an onion, remove it from the cord by cutting the tops.

NOTE: A former art teacher, I used to save the skins from yellow onions. When boiled, they make a lovely yellow dye that can be used on fabrics, hand-spun wool yarns, and even to dye Easter eggs!

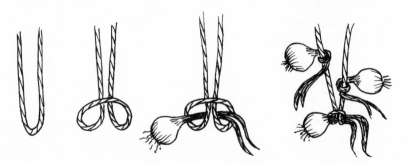

Onions in the Kitchen

STORING: Green onions should be stored in the refrigerator right away. They can be placed in plastic bags or containers. Farm folks sometimes clean a handful and store them bulb-side down in a cup with a little water to keep them crisp and hydrated until serving them as a finger food with salt for supper.

Mature onions and shallots, once mature and dried, store well at room temperature or slightly cooler, with the ideal being dry air in temperatures between 35 to 50 degrees F.

Place the bulbs in mesh bags or use baskets or other containers that allow air circulation, or make an onion braid as described above—never store onions in sealed containers unless they are refrigerated.

When using the onions, select the bulbs with the thickest necks first, as they are less likely to keep as long as onions with thin necks.

The milder and sweeter the onion, the less time it will keep at room temperature. If you can't use fresh sweet onions in a week or two, store them in the refrigerator in a tightly sealed glass jar or other vapor-resistant container.

STORAGE PROBLEMS: Too much moisture will cause the onions to grow roots, and too much heat will eventually cause the bulbs to grow tops; either will cause the bulbs to deteriorate.

Sprouting in storage can also be due to harvesting immature bulbs (not letting the tops die back and leaving them in the ground for two weeks) or to improper curing. Directions for ripening and curing are found above in "Harvesting."

FREEZING: Don't freeze green onions unless they are chopped. Pack into containers, seal, label and date, and freeze.

You can freeze mature onions, but they store so well in their natural state, why bother?

To freeze mature onions:

- Clean onions and peel off outer layers, if tough or dry.
- Leave whole, slice, or dice as desired.
- Blanch onions for three to seven minutes, depending on the size, until tender.
- Be sure to package them well, double- or even triple-bagging them in heavy freezer bags, or use bags as well as a freezer container, to prevent the odor from affecting other frozen foods.
- Seal, label and date, and freeze.
- Even with careful packaging, do not place onions in the freezer next to foods such as fruits.

EATING ONIONS

Raw or cooked, there aren't many soup, salad, or main course recipes that don't include some form of onion. Their flavor depends not only on the variety you plant, but also on your soil and growing conditions.

PREPARING: Remove the outer, dry layer of skin and cut off the tops and the roots. Use whole, sliced, diced, or chopped.

To easily peel small onions, boil them in water for about one minute, then quickly plunge them into cold water. The outer skin will now be loose and it can be easily slid right off, especially if you trim off just a bit of the root end.

PREPARING ONIONS WITHOUT TEARS: Do onions make you cry? I have a terrible problem with this and have tried everything.

Here are my very best solutions:

- Chilled onions are less troublesome to sensitive eyes than room-temperature onions. Keep a tightly lidded glass or plastic container in the refrigerator for storing a few unpeeled onions.
- Remove the chilled onions and peel them at the sink under a trickle of cool running water. Return any unused, peeled onion to the fridge in a clean glass jar with a tight sealing lid for later use. This method really cuts down on the tearing, although it doesn't entirely eliminate it. I recommend this when you're doing only a small amount of mild onion.
- Or peel, cut, and chop onions on the stovetop in front of a down-draft exhaust fan on high speed. It works great every time! (Don't attempt to do this if you have an overhead exhaust fan, because the fumes will be drawn right past your eyes, which is what you want to avoid.) This method is wonderful when doing a large batch of pungent onions!

FLAVORING: Onions go well with allspice, bay leaf, cinnamon, cardamom, coriander, caraway seed, chili powder, cloves, ginger, marjoram, mustard, nutmeg, oregano, parsley, sage, thyme, salt and pepper, bacon, brandy, and wine.

COOKING: Methods include boiling, broiling, stuffing, baking, creaming, steaming, frying, roasting.

Green Onion Appetizers

An old farmer's method of eating young green onions was to cut off the roots and remove the outer skin layer, and place them in water standing upright in a cup or other straight-sided container. They would be chilled in the refrigerator before serving. To eat them, sprinkle salt on a plate and dip the white ends in the salt, eating the onion and most of the green tops.

Skillet Onions

Sliced onions cooked in a generous amount of butter or olive oil in an open skillet are just wonderful. They can be served when their color is anywhere from a light golden brown to a deep rich brown—the longer you cook them, the better they get! Fabulous when served with a steak or hamburger. Be sure to use the down-draft exhaust fan if the onion fumes bother your eyes.

Skillet Onions on the Grill

Cook the Skillet Onions, above, on the grill in a heavy cast-iron skillet with a generous amount of butter or olive oil—this can be done at the same time you're grilling the meat, and you don't have to worry about the fumes.

Fried Breaded Onions

Very quick and so good!
1. Peel onions and cut crosswise into ⅜-inch slices.
2. Heat ¼ cup olive oil in a large skillet on medium-high heat.
3. Place 1 cup ground pork rinds in a pie tin and add pepper to taste. (Make crumbs by placing pork rinds or soda crackers or stale bread in a food processor.)
4. Place 1 egg in a second pie tin and whisk until yolk and white are blended.
5. Carefully dip onion slices in the egg and then in the crumbs and fry in the heated skillet about 3 minutes, or until the crumbs are browned. Turn slices and fry another 3 minutes until the other side is browned. Serve hot with a dollop of sour cream or plain yogurt, if desired. (Discard any unused egg or breading.)

NOTE: Try a combination skillet by using this recipe with breaded and fried tomatoes and onions alongside zucchini. Wonderful!

Quick and Easy Creamed Onions

1. Select small or medium-sized onions. Cover and simmer the peeled whole onions until tender when pricked with a paring knife.
2. While the onions are simmering, in a separate pan, gently simmer 1 cup or more of heavy whipping cream on low heat, without stirring—it will thicken by itself.
3. Drain the water from the onions and combine with the thickened cream. Salt and pepper to taste, and serve. Wonderful!

Onions Baked in Wine and Butter

Excellent!
1. Peel 6 medium onions and cut a thin slice off the root end and the top. Place close together in a casserole. Or, to speed up cooking time, cut the onions into quarters or eighths.
2. Melt ¼ cup butter. Add ½ cup water and ½ cup dry white wine. Stir in 1 teaspoon instant beef granules until dissolved. Pour over the onions. Sprinkle with minced parsley (optional).
3. Tightly cover the casserole and bake in an oven at 350 degrees F until onions are tender, perhaps 1½ hours for the whole onions, perhaps 50 minutes for the quartered onions. Serve hot.

PARSNIPS IN THE GARDEN

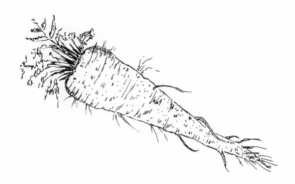

Parsnips are related to parsley, carrots, and celery and they are very easy to grow. They look like a giant, white carrot, with lots of top foliage and long, thick, tapering, crisp roots. Unlike carrots, parsnips are not eaten raw, as they have a coarser texture. When cooked, the texture becomes more like that of potatoes, but parsnips have a delicate, sweet, almost nutty flavor that gets better if they are harvested after frost. They are the only vegetable crop to survive overwintering in the frozen ground without mulch, even in the coldest areas, and it can actually be harvested early the next spring, tasting better than ever!

LOCATION: Place the parsnips where they can grow undisturbed for months, and where neither carrots nor parsnips grew the previous year.

GROWING RANGE: Everywhere in the United States and most of Canada. They're especially suited for areas where they can mature in cool weather. The flavor is improved if they can experience a hard freeze before harvest.

SOIL REQUIREMENTS: Parsnips need soil that's well drained yet able to hold moisture; it should be loose and deeply tilled, as parsnip roots can go two down feet. Any soil can be used if you mix in lots of compost. Too much nitrogen in commercial fertilizers results in forked roots.

MOISTURE: Water often until the plants are established, then only during prolonged dry spells. Parsnips will split if they get an influx of water after a drought.

LIGHT: Full sun to part shade.

PLANTING SEASON: Very early spring for short growing seasons, because parsnips need a long growing season of at least four or five months. For warm climates, parsnips should be planted in the fall for a winter crop.

HOW TO PLANT: Direct-seed outdoors. Transplanting is not recommended because it causes the root to fork.

- Be sure to buy fresh seed each year; older seed loses its viability.
- Plant spring parsnips in the East and the North two or three weeks before the last frost date; plant fall parsnips in the West and the South.
- Prepare the planting bed by tilling it thoroughly and deeply, adding plenty of rotted manure or compost to provide nutrients, and especially to make the soil loose and airy for the roots to penetrate easily.
- Soak the seeds in warm water for at least twenty-four hours to improve germination.
- Start when the soil temperature is at least 36 degrees F, although germination is best between 50 and 70 degrees F.

- Plant the seeds half an inch deep and one inch apart in two-and-a-half-foot rows, although the rows could be as close as eighteen inches to conserve garden space. Cover the seeds with fine soil or use sand or even peat, because the tender shoots have difficulty breaking through coarse, crusted dirt.
- Or plant the parsnips in wide rows and later thin so that each plant is spaced four to six inches in all directions.
- Water the seed well; keep it moist for at least three to four weeks because germination can take that long.
- If desired, cover the row with black or clear plastic until germination occurs, to warm the soil and keep the moisture in. Do not allow the soil to dry out at this time.
- When the seedlings have three leaves, thin the plants so that they're spaced six inches apart.

ONGOING CARE:

- **Tilling,** to keep the soil loose.
- **Covering** the parsnips' shoulders with soil, if they become exposed.
- **Covering** the row with at least twelve inches of mulch after a hard fall frost, for winter harvest.
- **Removing** any parsnips that are one year old. They can be eaten after overwintering in the ground if they have not resprouted.

VARIETIES INCLUDE:

- **All American**, a ten- to twelve-inch parsnip with three-inch-wide shoulders. It has sweet, fine-textured, tender, white flesh with a small core. 95 to 125 days.
- **Harris Early Model** has sweet, smooth, fine-grained roots without cores. 110 to 120 days.
- **Hollow Crown** prefers loose, airy soil. Twelve-inch-long roots with three-inch shoulders, sweet and nutty flavor after frost. 95 to 105 days.
- **Premium** develops shorter roots, so it's a good choice in shallow soil. 80 to 110 days.

YIELD: One root per seed, two roots per foot of garden row; or about eight pounds of roots from a ten-foot row.

HARVESTING: In areas without hard frosts, start the harvest two or three weeks after having the near-freezing temperatures of winter.

In other areas, wait to start the harvest after a hard frost, which will increase the sugar content for a sweeter flavor.

If heavily mulched, perhaps by covering the row with straw or hay bales, parsnips can be harvested all winter.

Even if the ground freezes, you can still dig the parsnips during a winter thaw. Or, harvest the parsnips very early the following spring before they sprout—which is actually the peak time for harvest because they'll taste their very best. After sprouting, the roots lose their flavor and become limp, tough, and stringy because they put their energy into growing the tops.

Parsnips in the Kitchen

STORING PARSNIPS: The roots can be kept in the refrigerator for a couple of weeks in a plastic bag. Parsnips can be stored right in the garden and harvested as needed, or they can be dug and stored in a root cellar or other cool place.

FREEZING PARSNIPS:
- Use firm roots, free from woodiness, or else remove the core.
- Remove the tops and scrub the parsnips well. Peel and slice, dice, or cut as desired.
- Steam or blanch for three minutes. Cool and Drain.
- Pack in freezer bags or containers. Seal, label and date, and freeze.

EATING PARSNIPS

PREPARING: Remove the top and bottom of the root, scrub the skin or peel it. If the root is wide, the core might be tough—if so, cut it out by quartering the root lengthwise.

FLAVORING: Celery seed, cinnamon, cloves, chili powder, curry powder, ginger, mustard, nutmeg, parsley, butter, salt and pepper, bacon, sherry, brandy, butter, Parmesan cheese.

COOKING: Methods include boiling, sauteeing thin slices in butter or olive oil, and deep-fat frying like French fries or potato chips. Parsnips are good mashed or creamed. Similar to potatoes, they can be baked alongside pot roasts with other root vegetables, or try adding them to stews during the last 15 or 20 minutes. Do not overcook parsnips.

Fried Parsnips with Parmesan

My favorite!
Cut the parsnips into strips, like French fries or Jo-Jo potatoes. Heat olive oil and fry the parsnips until golden brown, about 3 minutes. Remove to drain on paper towels. Sprinkle with Parmesan cheese. Serve hot.

Baked Parsnips

First boil the parsnips until tender (not soft). Drain and cool. Cut the parsnips into quarters the long way, then slice them into 2- or 3-inch lengths. Place them in a casserole coated with vegetable spray. Drizzle the parsnips with melted butter and lightly salt them. Bake uncovered at 375 degrees F until lightly browned, about 25 minutes.

Steamed Parsnips

Steam the parsnips until they are tender, perhaps 15 minutes. Puree the parsnips in a food processor and add butter, milk, salt, and nutmeg to taste. Serve warm.

Breaded Parsnips

The Farmer's Favorite!
1. First cut the parsnips into lengthwise slices 2 or 3 inches long and ¼ inch thick.
2. Boil the parsnips until tender (not soft). Drain and pat dry.
3. Heat ¼ inch of olive oil in a skillet on medium-high heat.
4. Place 1 cup ground pork rinds or soda crackers or bread crumbs in a soup bowl and add salt to taste. (Make crumbs by placing pork rinds, crackers, or stale bread in a food processor.)
5. Place one or two eggs in a second soup bowl and whisk until yolk and white are blended.
6. Dip parsnip slices in the egg and then in the crumbs and fry in the heated skillet until the crumbs are browned on both sides. Drain on paper towels. Serve hot.

Easy Parsnip and Cauliflower Soup

Delicious!
1. Simmer together until vegetables are tender:

> 1 ½ cup shredded parsnips (2 good-sized roots), packed
> 1 ½ cups chopped cauliflower
> 1 tablespoon dry parsley
> 4 cups water
> 4 chicken bouillon cubes

2. Stir in 2 cups cream and heat through. Salt to taste and serve.

PEAS IN THE GARDEN

I love the sight of peas growing on a fence and the touch of their cool, smooth vines. What can be better than homegrown peas eaten fresh right in the garden?

Peas have been in the human diet for thousands of years and are part of our history. Archaeologist Heinrich Schliemann found a storage jar in Troy containing four hundred pounds of dried shelled peas that were three thousand years old. In Thailand, peas were found at Spirit Cave that were dated to 9750 B.C. At one time, peas were eaten only dry and were a staple on long sea voyages; now we eat them almost entirely fresh. Thomas Jefferson raised them at Monticello, and fresh peas were his favorite vegetable. Peas were the first vegetable to be canned and also the first vegetable to be successfully frozen.

There are an astonishing number of pea varieties, and doubtless there are some that are just right for you. Because peas quickly turn their sugars into starch, the taste of fresh garden peas cannot be bought in a grocery store.

TYPES OF PEAS:

- Extra-early, early, midseason, and late-harvest.
- Vining plants that need support (some get up to six feet tall) or dwarf plants that need little or no support.

226

- Shell peas (which you remove from their pods), and edible pod peas (you eat both the pods and the immature peas inside).
- Shell peas, sometimes called garden peas, come in two forms: smooth seeds and wrinkled seeds. The wrinkled are the longest-maturing and the sweetest.
- Snow peas are edible pod peas and can be eaten raw or cooked. Highly recommended!
- Snap peas can be eaten as edible pod peas when they are young and flat, or they can be used as shell peas after the pods have grown fat. They are a cross between the shell pea and the snow pea.

LOCATION: Don't grow peas where they grew for the previous two years. Try to plant peas in the garden where corn grew the year before. Corn is a heavy nitrogen feeder and peas replace nitrogen to the soil.

Consider planting peas near taller crops, like corn, for some sun protection during the heat of the day. The taller crops will also protect the peas from high winds, which can be damaging.

GROWING RANGE: Everywhere.

SOIL REQUIREMENTS: Peas will grow on most soil and are quite tolerant of poor soil, so long as it is well drained and you loosen the ground by tilling it well. Pea roots need oxygen and dislike compacted soil. You can work in a little well-rotted manure or compost, but go easy on fertilizers as too much nitrogen will favor foliage at the expense of the pea crop. The soil should be warm for early spring crops, but peas prefer cool soil in summer.

MOISTURE: Peas like a little moisture but they don't like too much because it prevents the roots from getting enough oxygen. If you don't get sufficient rains, give them half an inch of water a week until they start blooming, and then increase to one inch a week. Peas can tolerate a little dryness until bloom time.

LIGHT: If you plant peas very early in spring, they need to be in full sun. If you plant them later, they might do better if planted in partial shade.

PLANTING SEASON: Peas are a cool-weather crop, so they grow best in early spring or fall. They can tolerate some frost but are intolerant of heat and prefer temperatures under 80 degrees F. Beyond that, no new pea pods will form.

In the South, plant the seeds in late fall and they will lie dormant until very early spring, when they will get a head start on the season, or plant them in late winter. Along the coasts in the West and the Gulf states, grow peas in the winter.

The rest of us need to plant our peas in the early spring. After the pea vines die in the summer heat, you may have time to start a second crop for fall if the weather is cool enough.

PREPARING A FENCE FOR VINING PEAS: The traditional farmer's wife used chicken wire fencing for pea supports, but chicken wire is stiff and hard to work with and the edges are sharp. I recommend buying quality plastic fencing, which is much like chicken wire but is easier to install and there are no cut edges to scratch you as you string the fence or harvest the peas.

Electric fence posts make installation easy. First insert the posts in the row, pressing down on the vanes with your feet. Because we have high winds in the spring, I like to space the posts every three to four feet; if you don't have to fight windy conditions, you could space the posts every six to eight feet. Using the top of the fence post much like a needle, weave it in and out of one end of the plastic fencing. Electric fence insulators anchor the fence at the top. Repeat the weaving technique with the next post in the row or use twist-tie fasteners. Instead of cutting the fencing, I slide the remainder of the roll over the last fence post and secure it by wrapping wire around it in a couple of places. That way I can vary the row length in future seasons without patching the fence together.

HOW TO PLANT: Peas grow best when they are direct-seeded in the garden.

- Plant the seed outdoors four to six weeks before the last frost date, when the soil temperature is at least 40 degrees F; above 50 degrees F is even better for germination. If nec-

essary, lay down black or clear plastic to warm the soil.
- You can plant early, midseason, and late varieties at the same time; or you can succession-plant one variety every two weeks for an extended harvest.
- Soak seeds for twenty-four hours before planting them to increase germination.
- Spread mashed eggshells over pea ground and till thoroughly before planting, to give the peas a calcium boost. (You do save all your eggshells for the garden, don't you?)
- Applying an inoculate either on the seeds before planting or in the planting row will provide the roots with a beneficial bacteria that helps the plant use nitrogen from the air. (Inoculate is available from nurseries and from seed catalogues.)
- If the peas will require a support, put it in place prior to planting.

For dwarf or bush peas: Plant the seeds one to two inches deep and two inches apart in two-and-a-half-foot rows.

For vining peas: Plant the seeds two to three inches deep and three inches apart on both sides of a fence.

For edible pod peas: Plant the seeds only one inch deep.

ONGOING CARE:
- **Protecting** the newly planted seed from birds, by covering the rows with mesh or some other deterrent. Although some gardeners say they have a problem with birds, I never have, probably because of my cat herd.

- **Watering,** when the soil is dry one inch below the surface, to prevent the soil from drying out but not to make it soggy.
- **Staying out** of the peas when they are wet. Like beans, diseases can be transmitted.
- **Mulching,** but wait until early summer. Mulch keeps the weeds down and the roots cool—peas prefer a soil temperature not much over 60 degrees F.
- **Weeding** while the weeds are still small so that pulling them doesn't injure the delicate pea plants.
- **Directing** the pea vines to their supports, if necessary, although peas that are planted close to their supports generally can find them on their own.
- **Covering** the peas with black mesh for shade if the weather gets hot, to keep the plants cool and productive. I was able to have productive vines this summer despite temperatures in the 90 degree F range, thanks to the mesh covering.
- **Harvesting** regularly, to keep the plants productive.
- **Cutting** the vines off at the ground instead of pulling them when they stop producing. This way, you're leaving the nitrogen-rich roots in the ground to add nutrients.
- **Planting** a second crop of dwarf peas when night temperatures are between 50 and 60 degrees F, if there is enough time before winter for the plants to mature. The seeds won't germinate in too-warm soil.

VARIETIES INCLUDE:

Shell peas:

- **Early Perfection Pea**, which is drought tolerant and short-season, ready for harvest in 66 days. Best with a short fence for support. Freezes well.
- **Green Arrow** vines get twenty-eight inches tall and have four-inch pods that stay sweet a long time and yield up to eleven peas per pod. 68 days.
- **Victory Freezer** is a bush-type plant that produces peas that freeze well and retain their color. 65 days.

- **Wando** is the most heat-tolerant of peas, on two-and-a-half-foot vines that can take some drought. Medium-height vines produce well. 70 days.
- **Maestro** produces a high yield of sweet peas over a longer time on strong, two-foot vines. Disease resistant. 61 days.
- **Novella** is self-supporting when planted together in a row, because the tendrils on the eighteen-inch plants twine with each other. It is nearly leafless, which makes harvest easier. 65 days.

Edible Pod Peas

Snow peas:
- **Oregon Sugar Pod II** is a snow pea with four-inch pods that is disease resistant and freezes well. Recommended. 68 days.
- **Dwarf Gray Sugar Peas** is an eighteen-inch snow pea with three-inch pods that cook well and freeze well. It's said not to require staking, but I recommend a short fence. 66 days.
- **Mammoth Melting sugar** has flavorful four-and-a-half-inch pods on three- to four-foot vines. Freezes well. 72 days.

Snap peas:
- **Super Sugar Snap** produces a heavy crop of plump pods and is resistant to disease. Vines grow four to six feet tall. 66 days.
- **Sugar Lace**, a snap pea variety which has fewer leaves and lots of tendrils and is nearly self-supporting, although a short fence is desirable. 68 days.
- **Sugar Daddy** produces slender, dark, sweet and tender pods that cook and freeze without splitting. 72 days.

YIELD: If you have a long season of cool weather, you can get about a pound of shelled peas per foot of row. I never get that much because our springs are too short.

HARVESTING: Harvest daily to prevent the peas from overripening and to encourage more blooming. Proper pea picking involves two hands.

Be careful to support the vine with one hand and pull the pod with the other, or else cut off the pods, to avoid damaging the delicate vines.

Shell peas are harvested when the pods are plump and glossy and the peas are large and sweet but there is still a little space between the peas in the pod; overripe peas are close together and starchy. Avoid eating from pods that look dried, spotted, yellowed, or flabby.

Edible pod peas should be harvested when the shells are not full. For snap peas, the peas inside should be developed and sweet but smaller than the shell type; snow pea pods should be flat and flexible with very tiny undeveloped seeds.

By the way, if shell peas become too ripe, you can shell them and allow them to dry thoroughly in a single layer. Then you can cook them as you would a dry bean. If you like dried peas, you can grow varieties especially for this purpose.

Peas in the Kitchen

STORING PEAS: If you will be using the peas within an hour or two, you can refrigerate them. Place either edible pod or shell peas in plastic bags or containers and refrigerator without delay. Store shell peas in their pods and shell the peas just before cooking.

It is far better, however, to pick the peas just prior to eating them, before the sugars start converting to starch. Or freeze them quickly after the harvest.

FREEZING PEAS:
- If possible, harvest and freeze the peas within one hour.
- Wash the pods. Shell (for shelled peas) or leave as is (for edible pods).
- Blanch for one minute. Cool and drain.
- Place in freezer bags. Seal, label and date, and freeze.

EATING PEAS

Peas are so good raw right out of the shell, that they might not make it out of the garden!

Raw peas can be added to many fresh salads. Cooked peas are wonderful in salads, soups, and casseroles.

PREPARING: Be sure to chill the peas quickly after the harvest, if you're not eating them right away.

Edible pod peas should be rinsed in cold water. Snip off the tips and remove the string, if necessary.

Shell peas, if needed, should be rinsed prior to shelling.

To shell peas, break the stem off the top of the pea and pull down on the string to remove it (if there is a string). You can rub your thumbnail down along the seam, gently press and the pod will snap open. Run your thumb inside and the peas will all fall out into a bowl in your lap. Traditionally, peas would be shelled while sitting on the farmhouse porch. The pods were collected for the pigs, who love them.

FLAVORINGS: Peas go well with basil, celery seed, chives, cinnamon, dill, marjoram, mint, nutmeg, oregano, onion, poppy seed, rosemary, sage, savory, parsley, butter, salt and pepper, nuts, cheese.

COOKING: Methods include boiling, steaming, and stir-frying.

Sauteed Peas

Either shell or edible pod peas can be quickly cooked in a little butter, which really brings out the fresh pea flavor. Don't cook them too long and don't cover the pan with a lid or you'll lose the lovely green color.

Easy Cooked Peas

To cook fresh shell or edible pod peas, bring water to boiling in a shallow saucepan, add the peas, cover, and turn off the heat. After one minute, drain the peas and top with a pat or two of butter, if desired. Serve.

Easy Creamed Peas

Simmer 1 cup heavy cream in a shallow saucepan until somewhat thickened. Add cooked and drained peas, perhaps 2 cups, more or less. Stir in a loose handful of fresh chopped mint leaves (optional). Serve.

Easy Curried Peas

Cook fresh shell peas and cool. Stir in mayonnaise, minced onion, and a dash or two of curry powder. Serve chilled, topped with hard-boiled egg slices, if desired.

Easy Cinnamon Peas

Saute 2 tablespoons minced onion in 3 tablespoons of butter until onions are golden. Add ⅛ teaspoon salt and two pinches of cinnamon. Stir into 2 cups of cooked and drained peas and serve.

Easy Cold Pea Salad

Combine frozen peas, chopped green onions, sliced water chestnuts, bacon bits, and cashews. Stir in enough sour cream to moisten. Serve chilled.

PEPPERS IN THE GARDEN

Peppers originated in tropical America and are relatives of tomatoes, eggplant, and the weed nightshade. Peppers became the first New World food to be taken back to Europe by Columbus. There are hundreds of varieties, with new ones being developed each year. Everyone should try growing a few.

I just cooked freshly harvested sweet peppers in a skillet with garden onions, tomatoes, and crumbled hamburger, and I couldn't resist popping several slices of pepper into my mouth as I worked. The flavor of homegrown is incomparable to store-bought!

TWO TYPES OF PEPPERS:
- **Sweet peppers,** which are sweet and mild. They can be picked when they are still green, or they can be allowed to ripen until they are yellow, orange, or red and taste even sweeter.
- **Hot peppers** like chili, cayenne, hot or red peppers, which are spicy hot. They, too, can be harvested when they are still green, or they can be allowed to ripen, which will make them even hotter.

LOCATION: Don't plant peppers where tomatoes, peppers, potatoes, or eggplant grew the year before.

Plant sweet peppers away from hot peppers as the two types can cross, affecting the crop.

Peppers don't like strong winds; position them so they get some protection if your area is windy, especially if the wind is cold.

Peppers grow well in containers, and they look attractive in the landscaping or flower beds.

GROWING RANGE: Peppers grow well where temperatures range between 65 and 85 degrees F. Make adjustments if your temperatures fall outside that range (using black plastic on the soil, providing shade during the hottest part of the day), and you can still have a good pepper crop. Peppers are very sensitive to frost. In hot climates, peppers are better grown in the fall and winter.

SOIL REQUIREMENTS: Any fertile, well-drained soil that has been thoroughly tilled and had well-rotted manure or compost mixed in will do. The sweet peppers prefer a richer soil than the hot peppers do. Peppers like having calcium added to the soil—till under crushed eggshells.

MOISTURE: Peppers need to be evenly moist; water if you don't get one inch of rain per week—more if your soil dries out quickly.

LIGHT: Full sun.

PLANTING SEASON: Peppers love warm weather rather than the expected extremely hot weather. They are very frost sensitive and so should be planted outside after the last frost date.

HOW TO PLANT: Transplant seedlings outdoors when the weather is warm and humid, not hot and dry, or the plant will abort its blossoms.
To grow seedlings from seed:

- Start seeds indoors six to ten weeks before transplant.
- Plant the seed a quarter-inch deep.
- Use room-temperature water when watering, tap water will cool the soil.

- Keep the pots warm, between 70 and 80 degrees F, or use bottom heat.
- Give the seedlings as much sun as possible.

To transplant seedlings to the garden:

- Transplant two or three weeks after the last frost date, when soil temperature is at least 60 degrees F.
- Harden off the seedlings for one week prior to transplanting.
- Choose a cloudy day to lessen the chance of seedling sun scorch, or else provide temporary shade.
- Put black plastic down to warm the roots. The seedlings can be planted in slits in the plastic.
- Plant the seedlings one inch deeper than they grew indoors.
- Space eighteen to twenty-four inches apart in two-and-a-half-foot rows. Most plants get about two feet tall.
- Use collars if cutworms are a problem in your area.
- If the night temperatures will approach freezing, cover the plants.

ONGOING CARE:
- **Weeding,** as needed.
- **Watering,** as necessary, especially during blossoming and fruiting.
- **Staking** the plants if the peppers are too heavy for the stems. This is especially true if you are growing the longer six- or seven-inch sweet peppers with thicker walls. If the plant tips over and the peppers come in contact with the moist earth, they might decay or be harmed by insects.
- **Harvesting** the first peppers on each plant in the green stage to encourage more fruiting.

- **Covering** the plants with black mesh, if the temperatures get very hot, to prevent leaf scald, or plant them near something tall that could give the plants shade during the heat of the day.

VARIETIES INCLUDE:

Sweet peppers

- **Bell Boy Hybrid**, which produces blocky, glossy green fruit with three or four lobes that turns bright red when mature. Sweet and juicy. 63 days.
- **California Wonder** has extra-thick-walled glossy green flesh that turns red. The fruits get five inches long and four inches wide. 68 days.
- **The Godfather** hybrid grows elongated seven-inch fruits that are three inches wide and are green, turning to red when mature. 64 days.
- **Golden Bell**, which turn yellow when ripe. My favorite! 68 days.
- **Orange Belle Hybrid II** is a compact plant that grows well in containers. The four-lobed fruits grow green and mature to a deep orange. 85 days.
- **Sweet Banana** is a long six-inch pepper that is a waxy yellow color and turns bright red when fully ripe. It's pungent, but not hot. 68 days.

Hot peppers

- **Jalapeño**, which produces deep green fruit that ripens to dark red. A very hot pepper. 70-80 days.
- **Long Red Cayenne**, which has five-inch-long yellow fruits

that turn bright red when mature. A very hot pepper that can be dried and ground and used for seasoning. 70-75 days.

- **Red Chili** peppers get green two-inch fruits that mature to red and can be dried. A very hot pepper. 70-80 days.
- **Hearts**, which makes a beautiful container plant or a nice accent in a flower bed because it produces thick clusters of small, pungent fruits that stand above the foliage. The color changes from green to yellow, red, and purple. 65 days.

YIELD: One pound per plant, depending on the growing conditions and the variety chosen.

HARVESTING: To pick a pepper, cut the stem with a knife. Leave the stem on the pepper so that it will store better.

Sweet peppers can be harvested at any size when they are green, but they are best when they are a mature bright green; that is, the flesh is no longer soft, thin, and pale green. Or they can be allowed to further mature, turning yellow, orange, bright red, or chocolate brown, depending on the variety. Green sweet peppers that are showing some signs of changing color will continue to ripen after they are harvested if they are kept at 75 degrees F.

Hot peppers can be harvested at any time or they can be allowed to become fully ripe for eating or drying. Hot peppers that ripen during cooler weather will be less spicy than those that ripen in warm weather.

To dry hot peppers, harvest the pods and hang them in an airy place. Some gardeners string them (using a needle to run strong thread through the stems) to hang in their kitchens for easy use.

Peppers in the Kitchen

STORING: Store peppers in a plastic bag in the refrigerator. Do not wash them first.

FREEZING: Peppers are so easy to freeze!

Sweet peppers

- Use tender, crisp, bright green, bright red, or bright yellow peppers.
- Wash in cold water, cut out stems, halve or quarter peppers, and remove all the seeds. You can slice, dice, or chop the peppers, if desired.
- Do not blanch. Just double- or, better yet, triple-package the peppers in freezer bags or containers so that the flavor doesn't permeate other foods in the freezer.
- Seal, label and date, and freeze. Do not place peppers next to foods such as fruits.

Hot peppers

NOTE: Be sure to use rubber gloves when working with hot peppers to prevent chemical burns.

- Use tender, crisp, bright green or bright red peppers.
- Wash in cold water and drain.
- Freeze whole in freezer containers lined with two freezer bags to prevent pepper flavor from permeating into other frozen foods.
- Even with careful packaging, do not place hot peppers in the freezer next to foods such as fruits.

Roasted peppers:

- Select ripe sweet peppers that are a deep red. Wash in cold water, remove stems and seeds, and cut into halves or quarters.
- Place on a baking sheet in a 400 degree F oven and leave until the skins blister, or place the peppers in a saucepan, cover them with water, and boil until tender.
- Cool, drain, and peel.
- Pack into freezer containers lined with freezer bags.
- Seal, label and date, and freeze. Do not store in the freezer next to foods such as fruits.

EATING PEPPERS

Raw or cooked, peppers are most often used to flavor other foods, rather than as a dish on their own, although sweet peppers are sometimes sliced and served raw on relish plates.

PREPARING: Wash peppers. Cut off the stem and stem cap. Remove the seeds and the membranes from the cavities inside the pepper. For hot peppers, do this only with rubber gloves, and be very careful to wash the pepper off the gloves before touching anything.

FLAVORINGS: Bay leaf, chili powder, curry, dill, garlic, ginger, mustard, thyme, bacon, mushrooms, lemon, cheese. Peppers are often used to flavor other ingredients.

COOKING: Methods include stir-frying, steaming, sauteeing, stuffing, and baking.

To stuff the peppers, carefully cut around the cap to remove the stem, the membranes inside, and the seeds. Boil the peppers about 3 minutes in salted water, then drain upside down before stuffing with a blend of rice, meat, vegetables, and herbs. Perhaps top with cheese.

Sauteed Sweet Peppers

Cut the peppers into strips and saute them in butter flavored with minced garlic and a little oregano for a great accompaniment to meats, especially beef.

Sweet Peppers with Tomatoes and Onions

1. Cut 3 sweet green peppers and 2 onions into strips and stir-fry in 2 tablespoons of butter until crisp-tender.
2. Sprinkle 1 teaspoon dried basil and 1 teaspoon wine vinegar over the peppers and onions. Salt and pepper to taste.
3. Add 2 coarsely chopped tomatoes and simmer on low for another 5 minutes until tomatoes are heated through. Garnish with black olives, if desired, and serve.

Easy Ratatouille

Place sweet peppers, eggplant, onion, zucchini, and tomatoes together in a pan coated with olive oil. Stew together until the vegetables are crisp-tender and serve hot.

Fried Sweet Peppers

1. Cut the peppers lengthwise into eighths. Beat an egg with a fork.
2. Dip the pepper strips into flour, then into the beaten egg, then into the flour again.
3. Pour vegetable oil in a pan and heat it to medium. Fry the peppers in the oil until they are browned. Serve hot.

Hot (or Sweet) Peppers and Potatoes

1. Use up to 1 pound of sweet peppers (less if using hot peppers). Cut the peppers in lengthwise strips and cut crosswise in half. Cut 5 potatoes into slices or cubes.
2. Heat ¼ cup of olive oil in a skillet and saute 1 clove minced garlic and 1 minced onion till light brown.
3. Add the pepper strips and the potatoes and 1 cup chopped tomato, tomato sauce, or tomato juice. Stir well. Cover and simmer over low heat for 30 minutes, or until potatoes are tender. Stir occasionally, and add a little more tomato juice or sauce, as is necessary. Serve.

POTATOES IN
THE GARDEN

My childhood memories include picking up potatoes that had been dug with an antique potato digger; but instead of pulling it with real horse power, ours was converted over to using tractor power. We'd place the potatoes in wire egg baskets, and when the baskets were almost too heavy to carry, we'd empty them onto large flat racks (the kind used to haul hay bales and for hayrides). Then the flat racks would sit outside under a shade tree until the potatoes were dried and ready for storage in an old man-made cave next to my grandparents' farmhouse.

This cave was used not only for storing root crops, but it was also an emergency shelter in case of bad storms, and indeed, my grandparents did emerge from it once after a tornado to find their house and barn were completely gone. The door had been blocked by a fallen tree, and they were trapped in the cave until their neighbors brought a saw to rescue them.

In the spring, whatever potatoes were left over would be brought back out of the cave and planted for seed. Of course there were always a few that had rotted, a smell that permanently imbedded itself into the cave walls, and I can remember the damp musty odor to this day.

There are lots of "old" farmer traditions associated with planting potatoes. For one thing, the "old" farmer advice was to plant potatoes on Good Friday. I must admit I still tend to follow this advice, even when Good Friday comes on a chilly March day.

Another "old" tradition followed by farmwives was to save potato peelings in the spring. By this time the potatoes in storage would have been thoroughly sprouted and good only for mashing. The peelings would be tossed onto the ground and covered with loose soil, and they'd sprout leaves and grow potatoes. One year I tried this in a large container in my living room and was able to harvest delicious "new" potatoes when outdoors it was still winter!

The old farmer's method for planting was to cut seed potatoes into segments, ensuring that each segment had an "eye" indentation, where the sprout would grow, and a generous amount of white flesh to provide food for the eye. These segments were placed about four to five inches deep in a deeply tilled soil bed. A four-foot wooden hand tool for planting potatoes was pressed into the ground. When you closed the handles on top, wooden lips opened a hole in the ground and you dropped a potato segment into the hole. You lifted the contraption and the hole filled in or you helped it fill in with your toe, and went on to the next planting spot.

The old farmer's way of planting cut-up potatoes four or five inches deep in well-tilled soil works fine, and I've done it many times. But one year I discovered that my seed potatoes had large sprouts on shriveled potato balls that were too small to cut. I had to do something with them quickly, and so I tried placing them directly on the ground, figuring what did I have to lose? It worked so well I've used the no-dig method ever since.

So now my preferred method of planting potatoes couldn't be simpler. After thoroughly tilling the soil, just lay the entire seed potato directly on the ground, spacing them about eighteen inches apart in all directions. Position each potato so that the side with the most eyes or sprouts is up. Cover the bed with eight or ten inches of mulch, and you're finished!

Straw works well but the very best mulch is about eight inches of leftover corn cobs, if you have them; ground up cobs or wood chips require only a five-inch depth. It's important that you maintain the layer of mulch so it's thick enough to prevent the sunlight from reaching the new potatoes, or they will turn vivid green. The green part should not be eaten.

LOCATION: Rotate the crop each year and do not plant where you previously had potatoes, tomatoes, peppers, or eggplants for the past three years. They like to grow where beans or peas grew the previous year.

Potatoes are not the most attractive plant, so you'll want to plant them in your garden or a separate potato patch, rather than incorporating them into landscaping or flower beds.

GROWING RANGE: Anywhere that the potato tubers have time to develop before the tops are killed by frost. Potatoes do especially well in the northern half of the U.S. and the southern half of Canada, but they can be grown elsewhere using the proper planting time.

SOIL REQUIREMENTS: Potatoes will grow in almost any soil; ideally fertile, well-drained soil that retains moisture but isn't soggy. Mix in well-rotted manure or compost and till the soil well to make it airy and easy for the potato roots to penetrate. Potatoes grow best in soil that's at least 42 degrees F; whole potatoes can tolerate even colder soil, cut potatoes do better in warmer soil. To get an earlier start, the soil can be warmed with black plastic.

MOISTURE: If your soil is well-drained, potatoes benefit from one inch of rain per week. In most climates, the potatoes will get enough moisture from occasional good rains, especially if they are covered with a mulch, but you should water deeply during dry weather.

Uneven moisture causes potatoes to grow into funny shapes with knobs. If there is a prolonged wet spell after a drought, potatoes may become hollow in the center or they might develop cracks in the surface.

LIGHT: Full sun.

PLANTING SEASON: Early spring in the northern United States and southern Canada; in warm climates potatoes should be started in fall or winter for a spring harvest. Potato leaves can be hurt by frost, but they usually come out of it. Since it takes a while for the sprouts to penetrate the soil or mulch they're planted in, potatoes usually emerge after the hardest frosts are over. Planting as early as possible generates a larger crop.

HOW TO PLANT: Potatoes aren't grown from actual seeds, instead they are cloned from the tubers, which contain indentations where sprouts will form, called eyes. It is best to buy certified seed potatoes every year for planting, rather than saving your own, to avoid disease. Do not use potatoes from the grocery store as seed potatoes; they probably have been treated to inhibit sprouting, and they might contain virus diseases that would be spread to your garden.

The no-work method: I highly recommend that you try my easy method of planting the whole potato on the ground, covered with mulch, as described above. It's a no-work planting method, there is little maintenance through the growing season, and it's the easiest way to harvest potatoes.

- Buy certified seed potatoes. If you can, allow the seed potatoes to sit in the sun for a few days before they are planted—this will bring them out of dormancy.
- Thoroughly and deeply till the soil where you'll plant the potatoes.
- Plant the potatoes two or four weeks before the last frost date or even earlier, as soon as you can work the ground.
- Place each potato directly on the surface of the soft, well-tilled soil and press it half into the soil. Space the potatoes eighteen inches apart in all directions, or plant them twelve inches apart in two- or three-foot rows.
- Cover the entire potato patch with several inches of mulch.

NOTE: Another benefit from planting whole potatoes is that it eliminates disease problems that come from the exposed cut potato surface. Other methods of planting potatoes:

- Instead of using the whole potato, as I do, cut it up so that there are two to three "eyes" and a good chunk of flesh in each piece. Some gardeners say to plant them immediately to prevent loss of moisture and increase viability, but the old farmer method was to lay them out in a single layer so that the flesh dries for about twenty-four hours. Till the soil deeply and thoroughly. Plant the potato segments cut-side down in five-inch furrows, spacing them twelve inches apart in two-and-a-half- to three-foot rows. Cover them with two inches of loose soil, gradually filling in the trench as the plant grows. Be sure to cover any exposed tubers with soil or mulch. Some gardeners keep mounding soil or mulch around the plant stems as they grow, forming hills—but be sure you don't bury all the foliage. Also be very careful not to harm the potatoes, which develop near the surface.
- Or, you can buy "sets" from garden catalogues that are already cut from the whole potato with one eye each. They've been treated to prevent disease and encourage growth. Plant them four inches deep, and space them twelve inches apart in three-foot rows.
- Or you can start potato seedlings in peat pots two or three weeks before transplant time. You can use purchased sets or cut up seed potatoes, planting one eye per pot. Transplant the seedling pot and all so you don't disturb the roots.

Ongoing care:
- **Watering,** if required.
- **Covering** the plants with old blankets if a hard frost is coming before the potatoes are mature.
- **Weeding,** as necessary. (This is completely avoided with a deep mulch.)
- **Mounding** dirt or mulch over any exposed potatoes to keep them from turning green.

- **Tilling** between the rows, if the potatoes were planted in the ground. Use a portable tiller to prevent damage to the developing tubers.
- **Removing** all the potatoes in the ground at harvest, even the very small ones, to discourage disease and insect problems.

VARIETIES INCLUDE: NOTE: There are hundreds of varieties of potatoes. Be sure to check with your local nursery or extension office for advice about which varieties are best suited to your area.

- **Russet Norkotah**, a dry, firm, meaty potato that's oblong and smooth with flaky white flesh and shallow eyes that makes this one the best choice for baking. Disease resistant. Midseason maturity.
- **Red Pontiac** has a great flavor and grows almost everywhere, yields well and keeps well. These oblong potatoes have crisp white flesh and shallow eyes in thin red skins that are easy to peel. Because the skins are so thin, allow the potatoes to firm up one to two weeks after the vines die down before harvest. A good all-purpose potato that stores well. Mid- to late-season maturity.
- **Red Norland** produces a high yield of round to oval potatoes early in the season, and the plants are disease resistant. Reds are considered the best choice for boiling. Stores well.
- **Kennebec**, a tan-skinned and white-fleshed oval potato with a fine flavor has medium starch. They are all-purpose potatoes with a mealy and flaky texture. The skins are thin and the eyes are shallow, which makes less work when peeling. Vigorous vines produce all-large potatoes that keep well and are disease resistant. Often planted here in farm country. Late midseason maturity.
- **Yukon Gold** is great for potato salad and for steaming, boiling, and frying. The tubers are slightly oval with tannish-yellow skin and flavorful buttery-yellow flesh that keeps its color when cooked. This one is a little earlier and it yields well although it doesn't produce a lot of tubers, so these can be planted closer together than other varieties. It stores well. Early midseason variety.

- **All Blue** has blue skin and flesh—and it keeps it's unusual color when cooked, but tastes like a regular potato.

YIELD: It varies quite a bit with the variety and growing conditions, but you should get at least several pounds from every plant.

HARVESTING: New potatoes are harvested from live potato plants. They are small, young, newly dug potatoes that are high in moisture and sugar content (they haven't become starchy yet), and they have thin skins. They can be harvested when the plants begin flowering, about three months after planting. They are delicate, so treat them gently. They taste delicious!

Fully-grown potatoes are harvested four to five months after planting, about three weeks after the tops have died down, usually after a frost, but before the ground freezes. If you can, leave the potatoes in the ground for a couple of weeks after the tops have died down to toughen the skins so they'll store better. The potato tubers are not harmed by frost (although it will kill the tops) and they will continue to develop.

The old farmer's harvest method involved digging the potatoes by hand—which is lots of work! If you planted your potatoes in the ground: Use a pitch fork or potato fork to loosen the soil a distance from the base of the plant, working all around in a circle, trying not to harm the potatoes. Then pull up the plant, potatoes and all, or dig through the soil with your hands. Search for any potatoes that got left behind. Try to treat the potatoes carefully, so that they don't get bruised or damaged—these won't keep well.

If you've used my simple method of planting the whole potato directly on the ground, covered with mulch, the harvest is very easy:

- To get the early "new" potatoes, just reach under the mulch and gently remove the quantity desired, being careful not to disturb the roots too much so that the vines can continue to develop the remaining potatoes.
- To harvest the fully grown potatoes, get a good grip on the potato vine and lift up—all the potatoes will come up with the roots! If the vine breaks, just pull back the mulch and pick up the remaining potatoes.

The biggest advantages to planting the potatoes on the ground show up at harvest:

- There is no digging required,
- The potatoes are easy to find, and
- The potatoes come out clean!

After the harvest, the potatoes need to be cured, sorted, and properly stored. See "Storing Potatoes," below.

Potatoes in the Kitchen

STORING POTATOES: To ensure that potatoes will store well:

- Use mature potatoes. Mature potatoes have remained in the ground until they are fully developed and until after the potato tops have died down. This allows them to develop a thicker skin, which is why mature potatoes are the best keepers for long-term storage.
- Cure the potatoes. Potatoes that are grown in the ground will sweat for two weeks. Spread freshly dug mature potatoes out in a single layer to dry and "cure" for two weeks at about 65 degrees F, until they quit sweating. They should cure in an airy place, but not in direct sun. Potatoes grown in mulch will take less time to cure.
- Do not wash the potatoes before storing them—they won't keep as well.
- Sort and remove any damaged potatoes, to prevent rotting. Damaged potatoes can be eaten; use them right away.

For short-term storage, mature potatoes will keep at room temperature for a week or two.

For long-term storage:

- Place the potatoes in slatted boxes, wire bins, or baskets to promote air circulation. Farmers of old used gunnysacks made of itchy burlap fabric that was coarsely woven and allowed the potatoes to breathe.
- Store the potatoes in a cool, dark place, like a cave or unheated basement room.
- The temperature should be 40 or 45 degrees F; a warmer temperature encourages sprouting.
- Do not use the refrigerator, because it is too humid.
- Never store potatoes in plastic bags or sealed containers.
- Don't store potatoes with fresh fruit, like apples.

NOTE: All potatoes lose sugar and gain starch as they age, when properly stored.

NOTE: Potatoes should be stored completely in the dark; if they get any light, green pigment will form under their skins. If only part of the potato skin is green, cut it off; if the whole potato has greened, it will be bitter, so throw it out. The green skins are somewhat toxic.

FREEZING POTATOES: Potatoes store so well, that I don't recommend freezing unless you have leftover mashed potatoes. Place these in a freezer container, seal, label and date, and freeze.

EATING POTATOES

Potatoes are one of the most versatile vegetables and can be prepared in countless ways.

They can be sliced; diced; chopped; shredded; mashed; creamed; scalloped; added to any number of soups, stews, and casseroles; added to bread dough, pancakes, pastries, and souffles; and even made into cold salads.

Potato varieties are used for different purposes:

- **Baking potatoes,** such as Russet, contain the most starch, which is why they bake up dry and fluffy. The cooked flesh tends to fall apart, so they don't work as well for potato salad or in soups and stews. (Any potato variety can be baked and will taste good.) The starchy potatoes also are the best for mashing and deep-frying French fries, and they work to thicken soups because they disintegrate into the liquid.

- **Boiling potatoes,** such as Red Pontiac or Red Norland, have the least starch, and the texture cooks up waxy and firm, which makes them ideal for salads, soups, and stews; for pan-fried or hash-browned potatoes; and for potato chips, scalloped potatoes, and potatoes au gratin. Baking potatoes would break down and become mushy for these purposes, especially if they are old and starchy. (Even waxy potatoes can be mashed, however.)
- Other potatoes, such as Yukon Gold or Kennebec, are good for both purposes because the starch content is in between that of baking and boiling potatoes.

PREPARING: Scrub the whole potatoes, but be very gentle with new potatoes because the skins are thin and delicate. Cut off any areas where the skin turned bright green from sun exposure, and remove any sprouts or bad spots. Remove the eyes and peel the potatoes if you wish, but the skin and the area just under the skin contain the majority of the potato's nutrients and also roughage. When using homegrown potatoes, I include the skins as much as possible.

FLAVORING: Potato seasonings include: basil, bay leaves, caraway seed, celery seed, chives, curry, dill, garlic, ginger, mustard seed, oregano, poppy seed, sage, marjoram, thyme, parsley, salt and pepper, butter, cheeses, sauces, bacon, onion, mushrooms, horseradish.

COOKING: Methods include grilling, frying, steaming, boiling, baking, stir-frying, broiling.

Raw potatoes darken when exposed to air. If you are preparing many potatoes, place the raw potatoes in a pan of cold water to prevent this discoloration.

Put a pat of butter in the water when potatoes come to a boil, to keep it from boiling over.

Mashed Potatoes and Skins

Wonderful—and nutritious!
Clean and halve or quarter the potatoes, but leave on the skins. Put them in boiling water and reduce the heat to medium, add a pat of butter to prevent the water from boiling over, cover with a lid, and cook until they are soft when pricked. Drain the potatoes, reserving or even freezing the nutritious water, which can be used for soups.

Mash the potatoes as usual. Most of the time the skins will shred up as the potatoes are mashed by hand or whipped in my mixer. If not, I fish them out and chop them up a bit—but only a very short time—in my food processor.

For light, fluffy potatoes, pour back a little of the potato water. Add milk or cream, butter, and salt as desired. Serve with additional pats of butter.

Easy Boiled Potatoes

1. Clean, cut up, and boil potatoes till tender. Toss them with:

    1/4 cup butter
    1 tablespoon lemon juice
    3 tablespoons minced fresh parsley
    1 tablespoon snipped fresh chives

2. Serve.

Easy Creamed Potatoes

1. Cut potatoes into bite-sized pieces to make 2 or 3 cups and boil until tender. Drain.
2. Simmer 1 cup cream until it begins to thicken. Stir in the potatoes and heat through.
3. Stir in seasonings:

    2 pats of butter
    salt as desired
    1/4 teaspoon white pepper
    1/8 teaspoon nutmeg
    about 2 tablespoons minced parsley

4. Serve.

Easy Baked Jo-Joes

A family favorite!

1. Preheat the oven to 400 degrees F.
2. Coat a jelly-roll pan or large cake pan with oil.
3. Scrub potatoes and cut into long wedges.
4. Place potatoes into a plastic bowl with a tight lid. Drizzle a little olive oil over the potatoes, cover, and shake the bowl up and down to coat jo-joes. Spread coated potatoes in a single layer on the jelly-roll pan. Or, spread the uncoated potatoes on the pan, spray with vegetable oil, turn the potatoes, and spray the other side.
5. Sprinkle your favorite seasoning on the potatoes: salt, pepper, garlic powder or garlic salt, herb blends like Italian seasoning, etc. Our favorite is cumin. Parmesan cheese can be added toward the end of the baking time.
6. Bake the potatoes twenty-five or thirty minutes, or until browned and tender inside when pricked, and serve. Delicious! Can use sour cream as a dip.

My Great Grilled Skillet Potatoes

Our all-time favorite potato recipe! The potatoes can be cooked on the grill right alongside the meat.

1. To make butter sauce, combine in a microwave-safe bowl:

> 1/4 cup butter
> 2 teaspoons dried basil
> 1 teaspoon paprika
> 1/2 teaspoon garlic powder
> 1/4 teaspoon pepper

2. Place the bowl in the microwave to melt the butter, about 15 seconds.
3. Generously coat a large cast-iron skillet with olive oil. If the skillet has a wooden handle, remove it.
4. Slice potatoes to fill the bottom of the skillet.
5. Drizzle the butter sauce over the potatoes. Sprinkle 1/2 cup Parmesan or Romano cheese over the potatoes.

6. Cover skillet with aluminum foil and seal the edges. Place on a pre-heated grill.
7. Cook about thirty minutes or until the potatoes are tender and lightly browned. Start the potatoes before the meat, and they'll be ready at the same time.

NOTE: If making a small batch in a small cast-iron skillet, you can halve the butter sauce recipe.

Potato Cakes

My mother often made this from leftover mashed potatoes.
1. Add 1 beaten egg to 2 or 3 cups of mashed potatoes. Stir together with the seasoning of your choice: minced garlic, minced onion, salt and pepper, garlic salt, etc.
2. Melt one stick of butter over medium heat.
3. Form potato cakes by rolling a large spoonful of the potato mixture in flour and gently flatten somewhat. Place the potato cakes in the heated butter and brown on both sides, turning carefully with a large spatula. Serve warm.

New Potatoes Steamed in Butter

Wonderful!
1. Gently clean about 1½ pounds of new potatoes, being careful not to remove the thin skin. Halve the potatoes that are over 1 inch in diameter.
2. Melt ⅓ cup butter in a large skillet. Add the potatoes and stir to coat them well with the butter. Sprinkle the potatoes with salt and pepper, as desired.
3. Cover the potatoes and cook them over low heat about 30 minutes, or until the potatoes are tender, shaking the pan from time to time.
4. Serve with any extra butter poured over the potatoes.

Mom's Easy Potato Soup

I grew up on this, and it's wonderful!

1. Dice up potato and onion and place in a saucepan with a little water. Simmer until just tender.
2. Add generous amount of butter and salt and pepper, as desired. Pour in milk until the mixture has the consistency of soup. Heat through and serve.

NOTE: You can add some minced celery or crisp, crumbled bacon, if desired.

Twice-Baked Potato Casserole

1. Scrub, quarter, boil, and mash 8 potatoes (about 2 to 3 pounds). Leave the skins on, if homegrown.
2. Place the potatoes in a large mixer bowl and add:

> 8 ounces cream cheese
> 8 ounces sour cream
> 1/2 cup butter
> 1/4 teaspoon garlic powder
> 1/4 teaspoon pepper

3. Beat together with the mixer until the potatoes are fluffy.
4. Coat a 2-quart casserole dish with vegetable spray. Spread the mashed potatoes in the dish. Sprinkle with 1 cup (4 ounces) shredded cheddar cheese.
5. Bake at 350 degrees F for 30 minutes or until cheese is lightly browned and the potatoes are heated through. Serve.

Mashed Potatoes and Bacon

1. Scrub, quarter, boil, and mash 8 potatoes (about 2½ pounds). Leave the skins on, if homegrown.
2. Fry about 1/3 pound of bacon until it's crisp. Drain on paper towels. Crumble. Add the bacon to the mashed potatoes along with:

1 cup shredded cheddar or American cheese
1/2 cup chopped celery
1/2 cup chopped onion
1/4 cup chopped green pepper
(NOTE: Place the celery, onion, and pepper in a food
processor and pulse until chopped.)

3. Mix well and turn the potatoes out into a casserole dish coated with vegetable spray. Top with more shredded cheese. Bake at 350 degrees F till heated through and cheese is lightly browned. Serve hot.

Mashed Potatoes and Pimento

1. To 4 cups hot mashed potatoes, add:

1 8-ounce package cream cheese
1 egg, beaten with a fork
2/3 cup chopped green onion, including tops, or 1/3 cup
finely chopped onion
1/4 cup pimento, chopped fine (can use canned)
Salt as desired

2. Mix together well and put into a casserole dish. Bake at 350 degrees F for 45 minutes.

Baked Potato Topper

1. Combine:

1 cup sour cream
1 clove garlic, minced
1 tablespoon olive oil
1 tablespoon wine vinegar
1 teaspoon Worcestershire sauce
1/2 teaspoon salt (or to taste)
1/8 teaspoon white pepper
Snipped chives or parsley

2. Serve over hot potatoes baked in their skins.

PUMPKINS IN THE GARDEN

In farm country, when you think of pumpkins, you think of crisp fall weather, colorful foliage, pumpkin pies, Jack-o-lanterns, harvest moons, and hayrides with your friends piled onto flat racks loaded with soft—but scratchy—straw. A bunch of our city-raised friends had never been on a hayride, so one fall we invited them to our home for dinner, which included pumpkin food, pumpkin decorations indoors and out, and a hayride around our farmland under the harvest moon. A good time was had by all!

Pumpkins are very easy to raise and they thrive on neglect—in fact, you'll probably find yourself overwhelmed by their vigorous growth! You can get varieties that produce pumpkins in almost any size, from the tiny three-inch Jack Be Littles, to huge monster pumpkins that weigh hundreds of pounds.

Jack-o-lanterns cut from pumpkins are very popular. But there are other ways to raise ornamental pumpkins, including cutting faces into the immature fruits that grow to become three-dimensional, and placing special forms around the immature fruits to force them to grow into desired shapes.

Not only are pumpkins great for decorations, but you can eat the pumpkins' flesh, their seeds, and even their blossoms.

LOCATION: Rotate pumpkins so that they do not grow where any squash, pumpkins, cucumbers, or melon were located the previous year. Choose a spot where they will have good air circulation, to prevent disease.

Plant pumpkins where they will have adequate space for their ten- to twenty-foot sprawling vines; or else plant the compact bush type that takes four to six feet of space.

To conserve garden space, you can plant pumpkins in with your sweet corn, and when the corn is harvested, remove the stalks so that more sun reaches the pumpkins.

NOTE: Pumpkins are a type of squash, and all squash, summer and winter, can cross-pollinate. This won't affect the current crop, but it will affect the seeds; if you plan to save the seeds to plant the next year, space the varieties some distance from each other or you might have peculiar offspring.

GROWING RANGE: Everywhere that they can get a growing season of at least 90 to 100 days. Unlike many other vegetables, pumpkins can't be harvested until they're mature, so be sure to select varieties that are suitable for your growing season.

SOIL REQUIREMENTS: Pumpkins accept almost any soil that drains well yet is capable of holding moisture. It should be loose and aerated, so till it deeply and mix in lots of well-rotted manure or compost. Add crushed eggshells.

MOISTURE: Pumpkins need lots of moisture. For the smaller pumpkins, rainfall will only occasionally have to be supplemented; the largest varieties might need extra watering.

LIGHT: Full sun, but they can tolerate some shade.

PLANTING SEASON: Late spring. Pumpkins are a warm-weather crop that needs to be planted after the last frost date. The plants can't tolerate even a light frost.

HOW TO PLANT: Pumpkins are direct-seeded in all but the shortest growing seasons.

To direct-seed pumpkins:

- Thoroughly and deeply till the soil, mixing in well-rotted manure or compost.
- If necessary, warm the soil bed with black plastic.
- Start the planting one week after the last frost date for your area or when the soil temperature is at least 70 degrees F.
- If desired, for easier watering, bury a perforated plastic one-gallon milk jug so all but two inches is in the ground.
- Plant four to six seeds one inch deep in clusters or hills, surrounding the buried milk jug, if you are using it.
- For vining pumpkins, space the hills at least ten to twelve feet apart; for compact plants, space the hills at least four to six feet apart.
- Remove the black plastic after planting and germination has occurred.
- Thin the seedlings to two or three plants per hill; eliminate all but one plant if you are raising giant pumpkin varieties.

To start pumpkin seedlings:

- Start the seed pots two weeks before the last frost date for your area.
- Plant the seeds one inch deep in peat pots.

- Harden off the seedlings for one week before transplant time.
- Transplant the seedlings outdoors one week after the last frost date for your area, when night temperatures remain above 55 degrees F.
- Carefully bury the peat pot in the soil, disturbing the roots as little as possible or the pumpkins won't take well to transplanting.

Ongoing care:

- **Mulching** is not necessary, unless desired, because the dense foliage discourages weeds and the mulch insulates the soil from all but the heaviest rains.
- **Watering** often and deeply unless you get ample rain. Direct the water to the roots, rather than the leaves, or water in the early morning so that the foliage dries in the sunlight.
- **Tilling** around the vines until they spread to cover the entire bed.
- **Weeding** will be minimal, once the plants are established.
- **Staying out** of the pumpkin patch when the vines are wet.
- **Drawing** a face on an immature pumpkin by cutting shallow slits to make an interesting jack-o-lantern; the pumpkin heals these slits by growing raised ridges, which gives the face a three-dimensional look.
- **Removing** all but one pumpkin per plant if you are trying to raise a giant pumpkin.
- **Fertilizing** with fish-emulsion if you want to grow the largest possible pumpkins.
- **Removing** all remaining blossoms and all the green pumpkins, and nipping off all the vine tips three or four weeks before the first frost date to encourage the remaining ones to grow larger and mature.

Varieties include:

- **Jack Be Little,** which bears cute bright-orange pumpkins that are two inches tall and three inches wide and have smooth skins. Although they are edible, they are mainly used for ornamental purposes. Each vine grows ten to fifteen feet long and yields about eight tiny pumpkins. If space is short, train this vine onto a fence or trellis. Properly cured, the pumpkins will last eight to twelve months. 100 days.

- **Small Sugar** bears pumpkins measuring about eight inches across and weighing about six or eight pounds, and they work well for pies and other recipes. The flesh is sweet and fine grained, the seed cavity is small, and the skin is bright orange and smooth. These pumpkins are attractive for arrangements or jack-o-lanterns. 82 days.

- **Hybrid Early Autumn** is the next size up, with intensely orange pumpkins in the ten- to fourteen-pound size, yet the flesh is fine grained and good for cooking and decoration. 100 days. This is a vining plant; for the same size pumpkin in a compact size, try **Hybrid Spirit**.

- **Hybrid Spirit** is an excellent-flavored compact semibush type that produces nine- or ten-inch pumpkins in the ten- to fifteen-pound range; good for cooking and decoration. It takes just four or five feet of garden space. 95 days.

- **Hybrid Frosty** has compact vines that produce fifteen- to twenty-pound pumpkins that store well. Fine for eating or carving jack-o-lanterns. 95 days.

- **Lumina** produces unusual white-skinned pumpkins that are eight to ten inches tall and weigh twelve pounds. They make "ghostly" carved or painted jack-o-lanterns, and the fine-grained flesh is good for eating, too. 90 days.

- **Connecticut Field** produces pumpkins that weigh fifteen to twenty pounds, and they have a flattened bottom to keep them from tipping, which makes this one a perfect choice for giant jack-o-lanterns. 110 days.

- For larger pumpkins, **Prizewinner Hybrid** and **Big Max** both yield huge pumpkins that weigh over 100 pounds, and **Dill's Atlantic Giant** (a squash type) will give you monsters in the 200- to 300-pound range, gargantuan 400- to 500-pound pumpkins, even a record-holding 1,000 pounds! These are probably what inspired the coach in Cinderella's story. 120 days. None are recommended for cooking.

YIELD: Varies greatly, depending on the variety chosen.

HARVESTING: Harvesting the pumpkins just before the first frost will give you the longest storage time; harvesting the pumpkins just after the first light frost will sweeten them but reduce the storage time somewhat. In any case, either cover the unripe pumpkins or bring them indoors before a hard frost, which will ruin them. One year I lost my entire patch due to an unexpected hard frost the night before I planned to harvest them. Many dozens went into the compost pile!

Signs that the pumpkins are mature and ready for harvest:

• The leaves have died and the vines are shriveling.
• The pumpkins turn from yellow to orange (unless they're a different-colored variety).
• The skins will lose their sheen and become hard; they are not easily dented with your thumbnail.

To harvest a pumpkin, cut it off the vine with a pair of nippers or a sharp knife, leaving three to six inches of stem on the pumpkin. If the stem is removed, the pumpkin won't keep well because there is an opening for rot to set in. Don't lift or carry the pumpkin by its stem.

NOTE: You can also harvest and eat the pumpkin blossoms. For information, see "Zucchini."

Pumpkins in the Kitchen

STORING: For longer storage, cure the pumpkins first, to harden the rinds.

To cure pumpkins:

• Store only pumpkins that properly matured before they were harvested.

- Sort out any damaged or bruised pumpkins, or pumpkins without a stem.
- Set the pumpkins in a warm, airy place, preferably between 80 and 85 degrees F, for one or two weeks.
- Or, cure them outdoors in the sun if the weather is dry, but you must cover them at night to protect them from frost.

To store pumpkins:

- Place them in a warm, dry place, between 50 and 60 degrees F.
- Don't crowd the pumpkins; they should not be touching, and air should circulate around them.
- Check occasionally for spoilage and remove spoiled pumpkins promptly.

Properly matured and cured, the pumpkins will keep for at least one or two months, often many more.

FREEZING:

- Use mature pumpkins. Wash and cut open to remove seeds and strings by scraping with a spoon; the stem can be left on. Cut into large pieces.
- Place pumpkin segments flesh-side down in a large cake pan or roasting pan. Segments can be laid on top of each other. Pour about a quarter-inch of water in the bottom of the pan.
- Bake pumpkin at 375 degrees F until flesh is soft when pricked with a sharp knife. Remove from the oven and cool.
- Remove the flesh by scraping the skin with a large spoon.
- Mash the pumpkin flesh or puree it in a food processor or with a cordless hand blender, or run it through a food mill.
- Pack the pumpkin in freezer containers. Seal, label and date, and freeze.

Pumpkin pies can be frozen successfully, but only after they've been baked. Or, you can freeze the unbaked filling without the crust and assemble and bake the pie after the filling has thawed. Either way, wrap well to prevent freezer burn.

EATING PUMPKINS

The best-tasting pumpkins are the smaller varieties. The pumpkin is cooked and served like potatoes, sliced, diced, or mashed, and the puree is used for breads, muffins, pies, etc.

NOTE: Pumpkin is interchangeable in recipes calling for winter squash.

NOTE: The blossoms can be fried, just as described for zucchini blossoms (see page 355).

PREPARING: Wash the pumpkin before using it. If the pulp seems watery or separates, pour it into a mesh strainer to drain before using it in recipes.

FLAVORINGS: Allspice, cinnamon, ginger, nutmeg, cloves, vanilla, pineapple, orange juice, sugar, brown sugar, sage, onion, salt, pepper.

COOKING: Methods include baking, steaming, boiling, frying in butter.

To make pumpkin puree, follow the baking directions, above, under "Freezing." Or you can remove the rind, cut the flesh into chunks, and steam or boil it and then mash it into a puree.

NOTE: The miniature Jack Be Little pumpkins can be baked whole in the oven. Cut off the top, scoop out the seeds, put in a pat or two of butter and your choice of the seasonings listed above (optional), and replace the lid. Place the pumpkins on a jelly-roll sheet or cake pan and bake at 375 degrees F for 45 minutes or until the flesh is tender when pricked. Serve whole. Eat the flesh by scraping it out with a spoon.

Roasted Pumpkin Seeds

When cooking pumpkins, save the seeds. Allow the seeds to dry and then rub off the membranes. Spread the seeds in a thin layer on a jelly-roll pan. Bake at 375 degrees F for 30 minutes. Drizzle melted butter over the seeds, stir, and return to the oven for 5 or 10 minutes, or until evenly browned. Remove from the oven and lightly sprinkle the seeds with salt. Cool and serve.

Mashed Pumpkin

Farm families served a scoop of hot pumpkin puree topped with a pat of butter and salt and pepper as a vegetable like mashed potatoes. It's good and tastes like a winter squash, which is what it really is.

Baked Sweetened Pumpkin

Place pumpkin puree in a casserole. Top with brown sugar, pats of butter, and cinnamon or nutmeg, if desired. Cover and bake till heated through.

Creamed Pumpkin and Saffron Soup

Great!

1. Place 4 cups of cooked pumpkin or pumpkin puree in a large saucepan. Add:

> 1 cup minced onion
> 2 cups chicken or vegetable broth
> 1 bay leaf
> a small pinch of saffron
> 1/4 teaspoon white pepper powder

2. Cover and simmer on low for 30 minutes.
3. Remove and discard the bay leaf. Pour the mixture into a food processor and puree it or use a cordless hand blender right in the pan.
4. Stir in 1 or 2 cups heavy cream and heat through. Serve, topped with a dollop of whipped cream, if desired.

Stuffed Pumpkins à la Julia Child

This fills two small sugar pumpkins or one average pumpkin.

1. Wash the outside of a pumpkin. Cut off a lid around the stem, taking care to make the cut at a diagonal so that the lid won't fall inside the pumpkin. Clean out the seeds and the seed membranes. Generously paint the flesh of the pumpkin and the lid with melted

butter. Sprinkle with salt and pepper. Return the lid to the pumpkin and place it on a jelly-roll pan. Bake it at 400 degrees F for about 35 minutes, or until the flesh is tender.

2. To make the stuffing, combine:

> 5 cups torn bread or use purchased dry stuffing
> I pound bulk sausage, cooked and crumbled
> I onion, chopped and cooked in the sausage fat
> 3 ribs of celery, chopped and cooked with the onion in
>   the sausage fat
> 2 eggs, beaten with a fork
> I tablespoon sage
> 2 or 3 tablespoons melted butter (or even more)

3. Remove the pumpkin from the oven. Remove the lid from the pumpkin and scrape the flesh from the lid. Stir this pumpkin flesh into the stuffing.

4. Spoon the stuffing inside the painted pumpkin(s) and replace the lid on the pumpkin. Bake an additional 30 minutes at 400 degrees F.

5. To serve, remove the lid and place a spoon in the pumpkin. Spoon out the stuffing along with some of the pumpkin, scraped from the rind.

Easy Pumpkin Ice Cream

Absolutely wonderful!

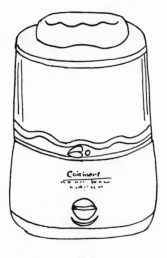

1. Puree cooked pumpkin to make 2 cups (see "Cooking," above). Add ¾ to 1 cup sugar and puree or beat well.

2. Stir in:

> 2 cups cream
> 2 tablespoons rum (optional)
> I teaspoon cinnamon
> ½ teaspoon ginger
> ¼ teaspoon ground cloves

3. Pour the mixture into your ice-cream maker and follow the manufacturer's instructions.

Old-Fashioned Pumpkin Pie

Positively wonderful! The Farmer raves over this!

1. Combine in a mixing bowl:

   > 1 cup sugar
   > 1 tablespoon flour
   > 1 teaspoon cinnamon
   > 1/2 teaspoon ground ginger
   > 1/2 teaspoon salt
   > 1/4 teaspoon nutmeg
   > 1/4 teaspoon ground cloves

2. Beat in 3 large eggs.

3. Stir in 1½ cups of cooked pumpkin puree and 1 cup heavy cream.

4. Pour the mixture into an unbaked pie shell in a 9-inch pie pan.

5. Bake in a preheated oven at 400 degrees F for 50 minutes or until a knife inserted in the center of the pie comes out clean. Serve with whipped cream.

RADISHES IN THE GARDEN

I must confess, I'm not particularly fond of eating radishes. But even though they aren't my favorite vegetable, I always plant them in my garden. Why? Because they are the very first seed to germinate in the garden and they can be eaten within three to four weeks! After a long, cold winter, it's a pleasure to harvest the bright red roots with their crisp white flesh in early spring, and these early crops are the sweetest and mildest of the year.

Everyone should plant radishes. They are very easy to grow, they'll give you an impressive crop with little effort, and they'll reward you with quick gardening success!

LOCATION: Radishes are traditionally the first row planted in the garden in very early spring. Although, technically, they shouldn't be planted where any members of the cabbage family grew the previous year, I usually just try to avoid planting them where I had radishes the year before and I don't worry about the rest.

Radishes don't have attractive tops that would look pretty in a flower bed, but they could be planted there because they grow so early in the spring and mature so quickly that they'll probably be harvested before flower planting season.

The radish plant actually requires very little room. The radish root is often only one inch in diameter, and it has a very small taproot, instead of a broad root system that fans out around it.

To save space, radishes can be interplanted in rows with other, slower-developing crops; they will mature and be harvested before their space is needed. Because the radishes germinate in only four to ten days, radish seed is sometimes planted in with other slower-germinating vegetables, like carrots, to mark the row.

Radishes can even be grown in the house. Plant them in loose potting soil, keep it moist but not soggy, give the radishes at least six hours of good light—and harvest them as they mature! I've done this throughout the winter, replacing each radish harvested by planting another seed. Works great using long, narrow window boxes indoors in a south exposure next to the winter-cooled window glass. Harvest not only the radishes, but also the tender greens for use in cream soups.

GROWING RANGE: Everywhere.

SOIL REQUIREMENTS: Almost any soil. It should hold moisture yet be well-drained and loose; till it well, mixing in well-rotted manure or compost. If your soil dries out quickly, cover the freshly planted row with a thin layer of peat moss to help retain moisture.

MOISTURE: Radishes should be evenly moist. A dry spell encourages the radishes to get hot and peppery. Rain after a dry spell can cause the radishes to crack or split. For quick growth and mild flavor, water often, even daily, using a fine spray at first to prevent washing out the seed.

LIGHT: Full sun (for spring or fall planting) to part shade (for summer sun protection).

PLANTING SEASON: Radishes are a cool-weather crop. Plant them as early in the spring as you can work the soil. A second crop can be planted in late summer or early fall to mature during cooler weather. Radishes can withstand a little frost in both the spring and the fall, but they cannot tolerate the heat and longer days of midsummer.

HOW TO PLANT: Radishes are direct-seeded in the garden in very early spring.

- Till the soil to a depth of at least six inches to prepare the seed bed, when the soil temperature is 40 degrees F or as soon as the soil can be worked in the spring.
- Plant the seeds a quarter- to a half-inch deep (depending on the variety) and one inch apart, in rows two and a half feet apart or as close as eight inches to conserve space; or plant the radishes in foot-wide rows, spacing the seed two inches apart in all directions.
- Gently firm the soil to keep the seed in place.
- Water with a fine spray mist.
- Succession planting every two weeks will extend the harvest into summer, perhaps by planting one-fourth of a row each time for eight weeks. Stop planting the radishes about one month before the hottest weather of summer.
- Toward the end of the hottest weather of summer, start planting radishes again; succession planting every two weeks until one month before freezing weather will extend the crop.

NOTE: Radishes are said to repel insects that are attracted to squash and cabbage. Gardeners sometimes plant a ring of radishes around these vegetables and leave them in the garden all summer, allowing them to mature and go to seed.

ONGOING CARE:

- **Watering,** as necessary, or do light misting daily for the very best radishes.
- **Weeding,** as needed.
- **Tilling** to keep the soil loose and aerated.
- **Harvesting,** starting early on with the largest radishes, or pull every other one in the row, as needed. If the radishes touch each other as they grow, their shape will be affected, but they are still edible.
- **Removing** any radishes that grow past maturity or that are growing in the heat of summer—these are not suitable for eating as they will be woody and strong-flavored. Or, leaving the mature radishes to go to seed and harvesting the green seed pods, which are delicious when added to salads.
- **Replacing** each harvested radish with a seed, to keep the row productive, if desired.

VARIETIES INCLUDE:

- **Cherry Belle** radishes, which are very early, ready to harvest in only 21 days. They are small, round, bright red, and very sweet. They are commonly served whole in lettuce salads. A favorite!
- **Champion** radishes are round and as large in diameter as silver dollars, yet still remain mild, sweet, and crisp. 26 days. Recommended.
- **Snowbelle** are round and white, and the size of silver dollars; they remain fine grained and flavorful even well past maturity. 28 days.
- **Easter Egg II** grow to an inch and a half in diameter, and their skins are red, white, pink, or lavender. 26 days.
- **Flamivil** or **French Breakfast** radishes have oblong, cylindrical red roots that are edged in white at their tips. They are mild when served at or before maturity, but hot, peppery, tough, and woody after maturity. 25 days.
- **German Giant Parat** grows to the size of a baseball (but can be harvested at marble size) without getting hot or woody. 29 days.

• **White Icicle** has short top growth yet produces four- to six-inch long tapered radishes that are pure white inside and out. They remain crisp and tender longer than any other radish, well past maturity. 27 days.

YIELD: One radish per plant; about 30 radishes per three feet of row.

HARVESTING: To harvest, just pull the radish up by its tops. Pull the largest radishes first to allow space for the remaining radishes. Some radishes will grow part way out of the ground, helping you to recognize that they're ready for harvest!

Start checking the size of the radishes for possible harvest about twenty days after planting. Radishes can be harvested before they reach full size, and a few varieties can be harvested past maturity, but unless the weather has stayed cool and moist, you won't want to eat radishes that are overripe.

Radishes in the Kitchen

STORING: To store for several weeks in the refrigerator, just cut off the green tops and put the radishes in a sealed container or plastic bag.

FREEZING: Do not freeze radishes as they are made up mostly of water and will be ruined.

EATING RADISHES

Most people know that raw radishes can be sliced and added to salads, cole slaws, and relish plates, or used as a garnish, but it's not well known that radishes can be cooked.

Also, tender radish greens can be cooked and pureed into cream soups.

PREPARING: Clean the dirt off the radishes and trim off the leaves and the taproot, but leave the colorful skin intact. They can be eaten whole or sliced thin or cut into fancy shapes to garnish platters or serving plates.

FLAVORING: Salad dressings, butter, curry powder, chives, salt and pepper, cheese, almonds, walnuts.

COOKING: Steaming, boiling, or stir-fry.

Radish Appetizers

The old way of serving fresh radishes was to wash them, remove the taproot, and cut off the tops, leaving 1 or 1½ inches of the stems on. These would be chilled in a bowl of water in the refrigerator. When served, the stems were used as handles, and the radishes were dipped in salt and eaten.

Skillet Radishes

Stir-fry whole or sliced radishes in a generous amount of butter or olive oil until tender. Serve with a sprinkle of fresh parsley.

Creamed Radishes

Place radishes in boiling water and reduce heat to simmer. Cook until tender. Place cream in a small skillet with a dash of curry powder and simmer until thickened. Drain the radishes and pour the cream over them. Serve with salt and pepper, as desired.

Creamed Radishes with Cheese and Chives

Place radishes in boiling water and reduce heat to simmer. Cook until tender. Place cream in a small skillet and simmer until thickened. Drain the radishes and pour the cream over them. Top with grated cheese and snipped chives.

Radish Salad

Thinly slice radishes and combine with shredded cabbage and diced celery. Serve with your favorite prepared salad dressing.

Radish Vinaigrette

Slice radishes and combine with celery, cooked and cooled green beans, and perhaps slivered almonds. Toss in a vinaigrette dressing, chill, and serve.

Easy Radish Dressing

1. Puree together:

> 1/2 cup mayonnaise
> 1/4 cup sour cream
> 2 tablespoons minced radish
> 1 tablespoon minced fresh parsley
> 1 teaspoon lemon juice
> salt, as desired

2. Serve over salad.

SOYBEANS IN THE GARDEN

In Iowa, we have two planting seasons, corn and bean, and we tend to think of all our garden planting in terms of these two seasons. The field corn goes in early, and just when The Farmer is finishing it, it's time to switch to planting soybeans, which need warmer soil to germinate, like other beans.

Soybeans not only taste great, but they take nitrogen from the air and fix it in the soil, which benefits anything planted on bean ground the next season. Since corn requires a lot of nitrogen, you can see why Midwestern farmers turned to planting soybeans the year following corn. Otherwise, they'd have to supplement with a lot more nitrogen fertilizer, adding significantly to production costs.

Soybeans originated in Asia and parts of Africa and since it is not found anywhere in the wild, it's assumed that it was developed at least three thousand years ago. There are many varieties grown only in China and protected as "national treasures." It's a fairly new crop in the United States, becoming widely grown during World War II.

Although not a complete protein, soybeans do contain the most complete protein of any plant. Unless they are cooked, soybeans contain a trypsin inhibitor, which blocks an enzyme essential to the digestion of protein.

Soybeans are used to make all kinds of things: tofu, soy sauce, margarine, salad oils, shortening, and even paints, inks, soaps, and synthetic rubber, to name only a few. It has been our country's biggest single exported agricultural commodity. Half of the thousand acres managed by The Farmer are planted to soybeans.

I've seen an awful lot of soybeans, up close and personal, you might say, as we used to have to "walk" them to pull the weeds that could contaminate the harvested grain or plug up the combine. The weeds also compete with the soybeans for soil nutrients and water, and if not caught before they go to seed, the weeds will spread rampantly. In the old days before modern farming practices, a clean field was a source of considerable pride and considerable work in the heat and humidity of summer.

Despite living among hundreds of acres of soybeans, I never liked the flavor until I discovered the edible varieties that taste much sweeter than the commercial-grade field soybeans. The difference is even greater than the difference between field-grade corn and sweet corn, so if you've been off-put by the results of cooking field-grade soybeans, I encourage you to give edible soybeans a try.

Since you will rarely find canned green soybeans, and fresh soybeans are not widely or often available, it's worthwhile to raise this delicious—and nutritious—crop in your home garden.

LOCATION: Like other members of the bean family, soybeans benefit the soil by adding nitrogen. Follow The Farmer's lead and plant soybeans in the garden where corn, a heavy nitrogen feeder, grew the previous year. Although The Farmer sometimes has to plant soybeans on soybean ground, rotating crops is the ideal because it prevents or discourages disease and insect problems.

GROWING RANGE: Nearly everywhere. If you live in a high altitude or have a short growing season, select very early varieties. Soybean plants, although tender, can tolerate a light frost better than other types of beans.

SOIL REQUIREMENTS: Soybeans tolerate a wide range of soils, even clay, so long as it's not waterlogged for long periods. The soil should be somewhat loose during germination or the beans will have a tough time emerging, especially if a crust forms on the surface. (This was a problem here this year; several farmers had to replant fields where their soybeans died trying to break through, which is costly.) Tilling will break up the soil. After germination, the beans don't mind heavy soil, but it should be kept tilled to allow moisture to be absorbed.

MOISTURE: Soybeans like to be evenly moist, especially during flowering. Ideally, soybeans should have one inch of water per week.

LIGHT: Full sun.

PLANTING SEASON: Do not plant until after the last frost date for your area. The soil must be warm for the beans to germinate; the seeds will quickly rot in cold soil. This spring we had freezing weather after the last frost date, and some farmers had to replant entire fields of soybeans.

HOW TO PLANT: Plant the seeds an inch and a half deep and four inches apart in rows spaced two and a half feet apart.

ONGOING CARE:
- **Tilling** to keep the roots aerated. If the tiller throws a little soil onto the lower plant stems, they will develop additional roots, a trick farmers use to get additional nutrients to the plants, resulting in increased yields.

SOYBEANS IN THE GARDEN

- **Weeding,** which is usually taken care of by the tiller. Only rarely will you have to hand-pull weeds within the soybean row after early summer.
- **Watering,** as necessary to ensure a steady supply of moisture, especially during blooming time.
- **Staying out** of the beans when they are wet, as this can cause the spread of a disease known as rust.

Growing up, we weren't allowed to "walk beans," which was what we called hand-pulling the weeds in large bean fields, until late morning, when the dew would have evaporated and there was no danger of rust. Nor could we work near sundown, if dew or ground fog would be forming. Unfortunately for us, it meant we worked in the heat of the day during the hottest months of summer! Most people used a "corn knife" to chop out the weeds or a "bean hook" to cut weeds off at the base, but my father wouldn't allow us to do that because the weeds might grow up again from the roots. We had to pull them out by hand, which was very hard work because weeds tall enough to be visible over the soybean plants had roots that "went to China." Whole crews would go into the fields, each person responsible for getting the weeds in two or four rows, depending on the size and quantity of the weeds. Rows might be half a mile long, and you wouldn't get drinking water until you got to the other end, or maybe until you finished a whole round going both ways.

Our children have never had to "walk beans" because by that time there was a wonderful new invention, the "bean rider." This device was powered by a tractor. The riders sat on seats with their legs dangling between the bean rows and they squirted a few drops of weed killer onto the offending plants—carefully, because if the smallest drop hit a bean leaf, the entire plant would die. This method was still costly because in addition to buying the chemicals, you had to hire a crew to ride, often four or six people in addition to the tractor driver.

To eliminate the labor cost, the "weed wiper" was invented. This device was also powered by a tractor, and consisted of arms extended out with a kind of rope attached. The rope was wet with a weed-killing chemical, and was set to stand above the crops, so that the soybeans weren't killed, but the taller weeds would be. This method wasn't perfect, because there were shorter weeds that didn't get hit. The timing was tricky because you had to wait until the weeds were tall enough to rise above the bean row, but then you ran the risk of the soybean plants getting so large that their stems meshed together, closing the row so that a tractor would ruin the crop.

Next, scientists figured out a way to develop soybean plants that are resistant to the chemicals and most farmers spray the entire field, soybeans and weeds. Now the fields look almost 100 percent weed-free, and today's crop of children has never experienced the joys of "walking" or "riding" the soybeans!

VARIETIES INCLUDE:

- **Extra Early Green**, which is a short-season variety producing a green soybean crop in only 70 days.
- **Early Green Bush**, a midseason variety. The sixteen-inch plants crop in about 85 days.
- **Frostbeater**, which, as it's name implies, withstands light frosts. Good for northern areas with short seasons. 70 days.
- **Fiskeby V** has eighteen-inch plants that bear high-protein soybeans in 91 days. Good even in northern climates.
- **Kanrich**, a long-season variety requiring 100 to 115 days. The plants are twenty-four inches tall and produce a heavy yield. Recommended for warmer climates.

If in doubt, get recommendations from your local Extension office as to the proper varieties for your particular area.

YIELD: It varies greatly, depending on the variety chosen and your growing conditions. Each plant will produce numerous pods, and each pod will contain two or three beans.

HARVESTING:

- **Green:** Starting at three months after planting (two months for the short-season varieties), the soybeans can be harvested in the green stage, when the fuzzy pods are just beginning to turn a bit yellow, and shelled like peas. Since all the beans don't ripen at the same time, pull off the pods with plump beans inside, leaving the flatter pods for later harvest. It is normal for each pod to have only two or three beans. Soybeans are tough, so you'll need to hold the plant stem in one hand and separate the bean pod from the plant with the other.

- **Dry:** Or soybeans can be harvested when the pods are dry and the beans are hard, but while the stems are still somewhat green. To wait longer risks having the bean pods split open, spilling their contents on the ground—before you get them picked. This is a big worry for The Farmer with his soybean crops. His combine cannot harvest beans on green stalks, because they are too tough to go through the machine. So it's a rush to harvest the beans after the plant is dry and brittle yet before the pods pop open. And all this must be done quickly, while the weather cooperates. Shelling homegrown dry soybeans is easy. Cut the plants off at the ground and place them in a large box. Be patient and the pods will open of their own accord, spilling out the dry beans, if stored in a dry room.

Soybeans in the Kitchen

STORING: Green soybeans can be kept in plastic bags in the refrigerator. Don't wash the soybeans first, and be sure that no moisture is in the bags. A few holes punched in the bags will help them breathe, or else leave the bag loosely sealed.

Dry soybeans can be stored like any other dried bean—in jars or plastic bags at room temperature. Don't allow moisture in the bag or jar.

FREEZING:

Green:

- Wash the bean pods in cold water.
- Boil the pods five to ten minutes. Rinse in cold water and drain.
- Squeeze the beans out of the pods. Or, freeze the entire pods—some people think they taste better this way, although they take up much more freezer space. (Later, the frozen pods can be thawed somewhat and then easily shelled.)
- Pack the beans in freezer bags or containers. Seal, label and date, and freeze.

Dry: It's not necessary to freeze soybeans harvested at the dry stage.

EATING SOYBEANS

Green: Fresh soybeans can be cooked and eaten alone as a vegetable, or added to soups, stews, and casseroles.

Dry: Cooked dried soybeans can be used cold in salads or hot in casseroles, stews, soups, etc.

NOTE: Neither the green nor the dried soybean should be eaten without cooking because it contains some antinutritional properties that are destroyed in cooking.

PREPARING: Rinse off the green bean pods or the dry beans before using them.

FLAVORING: Tomatoes, molasses, onion, green onions plus tops, bacon, liquid smoke flavoring, celery, soy sauce, pimento, cayenne pepper, celery seeds, chili powder, chives, cumin, curry powder, garlic, gingerroot, oregano, paprika, sesame seeds, turmeric, parsley, poppy seeds, mustard seeds, mustard powder, sliced green olives stuffed with pimento, Parmesan cheese.

COOKING: Simmer the soybeans in liquid on low heat; higher heat makes the beans tough.

Since the soybean doesn't soak up seasoning as it cooks, you can get better flavor if the cooked beans are pureed, or else add flavorful ingredients to the cooked soybeans.

NOTE: When the recipes specify "cooked" soybeans, you can use either the cooked and shelled green soybeans or the cooked dried soybeans. Both the green pod and the dried soybeans need to be cooked before they can be used in recipes.

Green soybeans: Steam or boil them in their pods for 10 or 15 minutes, rinse in cold water, and then shell out the beans. Discard the pods. The shelled soybeans are now ready for use in a recipe.

Dry soybeans: The dry soybeans should be soaked in water for several hours and then simmered in water. Or, you can just cook them longer without soaking.

If you soak the dry soybeans at least two hours and then freeze them, you will shorten the cooking time by about two hours. Freeze them at least overnight for best results.

The easiest way to cook dry soybeans is to place them in hot water in the Crock-Pot and cook them overnight, or for eight hours or so.

Pureed Soybean Patties

The cooked dry soybeans can be pureed and mixed with chopped vegetables and your choice of the flavorings above. If the mixture needs something to get it to stick together, add an egg to the puree; if it's too runny, add a little soybean flour. Roll flattened spoonfuls in sesame seeds, ground pork rinds, or bread crumbs and fry them in butter or oil.

Roasted Dry Soybeans

After they are cooked and dried on paper towels, the soybeans can be spread out on a greased jelly-roll sheet and roasted in the oven at 350 degrees F for 30 minutes or until deep golden brown and crisp. Stir them from time to time as they are roasting.

• Flavor the roasted soybeans with salt, a flavored salt, or your favorite herbs and spices and eat out of hand.

- Grind the roasted soybeans into a flour and mix it with butter or peanut butter as a spread for crackers.

Chilled Soybeans with Salad Dressing

Delicious and easy!
Cook the soybeans as instructed above. Chill the cooked soybeans. Then marinate them in French, Thousand Island, or Buttermilk Ranch dressing. Serve cold as is or add the soybeans to salads.

Chilled Soybean Salad with Celery and Onion

Very good!
1. Combine 2 cups cooked soybeans, 1 cup diced celery, and ½ cup minced onion. Blend in enough mayonnaise to make the ingredients stick together.
2. Serve the soybeans on a bed of lettuce. Top with diced tomato.

Polynesian Soybean Salad

A favorite!
1. Combine:

> 1 ½ cups cooked soybeans
> 1 sweet green pepper, diced
> 1 sweet red pepper, diced
> 8-ounce can of pineapple tidbits, drained
> ¼ cup catsup
> 2 tablespoons honey
> 2 teaspoons cider vinegar
> 2 teaspoons soy sauce

2. Chill and serve.

Green Soybeans Cooked in Milk

Quick, easy, and tasty!
1. Cook and shell the green soybeans as described above.
2. In a saucepan, combine 2 or 3 cups fresh shelled soybeans with ½ cup milk. Stir to coat all the beans with the milk. Start the heat on

high, then reduce the heat and simmer for 15 to 20 minutes. Add ½ teaspoon salt and serve with a dash of paprika.

Red and Green Soybeans Cooked in Milk

One of our very favorite soybean recipes!
Follow the instructions for Green Soybeans Cooked in Milk, above. Just before serving, stir in chopped sweet red pepper or chopped canned pimento, and top it with shredded cheese—we prefer a cheddar cheese blend.

Soybean, Beef, and Bacon Casserole

Excellent dish!
1. Fry 4 or 5 strips of bacon in a large skillet until crisp. Remove the bacon to paper towels, cool and crumble.
2. Pour off—but do not scrape—the bacon grease from the skillet. Add half a chopped sweet green pepper and half a chopped onion and fry them in the skillet until they're browned.
3. Add 1 pound ground chuck or hamburger to the skillet and brown and crumble it. If the meat releases grease, drain it off.
4. Add 2 cups cooked soybeans and 2 cups tomato sauce.
5. Cover and simmer on the stove for 1 to 2 hours or cook it in the Crock-Pot all day on low or bake it in the oven at 325 degrees F.
6. Add the crumbled bacon and serve hot.
   NOTE: If desired, sprinkle on a little chili powder to taste.

Easy Soybean Soup

Excellent!
1. Place 1½ cups green or cooked dry soybeans in a saucepan with 4½ cups water plus 3 chicken bouillon cubes. Bring the mixture to a boil, then cover and reduce the heat to a simmer for 20 to 30 minutes.
2. Melt 6 tablespoons butter in a skillet. Lightly brown 1 cup chopped onion and ¾ cup chopped celery. Add to the simmering soybeans.
3. When the soybeans are soft, puree them with the cordless hand blender right in the saucepan or use a food processor. If the soy-

beans do not completely puree, simmer them for another 10 minutes and try again, repeating if necessary. Add a little more water if the soup gets too thick. Serve hot.

Basic Cooked Soybeans

These recipes are from the late, great Adelle Davis.
NOTE: You can add beef, chicken, ham or sliced hot dogs or sausage to any of the recipes below.

USING DRY SOYBEANS:

- Soak 1½ cups dry soybeans in 2 cups water. Freeze overnight.
- Place the frozen soybeans in a kettle (thawed or not). Add 1 cup soup stock (beef, chicken, or vegetable) and simmer, covered, 2½ to 4 hours or until the beans are nearly tender. Add more liquid if necessary.

USING GREEN SOYBEANS:

- Simmer 2½ cups shelled green soybeans, covered, in 2 cups broth for 20 minutes.

After preparing either the dry or green soybeans,

1. Add:
   1 cup tomato sauce
   1 onion, chopped
   2 tablespoons olive oil
   1 tablespoon Worcestershire sauce
   1 bay leaf
   ¼ teaspoon black pepper
   1 or 2 garlic cloves, minced
   salt, as desired

2. Continue cooking until the soybeans are tender. Remove the lid and add 2 to 4 tablespoons of fresh parsley, minced, or 1 to 1½ tablespoons dry parsley. Simmer, uncovered, to allow moisture to evaporate.
3. Serve hot or cold or use as a base for one of the variations, below.

"Baked" Soybeans

1. To Adelle Davis's recipe, add:

   2 to 4 tablespoons dark molasses

2. Continue to simmer until more moisture has evaporated and the consistency is like baked beans.
3. Five minutes before serving, add:

   1 cup chopped onions
   1 tablespoon dry mustard powder.

Chinese Soybeans:

1. To Adelle Davis's basic recipe, add:

   1/4 cup dark molasses
   1 cup chopped onions
   1 tablespoon minced gingerroot
   1 diced apple
   2 tablespoons soy sauce
   salt to taste

2. Simmer together and serve when the apples and onions are tender-crisp.

Creamed Soybeans

1. To Adelle Davis's basic recipe, add:

   2 diced pimentos or 2 4-ounce jars chopped pimento
   2 shredded carrots
   3 tablespoons minced fresh parsley
   pinch of basil

2. Simmer together to reduce liquid, then add:

   1 cup or more of undiluted evaporated milk

3. Serve sprinkled generously with Parmesan cheese.

Savory Soybeans

1. To Adelle Davis's basic recipe, add:

> 2 shredded carrots
> 1 cup chopped onions
> 1 diced rib of celery
> a pinch each of rosemary, savory, and marjoram.

2. Simmer a few minutes and serve.

Spanish Soybeans

1. To Adelle Davis's basic recipe, add:

> 1 cup chopped sweet bell peppers
> 1 or 2 teaspoons chili powder
> 1/4 cup catsup or Unketchup
> 1 cup chopped onions

2. Simmer together a few minutes, then add 1/4 cup shredded cheese: American, Jack or Parmesan. Serve.

"Smoked" Soybeans

1. To Adelle Davis's basic recipe, add:

> 1 cup chopped onion
> pinch of savory
> dash of liquid smoke flavoring

2. Fry three pieces of bacon until crisp, then crumble and add them to the soybeans. Serve.

SPINACH IN THE GARDEN

I love spinach—not only for it's wonderful flavor and bright color, but also because it is so high in nutrition, especially when eaten raw! It's easy to grow and produces a quick crop.

TYPES OF SPINACH:

- **Savoyed,** or wrinkled-leaf varieties. This type has thicker, less-flavorful leaves than the smooth-leaf varieties, plus dirt tends to accumulate in the wrinkles, making it harder to wash. This type is better cooked than used in salads, because the leaves are a bit tough and dry. Choose this type for growing into winter, when it is most productive. The best reason for growing this spinach is that it can withstand weather as low as 10 degrees F, and it can even be harvested in the snow, as I learned while young.

  As a child, I was halter-training a pony named Little Red near my garden one winter, but she stubbornly refused to follow me. Instead, she stuck her head down in the snow bank and came up with a mouthful of still-green savoyed spinach, with one big leaf caught in her halter like a dangling earring!

- **Semi-savoyed.** These varieties have a slightly crinkled leaf that is less thick than the savoyed varieties and grows well in spring or fall.

- **Smooth-leaf varieties.** These are tender, moist, and good fresh or cooked.

LOCATION: Don't grow spinach where spinach, beets, or Swiss chard grew the year before.

Spinach is usually planted in narrow or wide rows in the garden, but it could also go into a flower bed, supplying bright green foliage until summer, when the spreading flowers would need the space just as spinach is in decline due to heat.

For midseason planting, you can plant the spinach near a taller crop so that it will receive shade during the hottest part of the day.

Using cold frames, spinach can be grown into winter in most areas.

GROWING RANGE: Everywhere.

SOIL REQUIREMENTS: Any well-drained soil with plenty of humus; till it well and add well-rotted manure or compost. Spinach has a higher need for nitrogen than most garden vegetables.

MOISTURE: Because spinach has shallow roots, it needs a continuous supply of moisture. Don't allow it to dry out, which might induce bolting. Water twice weekly if you don't have sufficient rain.

LIGHT: Full sun to partial shade, so long as it gets four to six hours of sunlight.

PLANTING SEASON: A cool weather crop, in most climates; grow it in spring and fall.

Spinach prefers to grow in temperatures ranging between 40 and 75 degrees F, and can take light frost but not heat. Longer day length and higher heat cause spinach to bolt, or go to seed.

If you have mild temperatures rarely over 80 degrees F, you can grow spinach continuously from spring through fall. If you have mild winter temperatures that rarely dip below 25 degrees F, you can grow spinach all winter.

HOW TO PLANT: Spinach is best direct-seeded in the garden.

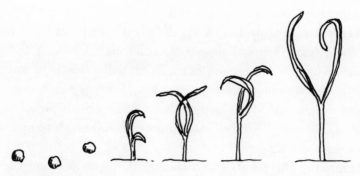

- Till the seed bed well to make the soil light and airy; mix in well-rotted manure or compost.
- Start planting four to eight weeks before the last frost date in the spring or as early as you can work the soil and the soil temperature is at least 35 degrees F. Use black plastic to warm the soil, if necessary.
- To hasten the germination, soak the seeds in water overnight (optional).
- Plant the seeds half an inch deep and an inch and a half apart in rows thirty inches apart, or as close as eighteen inches to conserve space, or plant in beds spacing it four to six inches apart in all directions.
- If you tilled the seed bed the previous fall, you can scatter the seeds in a wide row when the ground is barely thawed and incorporate the seeds by raking them into the soil, later thinning them for proper spacing.
- Succession planting every two weeks will increase the harvest season.
- Plant again six to eight weeks before the first frost date in the fall for a second crop, but plant the seed thicker to compensate for the lower germination rate in the warmer soil, then thin back to normal spacing.

ONGOING CARE:

- **Thinning** every other plant so that the remaining crop is three to six inches apart. (Eat the thinnings.)
- **Tilling** deeply to keep the soil loose and airy for the deep taproot of spinach.

- **Watering** to ensure an even soil moisture.
- **Harvesting** regularly to keep the plants productive and to get the leaves before they get old and tough.
- **Covering** the plants with black mesh will extend the harvest season into summer. I've successfully grown spinach under our nine-foot black-mesh satellite dish, which I've been able to harvest well into summer despite high temperatures and long days.
- **Removing** the plants when the weather gets hot and the plants begin to go to seed. The leaves get tough and taste strong and won't be worth eating. Till them under to add nutrients to the soil.
- **Starting** a second crop in midseason, for fall and winter harvest, perhaps selecting the wrinkled-leaf variety to withstand cooler temperatures.
- **Mulching** around the plants before winter, or covering them with plastic tunnels, to extend the harvest. In mild areas, the spinach will grow unprotected all winter; the following spring the plants will go to seed quickly, so remove them and start over.

VARIETIES INCLUDE:
- **Bloomsdale Longstanding**, a savoyed variety with dark, glossy leaves that withstands the cold well; outstanding as a fall and winter crop, early to harvest. 42 days.
- **Melody**, which has dark green, savoyed leaves. 42 days.
- **Avon**, with succulent, semi-savoyed leaves, is quick growing and works well for spring or fall planting. 44 days.
- **Tyee**, a large semi-savoyed that grows rapidly, produces well, and is slow to bolt. 42 days.
- **Medania**, a smooth-leafed variety that is slow to bolt despite heat and drought. 65 days.
- **Olympia**, a smooth-leafed variety with erect leaves; withstands some heat and drought without bolting. 40 days.
- **New Zealand** spinach, with smaller, smooth leaves, is not a true spinach but it grows the same and tastes the same when it is cooked. It tolerates heat better than regular spinach and can be harvested all season. 70 days.

• **Basella Malabar** is a red-stemmed spinach that is a vining plant that gets up to twenty feet long and needs a trellis or fence for support. Start the harvest by plucking leaves when the vine is about three feet tall. Good fresh or cooked.

YIELD: Five to ten pounds on a ten foot row.

HARVESTING: You can start when plants are about six weeks old and have five or six leaves; the harvest can continue until just before seed stalks develop. Break off two or three outer leaves, leaving at least half of the plant foliage so that it can grow more. By picking individual leaves, you can harvest the plants every ten days. When the plants first show signs of bolting, harvest the entire row by cutting the plants off close to the ground.

Spinach in the Kitchen

STORING: Store it in perforated plastic bags in the crisper drawer in the refrigerator, either unwashed, or washed and dried in a salad spinner. Moisture on the leaves will cause it to go bad.

For freshest flavor, try to use the spinach the same day it is harvested.

FREEZING:
• Wash spinach in cold water, discarding tough leaves.
• Steam or blanch in boiling water for two minutes. (Steaming is better because it preserves more nutrients.)
• Drain and cool.
• Pack into freezer bags. Seal, label and date, and freeze.

EATING SPINACH

Spinach is wonderful raw, in salads, or cooked. It's good in stir-fries and casseroles, creamed or added to soups.

PREPARING: Rinse well in cool water, discarding wilted, yellowed, or damaged leaves. Spin dry in a salad spinner or pat dry with towels. The spinach can be left whole or chopped. After cooking, it can be pureed.

If the spinach leaves are older or thickened, you might have to remove the stems. If so, just tear the leaf part off, cut it off with a quick whack from a chef's knife, or try this: fold the leaf in half lengthwise along the stem, hold it in one hand, and pull the stem off with the other.

FLAVORING: Spinach can be seasoned with basil, mace, marjoram, nutmeg, oregano, parsley, salt and pepper, butter, onions, bacon, lemon. It's great with cream, eggs, cheeses and other vegetables.

COOKING: Methods include steaming, boiling, stir-frying, baking, sauteeing in butter or olive oil.

NOTE: When cooking spinach in water, use the least possible amount, or try cooking it without any water at all—covered and on low heat, it will cook in its own moisture in a few minutes. Be careful not to overcook spinach, no matter which method you use, as it will lose flavor, nutrients, and its nice bright color.

NOTE: Don't cook spinach in aluminum pans because the spinach will turn gray and develop an acid taste.

Egg Spinach

Buttered steamed or boiled and drained spinach is great with the addition of some sliced or chopped hard-boiled egg.

Lemon-Nutmeg Spinach

Buttered steamed or boiled and drained spinach is great with a squeeze of fresh lemon juice and a sprinkle of nutmeg. (Freshly ground nutmeg has the best flavor.)

Lemon-Sesame Spinach

Buttered steamed or boiled and drained spinach can be dressed up with fresh lemon juice and a sprinkling of toasted sesame seeds.

Bacon Spinach

Fry a couple of pieces of bacon. When crispy, remove the bacon to drain on paper towels, and wilt the spinach in the bacon fat. Serve with the crumbled bacon bits.

Wilted Spinach

Stir fresh spinach in a large skillet with a little butter or olive oil.

Creamed Spinach

A favorite!
1. Melt ¼ cup of butter in a large skillet. Add about 1 pound of fresh spinach and stir until the spinach is wilted and deep green. Salt as desired, and add ¼ teaspoon white pepper.
2. Place the spinach in a food processor. Puree.
3. Pour in 1 cup heavy cream and blend well.
4. Serve in bowls with a sprinkle of nutmeg.

Creamed Spinach Parmesan

1. Melt ¼ cup of butter in a large skillet. Add about 1 pound of fresh spinach and stir until the spinach is wilted and deep green. Salt as desired, and add ¼ teaspoon white pepper.
2. Place the spinach in a food processor. Puree.
3. Pour in 1 cup heavy cream. Blend well.
4. Serve in bowls topped with a spritz of freshly squeezed lemon juice and a generous grating of Parmesan cheese.

Spinach with Cream Cheese

Cook about 1 pound of spinach in a large skillet in a little butter until the spinach is wilted. Add one 8-ounce package of Philadelphia cream cheese to the skillet and stir into the spinach. Serve with a sprinkle of ground nutmeg, if desired.

Mom's Spinach Casserole

1. Wilt 8 cups of fresh spinach in a little butter in a large ovenproof skillet.
2. Stir in one can of cream soup—any flavor, like chicken or celery.
3. Top with shredded cheese, like cheddar.
4. Sprinkle with crumbled pork rinds or soda cracker crumbs.
5. Bake at 350 degrees F until the cheese melts and the casserole is hot. Serve.

Easy Spinach Salad

1. Combine the following and chill at least 2 hours:

> torn fresh spinach to make 4 cups
> 6 green onions, sliced, including tops
> 3 hard-boiled eggs, sliced
> 8 slices bacon, fried crisp, drained, and crumbled
> 1 sweet pepper (any color), chopped or sliced

2. To make dressing, combine:

> 1/2 cup olive oil
> 1/4 cup cider vinegar
> 3 tablespoons lemon juice
> 1/2 teaspoon salt (optional, or less, to taste)
> 1/4 teaspoon lemon zest
> 1/8 teaspoon dry mustard

3. Just before serving, pour dressing over the spinach and toss.

SUMMER SQUASH
IN THE GARDEN

Summer squash is one of my favorite vegetables, and yellow straightneck or crookneck are my very favorite summer squash varieties.

Unlike winter squash, which is harvested after the vegetable is mature and ripened and hard-shelled, summer squash is eaten when it is young, tender, and immature. Their thin skins are eaten along with the delicious flesh.

Like all squash, the plants produce bright yellow flowers that are either male or female types. The female flowers can be recognized because they have a swelling at their base; once pollinated, this becomes the squash. Squash flowers are good to eat, and you can harvest a few male flowers at any time without harming squash production; or, if you're getting more squash than you can use or give away, harvest some female blossoms, too. For instructions on how to prepare the blossoms, see "Zucchini."

Summer squash has a wonderful flavor unmatched by any other type of squash, and it's so easy to grow—it should have a place in every home garden!

LOCATION: Choose a spot with good air circulation where no members of the squash family, including pumpkins and cucumbers, as well as melons, grew the previous year.

NOTE: All squash, summer and winter, can cross-pollinate. This won't affect the current crop, but it will affect the seeds; if you plan to save the seeds to plant the next year, space the varieties some distance from each other or you might have peculiar offspring.

GROWING RANGE: Everywhere. In extremely short-season areas, warm the soil and start with seedlings.

SOIL REQUIREMENTS: Any soil that is light and well drained. Till thoroughly and mix in well-rotted manure or compost.

MOISTURE: Moderate; water if the soil gets dry or you have extremely hot weather.

LIGHT: Full sun.

PLANTING SEASON: All squash is a warm-weather crop and should be planted after the last frost date.

HOW TO PLANT: Summer squash is usually direct-seeded in all but the shortest growing seasons as they do not like to be transplanted.

- Thoroughly and deeply till the soil, mixing in well-rotted manure or compost.
- If necessary, warm the soil bed with black plastic.
- Start the planting one week after the last frost date for your area or when the soil temperature is at least 60 degrees F.
- If desired, for easier watering, bury a perforated plastic one-gallon milk jug so all but two inches is in the ground.

• Plant four to six seeds one inch deep in a twelve-inch circle or hill, surrounding the buried milk bottle, if you are using it. Space the hills four feet apart.

• Or plant the summer squash in a row, spacing the seeds twenty inches apart in rows four feet apart. This is my favorite method and I plant several types of summer squash as well as zucchini in the row.

• If you're using the black plastic, remove it after planting and germination have occurred, or puncture it well so that water can penetrate.

To start seedlings:

• Start three weeks before the last frost date for your area.

• Plant the seeds one inch deep in peat pots.

• Harden off the seedlings for one week before transplant time.

• Transplant the seedlings outdoors one week after the last frost date for your area, when night temperatures are above 60 degrees F.

• Carefully bury the peat pot in the soil, disturbing the roots as little as possible or the seedling won't take well to transplanting.

• Follow direct-seeding directions, above, for spacing.

Ongoing care:

• **Covering** the young plants if there is a threat of frost. (Full-grown plants can tolerate a light frost.)

• **Thinning** each hill back to two or three plants.

• **Weeding** near the squash will not be necessary after the first two or three weeks, as the plants have a dense foliage that discourages weeds.

• **Watering**, as needed, directing the water to the roots, not the plants, or water overhead early in the day so the plants will dry out quickly in the sun.

• **Staying away** from the plants when they are wet, to avoid disease.

- **Harvesting** regularly, to stimulate the plant to keep producing until winter. If you allow one squash to stay on the plant too long, the entire plant might quit flowering.

VARIETIES INCLUDE:

- **Crookneck Yellow Squash** is a bush-type plant that produces an abundant yield of delicious, curved, bright yellow squash with slightly warted skin. 50 days.
- **Early Prolific Straightneck Yellow Squash** is a personal favorite because it's ready early. It sets smooth-skinned.yellow squash that is straight, as opposed to curved, on bushy plants. 42 days.
- **Butter Scallop** is a bush-type plant that produces flattened, yellow-skinned squash that look like flying saucers with bumps along the perimeter. 50 days.
- **White Pattypan** is a bush-type plant with scallop-type squash that have white skins and a slightly nutty flavor. 47 days.

YIELD: Depending on the variety and how well you keep up the harvest, you can get dozens of squash off one hill.

HARVESTING: Be sure to pick the squash while they are young and their skins are still tender, usually when they are under six or seven inches for crooknecks or straightnecks, under three inches for scallop or pattypan. If they are overlarge or their skin gets tough, just toss them to the hogs or put them in the compost pile because they will have poor flavor.

Check the plants every other day as squash grows quickly.

You can harvest and eat the yellow blossoms. For information, see "Zucchini."

Summer Squash in the Kitchen

STORING: If you'll use them in a day or two, you can leave them on the counter. Otherwise, store them in the refrigerator.

FREEZING:
- Young and tender squash can be frozen with their skins on, and produce the best results. Older squash can be frozen after it's peeled, but it tends to turn rubbery.
- Wash the squash. Remove the stem end. Slice or dice, as desired.
- Steam or blanch for three minutes. Cool and drain.
- Pack into freezer containers or bags and seal. Label, date, and freeze.

Or steam or boil sliced or diced squash in a little water until tender. Cool and drain, then mash or puree the squash and freeze in containers, leaving about half an inch headspace.

EATING SUMMER SQUASH

PREPARING: Wash the whole squash, cut off the stem and blossom ends. Leaving the skin on, cut up as desired for cooking. The squash seeds are immature and eaten along with the flesh and skins.

If the squash has become a bit too large and mature, you can still eat it if you remove the skin—however, it won't be as tasty as tender young squash.

FLAVORINGS: Summer squash goes well with basil, celery seed, curry, dill, ginger, garlic, marjoram, mint, oregano, mustard seed, rosemary, parsley, summer savory, butter, olive oil, salt and pepper, Parmesan cheese, bacon, onion.

COOKING: Methods include steaming, boiling, stir-frying, sauteeing.

Basic Summer Squash

Summer squash has such a delicate flavor, that my favorite method of preparing it is to steam it or boil squash slices in a small amount of water until tender, drain them, and serve them lightly salted with a pat of butter.

Summer Squash with Lemon Butter

Steam or boil sliced summer squash just until tender. Add lemon juice to melted butter and pour over the squash. Serve with salt and pepper, as desired.

Summer Squash with Dill

Steam or boil sliced summer squash just until tender. Serve with a dollop of sour cream or plain yogurt, topped with a sprinkle of dill.

Summer Squash Broiled with Parmesan

Steam or boil sliced summer squash until tender. Drain and place the squash in an ovenproof pan. Drizzle the squash with melted butter and sprinkle with Parmesan cheese. Place the squash under a preheated broiler for a minute or two until lightly browned. Serve.

Summer Squash Skillet

Melt butter in a skillet and saute a little minced garlic and onion. Add sliced summer squash and tomato slices cut in half. If desired, sprinkle a little marjoram, salt and pepper over the vegetables. Cook until the vegetables are tender, stirring often, about 5 minutes. Sprinkle with Parmesan cheese and serve hot.

Summer Squash Soup

Quick and delicious!
1. Dice 2 large squash and 2 onions; saute in 1 stick of butter until tender. (You can use less butter, if desired.)
2. Add 1 quart of chicken broth and simmer for 10 minutes.
3. Use the cordless blender to puree the vegetables in the pan, or else use the food processor or a blender.
4. Add 1 cup cream (or milk) and heat through, but do not boil. Serve hot, garnished with snipped chives.

Baked Squash Casserole

Great!
1. Saute 1 cup minced onion in 2 tablespoons butter.
2. Boil summer squash in a little water until tender. Drain and puree in a food processor to make 3 cups.
3. Combine the squash and the onion and add:

> 1/2 cup sour cream
> Salt and pepper, as desired

4. Place in a casserole that has been coated with vegetable spray.
5. Bake at 350 degrees F for 10 or 15 minutes or until hot and bubbly. Serve.

WINTER SQUASH IN THE GARDEN

Older varieties of winter squash were described by native Americans as one of "the three sisters," the other two being corn and beans. All three were diet staples, which they planted together in gardens. It went something like this: in the corn patches, every eighth seed would be a bean, and every fifth row would be planted to squash. Climbing beans grew up corn plants, vining winter squash grew below.

It's interesting that in Central and South America, winter squash, including pumpkins, were originally raised to eat their seeds; now we mainly raise them to eat their flesh.

Although most winter squash originated as vine plants, varieties are now available in bush form. This is good news for gardeners short on room, as the vining type can spread as much as twenty feet!

To conserve space, all but the largest squash can be grown on a trellis, using mesh or cheesecloth slings to support the fruits. Or, you can make four-legged teepees from well-anchored eight-foot poles with rope wrapped around the legs for support, and let one plant go up each leg. Old stepladders work, also. No matter which method you use, you'll need to tie the vines to the support with strips of cloth or old pantyhose. Instead of using slings, hay bales can be positioned as platforms under large squash.

TYPES OF WINTER SQUASH:

- **Acorn,** which has smooth, greenish-black rinds and yellow-orange flesh that's somewhat coarse. Great baked in the shell.
- **Buttercup,** shaped like a turban, also stores well for a long time because it has thick, hard flesh. Very sweet, mild, rich flavor with dry, smooth texture. Good for pies.
- **Butternut** has oblong nine- to ten-inch fruit with beige skins and orange flesh and has a small seed cavity in the bulbous end. It's got a dense, creamy texture and medium-sweet flavor. Butternut is resistant to disease and insects, including the squash borer.
- **Hubbard** has gray or bluish-gray rinds and smooth, sweet, nutty flesh that bakes well. Stores for a long time.
- **Spaghetti** has oval fruits filled with flesh that's much like spaghetti, and it is a vegetable substitute for pasta without all the starchy carbohydrates. It has a bland flavor, and must be dressed up with butter, a sauce, or a dressing to make it good.
- And many more!

Although they share similar growing conditions, winter squash has such a wide variety of sizes, shapes, colors, and flavors, that you'll want to try them all to determine your own favorites.

LOCATION: Choose a spot with good air circulation where no members of the squash family, including pumpkins and cucumbers, as well as melons, grew the previous year.

Vining types need lots of space to sprawl. Bush types and semi-bush types take much less space and are preferred for smaller gardens.

NOTE: All squash, summer and winter, can cross-pollinate. This won't affect the current crop, but it will affect the seeds; if you plan to save the seeds for planting the next year, space the varieties some distance from each other or you might have peculiar offspring.

GROWING RANGE: Winter squash grows well everywhere; just be sure that the growing season is long enough for the squash to mature. In short-season areas, warm the soil and start with seedlings. The squash can take heat but not frost.

SOIL REQUIREMENTS: Light, well-drained soil. Till thoroughly and mix in well-rotted manure or compost and add crushed eggshells.

MOISTURE: Winter squash needs even and plentiful moisture. Water when the soil is dry one inch below the surface.

LIGHT: Full sun, but they are somewhat tolerant of a little shade.

PLANTING SEASON: All squash is a warm-weather crop and should be planted after the last frost date.

HOW TO PLANT: Winter squash is usually direct-seeded in all but the shorter growing seasons, which require a head start for the squash to have time to ripen on the vine.

- Thoroughly and deeply till the soil, mixing in well-rotted manure or compost.
- If necessary, warm the soil bed with black plastic.
- Start the planting one week after the last frost date for your area or when the soil temperature is at least 60 degrees F.
- If desired, bury a perforated plastic one-gallon milk jug so all but two inches is in the ground, to fill for easier and deeper watering.

- Plant five or six seeds one inch deep in a twelve-inch circle or hill, surrounding the buried milk jug, if you are using it.
- Space the hills four feet apart for bush types; at least six to eight feet, or more, for vining types.
- Remove the black plastic after planting and germination have occurred, if you're using it.

To start seedlings:

- Start the seeds in pots four weeks before the last frost date for your area.
- Plant the seeds one inch deep in peat pots.
- Harden off the seedlings for one week before transplant time.
- Transplant the seedlings outdoors one week after the last frost date for your area, when night temperatures are above 60 degrees F.
- Carefully bury the peat pot in the soil, disturbing the roots as little as possible or the seedling won't take well to transplanting.
- Follow direct-seeding directions, above, planting one or two seedlings per hill.

ONGOING CARE:

- **Covering** the plants with row covers, if desired, will keep them warmer and give them a better start. Remove the fabric when the first female flowers appear so that bees can pollinate them. Or, you can hand-pollinate.
- **Thinning** acorn squash hills down to three plants; all other winter squash should be thinned to two plants per hill.
- **Mulching** around the plants, to retain moisture and keep down weeds,

after the plants are one foot tall and the soil is well warmed.

- **Pollinating** by hand by rubbing a male blossom against the females; if your female flowers are not growing into squash; it may be because of a lack of bees.
- **Watching** for squash bugs, and eliminating them as soon as you find them, to prevent an infestation. If you have only a few, you can pick them off by hand. I've even used the shop vacuum on them before applying an organic control. If the population gets out of hand, you may need to use a chemical control or risk losing the entire crop.
- **Removing** all flowers after midsummer, so that the plants put all their energy into developing the existing crop before winter. You can eat the blossoms—they're delicious! For information, see "Zucchini."
- **Harvesting** all ripe squash just before the first frost.
- **Covering** the immature squash to protect it from fall frost, so they can continue to develop.

VARIETIES INCLUDE:

Acorn Squash

- **Table King** and **Table Queen** are both bush-type plants that produce 1½-pound, six-inch-long and five-inch-wide, dark green squash with yellow-orange flesh and a small seed cavity. Six to eight squash per plant. Excellent to eat and to store! 76-80 days.
- **Cream of the Crop** is a semi-bush-type plant that produces creamy-white-skinned acorn squash with buttery golden flesh that weigh three pounds. 85 days.
- **Heart of Gold** is a semi-bush plant that produces acorn squash that are heart-shaped and have mottled creamy-white skins with dark green stripes. 90 days.

Butternut

- **Waltham Butternut** is a vining plant. The nine- or ten-inch-long squash have solid orange flesh, weigh about three pounds, and have thicker, straighter necks and an excellent flavor. 95 days.

- **Early Butternut** is a semi-bush vining plant that produces creamy-skinned squash ten to twelve inches long that have rich, meaty, orange flesh and seed cavities in the wider, blossom end. 82 days.
- **Butter Boy** is a vining plant with extra-sweet, nutty-flavored 2½-pound squash with tan skins and reddish-orange flesh. 80 days.
- **Butterbush** is a bush-type plant that saves a lot of space over the usual butternut vines. The squash are eight to ten inches long and weigh a pound and a half, and have deep orange-red rich-flavored flesh. 75 days.

Spaghetti

- **Vegetable Spaghetti,** a vining plant that produces smooth, oblong, yellow-skinned squash that resembles spaghetti pasta and can be substituted for it in cooking. 100 days.
- **Pasta Hybrid** produces large, ten- to twelve-inch-long by seven-inch-wide squash. 92 days.
- **Small Wonder** produces small spaghetti squash that are just right for single servings. 70 days.

Other Winter Squash

- **Jumbo Pink Banana** produces squash that get three to four feet long and weigh up to seventy-five pounds! 105 days.
- **Golden Hubbard** produces sweet ten-pound squash with a bumpy red-orange skin and fine-grained flesh. Keeps well. 95 days.
- **Buttercup** squash weigh three to five pounds, and are shaped like turbans with gray-flecked green skins and orange flesh. A good keeper. 105 days.

- **Lakota** is an heirloom hubbard-type squash grown by the Sioux. The eight- or nine-inch squash has a bulbous shape, orange skins striped in dark green, and the flesh is sweet and nutty and bakes well. 85 days.
- **Delicata,** or **Sweet Potato Squash,** produces unusual seven- to nine-inch ribbed squash that are rich and moist like sweet potatoes. 100 days.

YIELD: Varies greatly depending on the variety grown, but usually a minimum of eight to twelve squash per plant.

HARVESTING: Wait to harvest after the leaves have died back and the squash have hard shells, but before the first frost. Winter squash get sweet when they have sunny days and cool fall nights. A light frost will further sweeten the squash, but will greatly shorten their storage time.

Check the hardness of the skins by pressing with your thumbnail. If it resists denting, it's ready to harvest. Cut the squash off the vines with nippers, leaving at least two inches of stem on the squash. Allow them to cure in the sun for a week, if possible, protecting the squash from frost.

Do not carry the squash by the stems. If the stem breaks off, use that squash first as it will be subject to rotting in storage.

NOTE: Acorn squash are the first to ripen, perhaps because they are smaller than other squash. They can be harvested earlier than the others, when their yellow spot turns orange.

Also, if you are eager to eat a butternut earlier, you can harvest it when the skin has turned from a greenish color to a tan or brownish color; you can tell that it's mature when the seeds inside are plump and well filled out. But leave the rest on the vine to ripen till frost so that they will store up more sugars.

Winter Squash in the Kitchen

STORING: Winter squash, when harvested mature, have a hard rind. Do not wash the squash before storage, but you can wipe it off with a damp cloth, if needed. Cure the squash between 70 and 80 degrees F for one week, except for acorn squash, which doesn't need curing.

To prevent storage mildew, try this: Wipe the squash's exterior with a mild chlorine solution, allow them to dry, and then coat them with vegetable oil.

Store winter squash so that they are not touching each other. In a cool, dry place at about 60 degrees F, they'll keep for at least a month or two; at 50 degrees F with low humidity, they will keep till spring.

FREEZING:
- Use mature squash. Wash and dry. Cut the squash into halves and scrape out the seeds and seed membrane with a spoon.
- Place the squash flesh-side down in a large cake pan or roasting pan or lasagna pan. You can stack the squash in layers; I usually do a large pile at one time.
- Add a quarter-inch of water if the squash is in a single layer or a half-inch of water if the squash is in more layers. Drape foil over the squash if you have more than one layer, otherwise leave it uncovered.
- Bake at 375 degrees F until the flesh is tender when pricked with a sharp knife.
- Remove squash from the oven and cool.

311

Scoop flesh out of shells with a large spoon. Mash or puree the flesh in a food processor or run it through a food mill.
• Pack the squash into freezer containers. Seal, label and date, and freeze.

EATING WINTER SQUASH

NOTE: Winter squash may be used in recipes calling for pumpkin.

PREPARING: Wash and dry the squash. Cut in half with an electric knife, being very careful as the skins can be very tough. Remove the seeds and seed membranes with a spoon.

FLAVORING: Winter squash seasonings include: allspice, cinnamon, cloves, curry, fennel, ginger, nutmeg, mustard seed, rosemary, parsley, butter, salt and pepper, nuts, orange, lemon, brandy, rum.

COOKING: Methods include steaming, baking, broiling, boiling.
To make squash puree, follow the baking directions, above, under "Freezing." Or you can remove the rind, cut the flesh into chunks, and steam or boil it and then mash it into a puree. Place halves in oven with butter, maybe sugar, etc.

Whipped Winter Squash

My favorite! It tastes sweet without added sugar.
1. To 2 cups of hot winter squash puree, add:

> 2 tablespoons butter (stir it in the squash until melted)
> 3 tablespoons crushed pineapple
> 3 tablespoons sour cream
> 1 teaspoon lemon juice
> 1/2 teaspoon cinnamon
> 1/4 teaspoon salt

2. Beat together until smooth. Serve hot.

Baked Squash Casserole

1. To 2 to 3 cups winter squash puree, add:

> 2 eggs, beaten
> 1/2 cup shredded cheddar cheese
> 1 cup minced onion
> 1/4 cup butter, melted
> 1 teaspoon ground sage
> 1/2 teaspoon salt (or to taste)
> 1/8 teaspoon pepper

2. Stir together and pour into a casserole dish coated with vegetable spray. Top with another 1/2 cup of shredded cheddar cheese and lightly sprinkle with paprika.
3. Bake at 400 degrees F for 25 minutes or until the casserole is bubbly and the cheese is lightly browned.

Baked Winter Squash Casserole with Nut Topping

The Farmer's favorite!

1. To 3 to 4 cups winter squash puree, add:

> 3 eggs
> 1/2 cup sugar
> 1/4 cup milk
> 1/4 teaspoon cinnamon
> 1/4 teaspoon allspice

2. Turn out in a casserole dish coated with vegetable spray.
3. Bake the squash in the oven at 350 degrees F for 30 or 40 minutes.
4. To make topping, combine:

> 1/4 cup brown sugar, packed
> 1/4 cup butter, mixed into the sugar with a fork until
>   crumbly
> 1/2 cup chopped pecans

5. Remove the squash from the oven, sprinkle on the topping, and serve.

Baked Winter Squash in the Shell

So easy, and delicious!

Butternut, acorn, or any winter squash (except spaghetti) can be baked and served in their shells. Just cut the squash in half, being very careful as you can lose control of the knife cutting the hard shells.

NOTE: It's easier to cut the squash if you use a sawing motion with a serrated knife or use an electric knife. If this is too difficult, first place the squash in the microwave for a few minutes, just until the shells are a little soft. Clean out the seeds and seed membranes.

Place the halved squash cut-side up in a cake pan or on a baking sheet. Brush the exposed flesh with butter and place a pat or two inside each seed cavity. Salt and pepper, as desired, or use one of the seasonings listed above, or sprinkle the squash with a little brown sugar, or put a spoonful of maple syrup in the cavity. Bake at 325 degrees F until the flesh is soft and the cut edges are lightly browned, perhaps 45 minutes. If the squash is small, like acorn, serve each person one-half shell. It can be properly eaten with a fork or a spoon, scraping the flesh from the shell.

Alternately, place the halved squash cut-side down in ¼ inch of water. When tender, flip the squash over, then brush them with butter and place a pat or two in each cavity. Return the squash to the oven (or use the broiler) until lightly browned. This will result in squash that are a little more moist, and they can be left unwatched for a longer time than just baking them right-side up as described above.

Spaghetti Squash in the Kitchen

STORING: Same as other winter squash.

FREEZING: Just follow the directions, below, for cooking the whole spaghetti squash. Using a large meat fork, rake the spaghetti-like flesh out of the peel, into a bowl. Pack the spaghetti squash in a freezer container, seal, label and date, and freeze.

EATING SPAGHETTI SQUASH

Cooked spaghetti squash can be served as a vegetable, or it can be substituted for spaghetti in pasta recipes.

PREPARING: Simply wash the outside of the squash in preparation for cooking it in the shell. Follow directions, above, for freezing spaghetti squash.

FLAVORING: Butter, salt and pepper, Italian or vinaigrette dressings, tomato sauce, cream sauce, and cheeses.

COOKING: Methods include boiling, baking, or microwaving.

To boil the spaghetti squash, prick through the rind in several places with a long meat fork. Place the squash in a large saucepan and cover it with water. Bring it to a boil and cook it until tender, about 30 minutes. Cut the squash in half. Remove and discard the seeds and scrape out the spaghettilike strands of squash with a fork.

To microwave the spaghetti squash, prick through the rind in several places with a long meat fork. Place it in the microwave on a paper towel. Microwave the squash on high for about 10 to 15 minutes or until the shell gives a bit when pressed. Let it rest for 5 or 6 minutes, then cut the squash in half. Remove and discard the seeds and scrape out the spaghettilike strands of squash with a fork.

To bake the spaghetti squash, prick through the rind in several places with a long meat fork. Place the squash on a jelly-roll sheet and bake at 350 degrees F for about 1 hour or until the shell gives a bit when pressed. Remove from the oven and cool a bit, then cut the squash in half. Remove and discard the seeds and rake out the spaghettilike strands with a fork.

The cooked "spaghetti" can now be used just like pasta, with your favorite sauces and meat and vegetable additions. Or, serve it as a vegetable side dish, tossed with butter, salt and pepper, as desired.

Spaghetti Squash with Garden Tomatoes

1. Use meaty beefstake or roma tomatoes. Coarsely chop several tomatoes into a saucepan.
2. Add some chopped garden onions, a little olive oil and a pat or two of butter, fresh minced parsley, minced garlic, salt, pepper, and Italian seasoning, as desired. Cook until tomatoes are just heated through.
3. Pour the tomato mixture over hot spaghetti squash (see above for directions) and sprinkle with Parmesan cheese. Serve.

SWEET POTATOES
IN THE GARDEN

Sweet potatoes are not a potato at all, nor are they a yam. They are actually a member of the morning glory family, and the part we eat is really the root.

There are hundreds of varieties, with oval or tapering roots, and they come in a variety of skin colors: pink, red, purple, brown, yellow. Their flesh can be white, cream, golden, and deep orange.

Sweet potatoes' flesh is said to be either dry or moist, based on the taste, not the water content. The moist-flesh varieties have more starch converted to sugar during cooking than the dry-flesh varieties.

Sweet potatoes need at least four months of warm or hot weather, and loose, crumbly soil—give them these two things and you'll have success. Sweet potatoes are interesting to grow and they can be used in a variety of recipes.

LOCATION: Avoid planting sweet potatoes on low ground where cold air and water pool.

Sweet potato vines are quite attractive and can easily be added to the landscaping or the flower beds. This year I planted sweet potatoes on landscaped berms, as ground cover around forsythia and bridal wreath bushes. Sweet potatoes also make a trailing container plant.

GROWING RANGE: Sweet potatoes can be raised everywhere that they can grow at least three months without frost. They love hot weather, and they are very frost sensitive; the roots can be damaged at temperatures below 40 or 45 degrees F.

SOIL REQUIREMENTS: Although sweet potatoes like sandy, well-drained soil, even poor soils will work fine if you till in peat moss and compost. The roots need a deep light soil so that they can grow unimpeded by hard impenetrable soil or subsoil

MOISTURE: Sweet potato slips need consistent moisture at first; if you don't get one inch of rain weekly, water the sweet potatoes until the plants are established. After that, watering will probably not be necessary except in the driest conditions. Soggy soil will rot the roots.

Sweet potatoes can tolerate dry soil but dislike soggy, wet soil. If you live in a wet area, consider using raised beds with sand mixed in.

LIGHT: Full sun.

PLANTING SEASON: Sweet potatoes are a warm-weather crop, so they should be planted after all danger of frost.

HOW TO PLANT: Sweet potatoes are started from purchased slips, which are shoots that are grown on the sweet potato, or you can start your own.

To start sweet potato slips:

- Select sweet potatoes that haven't been waxed or treated to prevent sprouting.
- Start six weeks before trans-
  plant time, which is two to
  three weeks after the last
  frost date.
- Place the whole potato in a
  lengthwise container and
  cover with two inches of moist
  sand, vermiculite, or sawdust.

- Keep the sweet potato in a warm and sunny window with temperatures at 75 or 80 degrees F.
- Shoots will appear. When they are six to nine inches long, cut them off of the potato.
- Remove the bottom inch of each shoot, and transplant them outside.

NOTE: You can do the same thing by placing a sweet potato vertically in a jar of warm water so that it is partially submerged, holding it in place with toothpicks inserted around the middle. Place it in a warm place, perhaps a sunny window. Each potato will produce two to four sprouts. Break off the sprouts when they are six to nine inches long and transplant them outside.

To transplant sweet potato slips outdoors:

- Wait until all danger of frost is past and the soil temperature is 70 degrees F, usually two or three weeks after the last frost date.
- Prepare the bed by tilling it thoroughly, mixing in a generous amount of peat moss.
- Warm the soil with black plastic about a week before transplanting the slips.
- Plant each sprout so that the roots are down and the top three leaves show at ground level. If desired, plant them in slits in black plastic to keep the ground warm and free of weeds.
- Space each sprout eighteen inches apart in three-foot rows.
- Water each slip well after planting, and keep it moist until established.

ONGOING CARE:
- **Mulching** under the vines, but only after the soil is well warmed, if you are not using black plastic.
- **Weeding**, to prevent competition, or the sweet potato roots will stay small.
- **Handling** the delicate plants as little as possible to avoid damage.
- **Lifting** the vines above the mulch occasionally, to discourage the joints from rooting and diverting the plant's energy away from the main crop.

- **Watering** only if the weather is very dry or when the leaves wilt during the day and they haven't recovered by night. Once established, the plants will produce a fair crop without watering, even in drought.

VARIETIES INCLUDE:

- **Georgia Jet** is fast-growing and gives a good yield, even where summers are short. It has red skin and sweet, moist, rust-orange flesh. Somewhat cold tolerant. Bakes well and stores well. 100 days, but can start the harvest in 40 days.
- **Centennial** has long vines that produce a large crop of bright orange-skinned sweet potatoes that have moist, deep orange flesh. Stores well. The most commonly planted variety. It grows well even in the North. 90 to 100 days.
- **Beauregard** has long vines and produces a large number of sweet potatoes with red-orange skin and moist orange flesh. Extra sweet and high-yielding. 90 days.
- **Porto Rico** has short vines that yield well in small gardens. The skins are copper and the moist flesh is very sweet and salmon-orange. Excellent for baking. Good in the South. 110 days.
- **Vardaman** has attractive purplish foliage that turns to green on short vines that work well in small gardens. Golden skins darken to orange. Easy to harvest and a very good keeper. 110 days.
- **Jewell** produces a big crop of sweet potatoes with red skin and deep orange flesh. Stores well. 100 days.

YIELD: Each plant produces four or more sweet potatoes, or about two pounds.

HARVESTING: Start checking on the roots about ninety days after they were planted. Since sweet potatoes don't ripen or mature, you can start the harvest when the roots are at least three inches long (these are called "baby bakers"), or wait till they are larger.

In hot climates, the sweet potatoes can grow huge and get fibrous, so it's better to harvest them smaller.

In short-season climates, allow the sweet potatoes to stay in the ground as long as possible, until just before the first frost—but not after the frost, because it can harm the roots that are close to the soil surface. Dig immediately if the vines have been frost-killed or the soil temperatures reach 55 degrees F.

To harvest sweet potatoes:

- Choose a day when the soil is dry; if they are harvested wet, the roots will shrink considerably.
- Cut off the trailing vines.
- Use a pitch fork or flat potato fork and loosen the soil over a foot away from the crown base of the vine. Work around the plant in a circle.
- Then lift the plant's crown, and the sweet potatoes will come up with it. Dig around in the soil with your hands to bring up any roots left behind. Do all this carefully, because the sweet potatoes have tender skin and damage easily, and damaged roots don't store well.
- Allow them to dry in an airy place out of the sun for two to three hours, then gently rub off the dirt. They are now ready to be cured. (See instructions under "Storing.")

Sweet Potatoes in the Kitchen

STORING: Before they can be used or stored, sweet potatoes must be cured. Do not refrigerate raw sweet potatoes.

To cure sweet potatoes:

- Allow newly dug sweet potatoes to dry out of the sun for several hours. Gently rub off the dirt.
- Spread them in a single layer for ten days in a warm, humid place with temperatures between 80 and 85 degrees F. Or place them near the furnace for two or three weeks to cure, if you don't have a warmer place.
- They are now ready to be used, or you can place the sweet potatoes into long-term storage.

For long-term storage:

- Sort out any damaged or bruised sweet potatoes, and use them right away, as they won't keep well.
- Spread the cured sweet potatoes out on newspaper in a dry, dark place at 55 or 60 degrees F with moderate humidity. Never store them in temperatures under 50 degrees F, which can cause spoiling, or above 65 degrees, which might cause sprouting. The roots will shrivel in low humidity.

FREEZING: It can be done easily two ways. Be sure that the sweet potatoes have been properly cured before freezing them.

Baked:

- Wash the sweet potatoes in cold water. Dry. Coat with oil.
- Bake at 350 degrees F until a little soft when pricked.

- Remove from the oven and cool.
- Wrap each potato in foil or freezer plastic and place in freezer bags.
- Seal, label and date, and freeze.

Pureed:

- Wash the sweet potatoes in cold water. Dry.
- Bake at 350 degrees F until completely soft.
- Remove the sweet potatoes from the oven and cool.
- Remove the peelings and mash the sweet potatoes or puree them in a food processor.
- Pack in freezer containers leaving a half-inch of headspace.
- Seal, label and date, and freeze.

EATING SWEET POTATOES

NOTE: Both the moist-fleshed and the dry-fleshed sweet potatoes are cooked the same.

PREPARING: Be sure that the sweet potatoes have cured for at least one week before using them.

FLAVORINGS: Sweet potatoes go well with allspice, cardamom, cinnamon, cloves, curry, fennel, ginger, nutmeg, mustard seed, rosemary, orange juice, pineapple, peaches, apricots, parsley, maple, raisins, butter, salt and pepper, nuts, orange, lemon, brandy, rum, pecans.

COOKING: Methods include baking, steaming, frying, boiling. Sweet potatoes can be baked in their skins, and eaten skins and all, like white potatoes. Sweet potatoes can be thinly sliced and deep-fat fried like potato chips.

Easy Glazed Sweet Potatoes

Peel, cut up, and boil sweet potatoes until tender. Drain. Melt together equal parts butter and brown sugar. Drizzle over the sweet potatoes and serve.

Mashed Sweet Potatoes

Peel, cut up, and cook sweet potatoes in boiling water. When tender, drain and mash the potatoes. Stir in a little milk (perhaps ¼ cup per pound of potatoes), butter (2 or 3 tablespoons per pound of potatoes), and salt to taste. Serve hot.

Baked Sweet Potatoes

1. Peel, cut up, and cook about 5 cups of sweet potatoes in boiling water. Drain and place the potatoes in an ovenproof casserole dish.
2. Combine ⅓ cup melted butter, ½ cup brown sugar, and one small can of crushed pineapple in natural juice. Pour over the sweet potatoes. If desired, top with a handful of marshmallows (optional).
3. Bake in the oven at 350 degrees F until heated through, bubbly, and the marshmallows are lightly browned. Serve.

Sweet Potato Soup

Superb!

1 Peel and dice one large sweet potato to make about 4 cups; you can use a sweet potato that is raw or one that has been oven-baked. Place the diced sweet potato in a covered saucepan with:

> 2 cups chicken broth
> 1½ to 2 cups chopped onion
> 1 tablespoon fresh gingerroot, grated
> ⅛ teaspoon cinnamon
> 1/16 teaspoon ground cloves

2. Bring the mixture to a boil, then reduce heat to a full simmer and cover. Cook for 10 minutes or until the onion and sweet potato are

soft. Puree the mixture in a food processor or use a cordless blender right in the pan.

3. Add 2 cups of cream and simmer uncovered until thickened, about 6 minutes.

4. Serve hot or well chilled. Top each serving with a dollop of whipped cream, if desired.

Sweet Potatoes and Applesauce

1. Cook and mash sweet potatoes to make 3 or 4 cups. Stir in:

> 1/4 cup butter, cut up (or use melted butter, if the sweet potatoes are cool)
> 1 cup applesauce
> 1/2 teaspoon cinnamon
> 1 cup miniature marshmallows (optional)

2. Cook on the stove or in the oven until heated through. Serve.

Sweet Potato Balls

An unusual appetizer!

1. Combine:

> 2 cups mashed, cooked sweet potatoes (NOTE: Do not use yams.)
> 1/3 cup flour
> 1 small egg
> salt and pepper to taste

2. Make a ball using about 1 tablespoon of the sweet potato mixture, placing 1 miniature marshmallow in the center of each. This recipe makes about 32 balls.

3. Roll each ball in chopped cashews or pecans, and/or shredded coconut.

4. Heat 1/2 inch to 1 inch cooking oil in a pan and fry the sweet potato balls until golden brown on all sides.

5. Remove to a paper towel and serve hot. They can be reheated on a cookie sheet in the oven.

SWISS CHARD
IN THE GARDEN

One of my very favorite vegetables, Swiss chard is a garden staple for me. I was raised with it, but The Farmer was not. He'd never even seen it before he married me! At first he frowned on chard and the other greens I grew each year because it reminded him of cattle feed. It took a while, but I can now say that he's a chard convert.

Swiss chard is a good substitute for spinach in the garden, it's a prolific producer that is taller than spinach, and it grows under conditions that spinach will not. I usually plant the white-stemmed variety, but there are varieties with brightly colored stems in vivid red, pink, orange, and yellow shades.

Swiss chard has abundant foliage that is usually heavily crinkled. It can be a rich green or a deep purplish-red. The stalks can be eaten separately and are much like celery. I plant it in the early spring and harvest it until very late in the fall. In fact, it is the last vegetable I bring in just ahead of heavy frost and snow.

Swiss chard is highly nutritious; it has a delicious, mild flavor; it is very easy to grow; and it yields abundantly. I highly recommend it for the home gardener!

LOCATION: Don't plant it where Swiss chard, beets, or spinach grew the previous year. It grows well on bean or pea ground, and Swiss chard can be planted in the pea row after the peas die back, for a later crop.

Chard is a beautiful eighteen- to twenty-four-inch-tall plant, especially the varieties with brightly colored stems, and it looks great mixed into the landscaping or flower beds. This year I grew a ring of it around my birdbath—a focal point in the center of my courtyard garden. It was strikingly ornamental—and edible, too!

Swiss chard is a good container plant, especially if grown in part shade and watered daily.

GROWING RANGE: Everywhere. Swiss chard is tolerant of frost and grows well in cold or hot weather. Although hot weather might induce it to bolt, I've never had it happen, even during the hottest summers.

SOIL REQUIREMENTS: Swiss chard tolerates most soils so long as it is well drained and moist, but not soggy. To increase fertility, till in plenty of rotted manure or compost.

MOISTURE: Swiss chard likes to have a steady supply of moisture, especially to get started, but then I often ignore it, and it will survive even during drought.

LIGHT: Full sun, or part shade so long as the plants get at least four to six hours of sun.

PLANTING SEASON: Swiss chard can be direct-seeded from spring until midsummer for a fall crop. If left in the ground over winter, roots send up a very early spring crop in mild climates.

HOW TO PLANT: Direct-seed Swiss chard outdoors in early spring.

- Thoroughly till the soil, mixing in well-rotted manure or compost.
- Plant early in spring, as soon as the ground can be worked, two or three weeks before the last frost date or when soil is at least 45 degrees F.

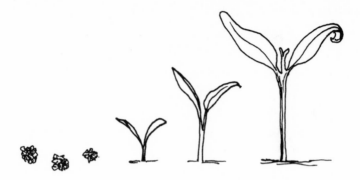

- Plant the seed one-half to one inch deep and spaced three to four inches apart in rows two and a half feet apart.
- Firm the seed lightly and water it.

ONGOING CARE:

- **Thinning** the row so that the plants are spaced six to nine inches apart, depending on your soil fertility and available moisture. Eat the thinnings.
- **Tilling** to keep the soil friable.
- **Mulching** is needed only in hot, dry climates, to retain moisture.
- **Watering**, as needed.
- **Leaving** the outer leaves on the plant if they get tough during the hottest part of summer—these will protect the newer inner leaves from heat and fall frost.
- **Cutting** out the flower stalk, if the plant should bolt.

VARIETIES INCLUDE:

- **Lucullus,** which has white stems, dark green leaves, produces vigorously, and withstands heat without bolting. 60 days. Highly recommended.
- **Rhubarb Chard** has bright red ribs. 60 days.
- **Burgundy Chard** has purplish red stems. 60 days.
- **Bright Lights Chard** is a mixed variety that produces stalks in several vivid colors. 55 days.

YIELD: At least seven to ten pounds from a ten-foot row.

HARVESTING: In early summer, after the plant has four or five true leaves, you can begin to carefully cut or break off a few outer leaves, but don't remove too many from any one plant. Once it is well established, you can cut the entire plant off about two inches above the ground. If doing the latter, the chard will grow back again, just like leaf lettuce.

I usually stop harvesting my chard during the hottest part of the summer, when the leaves and stems get tough and strong-tasting. I leave these stems on the plant, however, because they shade the developing shoots from the hot sun, and later these tough leaves blanket the plant from light frosts. After the summer heat abates, I harvest the inner leaves toward the center of each plant so as not to disturb the protective outer leaves.

For the last harvest of the season, I break off and discard the tough outer leaves and use a knife to cut off the entire row just above the ground, saving everything, including the tiny new shoots, which are

very succulent. I'm often doing this on a gray November day, sometimes with snowflakes swirling around me. If I should miscalculate and we get a subsequent warm spell, the roots will start sending up new shoots, which are very tender and taste wonderful, just like new spring growth.

Lucky you if you live in a mild climate, because your spring-planted chard will produce for you through winter until late spring the following year before going to seed!

Swiss Chard in the Kitchen

STORING: Chard will keep a long time fresh in the refrigerator. Just gather the leaves into large bundles with the stalks running the same direction, and place the bundles in large plastic bags. Do not wash it first. Whenever you want chard, just remove the quantity needed and return the rest to the refrigerator. I kept our old refrigerator just to hold excess produce like chard, and usually store two large bags in the late fall, freezing the rest.

FREEZING:
- Wash and prepare the Swiss chard as described below. It's best to remove the stems because they tend to blacken when frozen (although they're still edible).
- Steam till wilted and quickly spread out on large dark towels to cool (this retains the most nutrients).
- Or blanch the chard for two minutes in boiling water, drain, and cool.
- Pack into freezer bags and squeeze out all possible air.
- Seal, label and date, and freeze.

EATING SWISS CHARD

You can use Swiss chard in any recipe that calls for spinach, although you will probably need to remove the stems. But don't throw away the stems, which can be substituted in recipes for asparagus or celery. They resemble celery in taste and texture and can be served as a steamed vegetable with a little butter, or they can be added to soups or stews.

PREPARING:

- I harvest an armload of leaves, which I soak in cold water in my extra-large kitchen sink. I swish each leaf in the water, shake it, and place it on a large terry towel to catch the drips.
- I then place a large cutting board on a dark-colored terry towel to catch any drips, and stack several clean Swiss chard leaves on the board. Using a large chef's knife, I first make some cuts through the leaves parallel to the stems about an inch to an inch and a half apart, then I cut them perpendicular to the stems the same distance. These chopped leaves can be steamed, boiled, braised, etc.

If desired, you can eat only the leafy part or only the stems. To separate the two, you can fold the leaf in half the long way and cut along the stems to separate them from the leaves. Or stack several leaves and use a chef's knife to cut on both sides of the stems. Then chop and eat each part separately. Sometimes the stem is old and tough, but the leaf is still edible, in which case you just discard the stem.

FLAVORING: Butter; salt and pepper; lemon juice; cheese, especially Parmesan; cream or cheese sauces.

COOKING: Boil, steam, or saute the Swiss chard in butter.

Swiss Chard with Raisins

1. Chop the chard leaves, including the stems. (Make enough to loosely fill the skillet to heaping twice, as it cooks down a lot.)
2. Melt 3 tablespoons butter in a large skillet. Lightly brown 1 teaspoon of minced fresh gingerroot. Add the chard and stir-fry it until the leaves are wilted.
3. Add ½ cup water and a small handful of raisins; stir well. Simmer, covered, until the chard stems are tender and the raisins are plumped. Serve.

Swiss Chard with Bacon

1. Wash and chop the chard as described above.
2. Fry several pieces of bacon in a skillet. When crisp, remove the bacon to a paper towel. Pour off excess grease, but do not scrape the pan.
3. Add the chopped chard to the skillet and stir-fry until wilted. Add the crumbled bacon and serve hot.

Crustless Swiss Chard Quiche

This is a favorite from my Back to Protein *cookbook.*
1. Chop fresh Swiss chard to make 2 or 2½ cups. Place it on the bottom of a buttered quiche dish or a deep pie plate.
2. Chop 1 medium onion and place it on top of the chard. Sprinkle on ⅔ cup shredded Swiss or mozzarella cheese and ⅔ cup shredded cheddar cheese.
3. In a bowl, combine:

> 9 eggs, beaten
> 1½ cups half-and-half or heavy cream
> ½ teaspoon salt
> ½ teaspoon pepper
> ⅛ teaspoon nutmeg
> ⅛ teaspoon garlic powder

4. Blend the egg mixture well and pour over the chard.
5. Bake 30 minutes at 350 degrees F, then sprinkle on some grated Parmesan cheese and return to the oven for 15 more minutes. Serve.

TOMATOES IN THE GARDEN

What can be better than a ripe, red, sun-warmed tomato eaten right off the vines in your very own garden?

Unfortunately, the fruit from these members of the deadly nightshade family were thought to be poisonous for many years. In fact, a British spy slipped some tomato into George Washington's food and sent a letter to England about his deed, anticipating George's imminent death!

The best-tasting tomatoes ripen on the vine. This develops the sugars in the tomatoes, which is what gives them their flavor—and it's what is lacking in store-bought tomatoes, because they are picked and shipped before they are ripe. Unfortunately, they are often chilled during shipping, which also destroys flavor. The only way to get great vine-ripened tomatoes is if they're grown locally—preferably by you!

Tomatoes are one of the most popular home-grown vegetables, and no wonder. Tomatoes are adaptable to all growing areas, extremely productive, highly nutritious, and they can be used in so many ways. That fresh tomato flavor is absolutely wonderful and is completely missing in the beautiful but tasteless tomatoes you buy in the store. Best of all, tomatoes are so easy to grow!

TYPES OF TOMATO PLANTS:

- **Determinate**, which means they set all their fruit at once and it all ripens over three to four weeks on compact plants that might not need support. These are the traditional choice of home canners who want a lot of tomatoes at one time. They take up less garden space because the vines stop growing once they set fruit, usually when they're three or four feet tall.
- **Indeterminate**, which means they produce fruit over a long period for a continuous harvest, from large, sprawling plants that require support. They can get over six feet tall.
- **Semi-determinate**, are in between determinate and indeterminate in size and fruiting season.

The fruits can be tiny cherry tomatoes on up to large, meaty beefsteak varieties. Besides the usual bright red, tomatoes can ripen to yellow, orange, and pink shades. The fruit can be very round, elongated, or squatty and wide. There are hundreds of varieties, with more being developed each year.

LOCATION: Do not plant tomatoes on soil where you've grown tomatoes, green peppers, eggplants, or potatoes the previous year or even two or three years, if possible. Avoid low-lying areas where frost can gather or water pools, and select a spot with good air circulation.

Don't give up on tomatoes if you are short of space. This year I'm growing two plants in with my flower beds on tall stakes; the bright-red cherry tomatoes look quite attractive there.

All types of tomatoes grow well in containers. I've even grown tomatoes successfully in my living room, which I harvest all winter long. The best types for winter gardening indoors are the smaller cherry tomatoes, but the others will work if they are properly supported and receive enough sunlight.

GROWING RANGE: Zones 3 to 11, but they can be grown even farther north if choosing short-season varieties and starting them extra-early indoors.

SOIL REQUIREMENTS: The soil should be fertile and well drained. To make the soil more fertile, till in well-rotted manure, commercial fertilizer, or a combination of the two. Tomatoes don't like soggy soil or standing water. If you live in a rainy climate, you might consider growing tomatoes in raised beds for added drainage.

MOISTURE: Tomatoes need at least one inch of rain per week; otherwise, water them well twice per week for best fruit production, more often if you have sandy soil or live in a hot climate. An influx of too much water after a dry spell, especially in hot weather, will result in cracked tomatoes or blossom-end rot.

LIGHT: Full sun.

PLANTING SEASON: Tomatoes are a warm-weather crop that cannot tolerate frost, so they must be planted on or after the last frost date in spring, and they will die at the first frost in fall unless protected.

HOW TO PLANT: Tomatoes are best started in the garden from transplants, either purchased from a nursery or homegrown to get exactly the varieties you prefer. If your growing season is very long, you can direct-seed on your last frost date or when the soil temperature reaches at least 60 degrees F, but you'll get an earlier harvest from transplants.

Growing tomato seedlings:

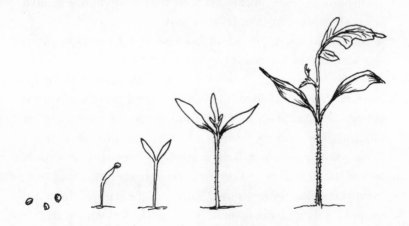

- Start seedlings in the house six to ten weeks prior to your last frost date.
- Plant the seeds one eighth- to one quarter-inch deep in peat pots.
- Keep the soil moist for germination; a sunny window should do it, or apply bottom heat if the indoor temperature isn't between 70 to 80 degrees F.
- Give them lots of light; if you don't have enough sunlight, use artificial light and position the seedlings so their tops are three inches below the light.
- As the tomatoes grow, transplant them every two or three weeks to a deeper depth to encourage root development along the stem, starting when they are three weeks old. Quart-sized plastic milk cartons are ideal because they are tall and narrow.
- An indoor temperature of no more than 70 degrees F is ideal for the seedlings.

Transplanting tomatoes:

- Prepare the planting area by tilling the soil deeply, mixing in eggshells for their calcium, as well as well-rotted manure or compost, and perhaps adding a commercial fertilizer.
- Harden off the seedlings outdoors for two weeks before transplant time, or they will go into shock, setting their development back or maybe even killing them.
- Transplant outside on the last frost date or up to one month later, after all danger of frost is past.
- A warm, cloudy day is ideal because it lessens transplant shock and gives the plants a better start.
- Plant the seedling at least two inches deeper than it grew indoors. New roots form along the buried main stem, providing the plant with increased nutrients and water. If your seedlings got a bit spindly and weak, burying them even deeper will encourage better, stronger growth and expose less of the delicate seedling to wind damage.
- Firm the soil and press down gently at the base of the plant to make a depression to hold water, and fill it with water.

- Plant the seedlings no closer than three feet apart in four- or five-foot rows. This gives you plenty of room to work freely around the plants.
- If cutworms are a problem in your area, apply cutworm collars.
- Consider laying black plastic or, better yet, red plastic, sheets under the tomatoes to keep the soil warm; the red color has been shown to enhance the production and flavor of tomatoes. The easiest way to do this is to lay down two strips—one on each side of the tomato row—with the edges right against the stem of the tomato plants. Anchor the plastic with boards, stones, or bricks so that it doesn't blow in the wind. Later, the plastic can be removed to allow more moisture to penetrate to the roots, or else puncture holes in the plastic.
- Put wind protection in place, if you live in a windy area. I place a gallon can that has both the top and bottom removed over each seedling for a week or two, until it gets established.
- Water daily, until the seedling can grow roots into the garden soil. The potting mix used for seedlings does not hold moisture for more than one day.
- Cover the seedlings if a frost is coming. If using the gallon cans, just put a small board over the top, or cover the row with a blanket, old sweatshirts, etc.

NOTE: If your seedlings got spindly and weak, they can still be used. Instead of digging a really deep hole, just remove all the side leaves and plant the stems sideways in trenches three or four inches deep with only the topmost leaves above the soil. The plant top will straighten and grow up like any other tomato. If all the plants are planted in furrows going the same direction, you will still be able to till between the rows but not between the plants, where you should lightly hoe by hand. Or put down black or red plastic, or, after the soil is well warmed, mulch, between the plants and over the furrow to help keep down weeds. The year my seedlings became weak and spindly beyond use, I used this method and had the biggest and best-ever crop of tomatoes all season!

ONGOING CARE:

- **Watering** often, daily until the seedlings get established, and then as needed to give the tomatoes adequate moisture.

- **Removing** the gallon cans as soon as the tomatoes grow above the top.

- **Placing** tomato supports in place as soon as the wind protection is removed; at transplant time if you don't use wind protection. There are a variety of tomato supports available for purchase; be sure to buy something substantial because some of them are too weak to be of any use. I prefer to use tomato cages, which can be made from galvanized wire mesh with large openings, the kind construction workers use to strengthen cement; stake these so they don't topple. Anchor the cages with stakes or electric fence posts wired to the cages. Even the determinate varieties benefit from support, especially if you live in a windy area.

- **Pruning** each indeterminate plant to maintain only one or two stems is recommended by some gardeners, especially for the far North, but I find it's unnecessary; it results in a reduced yield and the loss of the leaf canopy opens the tomatoes to sun scald.

- **Shading** the plants with black mesh and using mulch, if you live in an extremely hot area.

- **Pinching** out the tops of the plants late in fall, when the days are noticeably shorter and tomato growth has slowed down quite a bit. This will stimulate the tomatoes already on the vine to ripen and the plant won't be wasting its energy developing new tomatoes.

- **Providing** frost protection, by covering the plants with blankets, quilts, or even plastic, if nothing else is available. Often, a few fall frosts might be followed by days or even weeks of warm weather, which allows continued tomato harvest.

- **Transplanting** slips: When winter is arriving, frost protection will no longer be adequate. At this time, you can transplant a tomato into a large pot indoors, or cut off a few branch tips or suckers—the sprouts that grow in between the main stem and the branches of the plant—and root

them in water or moist potting soil. You may have to provide artificial lights, if your daylight gets too short.

How to Get Early Tomatoes—
A Few Farmer's Wife's Tricks!

I'm always anxious to pick my first tomato, and in our area it usually doesn't happen until July. But I've learned how to have my first harvest no later than mid-June:

- Start the seedlings in the house a little earlier than recommended above.
- Select the right seed. The cherry-type tomatoes ripen first, and I recommend using the Sub-Arctic Plenty variety because it withstands cool weather and even light frosts.
- Repot the tomato seedling several times indoors, each time placing it deeper in the soil to encourage root development along the stems.
- Use black or clear plastic to warm the soil before and after planting the seedlings outside.
- Plant the seedlings two weeks before the recommended time.
- Give the plants extra-good protection from wind and frost, using an old quilt or several layers of blankets at night.

- Locate the seedlings where they'll get the earliest morning sun, and uncover them promptly to get the earliest sunlight, if you used frost protection overnight.
- After you see three clusters of tomatoes on the plant, use a corn knife or an old kitchen knife to cut a quarter circle into the soil about four inches from the base of the plant and eight inches deep, which cuts part of the plant's root system (be careful not to cut the stem if trench-planting). When plants suffer an injury like this, they hasten to produce fruit even though the lengthening days would ordinarily tell them they still have lots of time. The plants slow down their growth and concentrate their energy on producing tomatoes, thinking they will have a shorter life span. This trick reduces the normal yield, so do this only on a few select plants. I do this about mid-May here in Iowa; you'll have to adjust the date for your area.
- Some gardeners use plastic tunnels on hoops as a mini-greenhouse over their tomato rows to give the transplants a head start in early spring, which would probably work well, although I've never done this.

VARIETIES INCLUDE: Cherry or salad tomatoes, which are very small and sweet and can be harvested early in the season. My favorites are:

- **Super Sweet 100** for its incredible sweet flavor, an indeterminate type ready in 65 days and a great indoor producer of hundreds of one-inch round and juicy fruits.
- **Sub-Arctic Plenty**, a determinate type that can withstand cold snaps and has two-inch fruits that can be harvested in only 51 days from transplant.
- There are many other fine varieties of cherry tomatoes, including **Christmas Grapes** (75 days), **Sugar Snack Hybrid** (65 days), and **Fourth of July** (49 days), the earliest.

Plum or paste-type tomatoes are smallish, meatier tomatoes with few seeds. These are preferred for sauces and tomato pastes. Varieties include:

- **Viva Italia**, which has sweet, meaty flesh with few seeds. A prolific determinate. 72 days.
- **Roma**, which has pear-shaped, meaty tomatoes with few seeds. Determinate. 75 days.

Everyone has their own favorites among the many hundreds available, and I always plant several. Here are a few other tomato varieties:

- **Celebrity**, which is a semi-determinate vine but is a variety to consider because it resists drought and disease and the eight-ounce fruit are crack-free. 72 days.
- **Beefmaster**, which produces large, meaty, nearly seedless fruit that can weigh two pounds and cut up into firm beefsteak slices large enough to cover an entire sandwich. This indeterminate needs strong support. 80 days.
- **Long Keeper**, a determinate that produces six- to eight-inch fruit that keeps six to twelve weeks after harvest. This is the one to choose to serve fresh tomatoes on Thanksgiving. Another variety to consider for winter storage is Red October Hybrid. 78 days.
- **Big Red Champion** produces early and tolerates drought and heat. Indeterminate. 70 days.
- **Heatwave II Hybrid** does well even in 100 degree F heat, producing seven-ounce fruit on compact plants in 68 days, as long as it has sufficient moisture.

Heirloom tomatoes are delicious, but they don't have the protection against disease that the newer varieties have. You still might want to consider:

- **Brandywine**, a very old tomato variety first introduced to me by a friend who insists "it's the best tomato you'll ever wrap your lips around." It's an indeterminate type that produces lots of deep-pink, irregular-shaped beefsteak tomatoes. 90 days.

YIELD: Each plant will give you dozens or hundreds of tomatoes. Even potted tomatoes grown in my living room in winter will yield two to three quarts of cherry tomatoes per week, if we have some bright days, and if there is snow cover to bounce more sunlight into the windows.

HARVESTING: For the best flavor, pick tomatoes only after the fruit has fully ripened on the vine, if possible.

Tomatoes ripen from the inside out, so when you see the first blush of orange on the skins, it won't be too long before they're ready to be picked.

To harvest, just release the tomato from the vine with a twisting tug—but be careful not to damage the plants.

Wear gloves and a long-sleeved shirt if you break out from contact with the vines, or be sure to wash your arms with soap and water as soon as you return to the house.

If winter is coming, you can harvest the tomatoes early, even when whitish-green, and they will ripen in the house, but they won't taste the same as vine-ripened tomatoes. The best flavor comes from tomatoes that have ripened at least partially on the vines. Light helps develop the color somewhat but is not essential to ripening. I set mine on layers of newspaper on the counter so that they aren't touching, and I check them often, because they sometimes rot while ripening indoors, although this problem is reduced if you choose the long-keeping varieties.

Tomatoes in the Kitchen

STORING: Fresh tomatoes should be kept in the open at room temperature, and should not be stored in sealed containers or plastic bags that don't allow them to breathe. Keep in mind that tomatoes continue to ripen even if stored in a dark pantry, so use them before they go bad.

Avoid putting uncooked tomatoes in the refrigerator as the raw tomato loses it flavor, although refrigerated raw tomatoes can be added to soups or sauces. The exception to this is raw cherry tomatoes, which can be stored in sealed plastic containers without losing their flavor—we snack on them like grapes.

Cooked tomatoes can be refrigerated with no loss of flavor.

FREEZING:

Basic Tomato sauce:

- Use firm, ripe, meaty tomatoes–romas are ideal.
- Wash and core the tomatoes. Either cut the tomatoes in half and place them in a saucepan or kettle or crush the tomatoes in the pan with a potato masher.
- Bring to a boil, then reduce heat to a simmer. Add additional ingredients, if desired—see recipe below. Or leave the sauce plain and add ingredients later after it's thawed and being used.
- Continue simmering until the liquid is reduced and the tomatoes are tender. Use a cordless hand blender in the kettle to puree the tomatoes, or remove from heat, cool down a little, and run the tomatoes through a food mill or puree in a food processor, then return the puree to the kettle and simmer until sufficiently thickened. If you want to remove all the seeds and the skins, use the food mill. However, leaving them in gives the sauce more body and it thickens sooner.
- Cool and pour premeasured amounts into freezer containers, allowing headspace.

- Seal, label and date, and freeze.

NOTE: The tomato seeds can be left in and pureed with the sauce, or you can squeeze them out when halving the tomatoes, or they will be removed in the food mill.

The tomato skins can be pureed into the sauce, which thickens it and adds nutrients, or they will be removed in the food mill. There is no need to go to the trouble to skin the tomatoes.

Easy Tomato Juice:

Work quickly to preserve the nutrients.

- Use firm, ripe tomatoes.
- Wash and drain.
- Place the whole tomatoes in a saucepan or kettle. If you wish, you can core and cut the tomatoes into quarters—but this is unnecessary.
- Crush the tomatoes slightly with a potato masher.
- Cover and put on the stove. Heat until the temperature of the tomatoes is between 185 and 195 degrees F (it will not boil). Cool.
- Run the tomatoes through a food mill or use the fruit and vegetable strainer/food grinder attachment on a KitchenAid mixer.
- Add salt to the juice, if desired, up to 1 teaspoon per quart of juice.
- Pour the juice into freezer containers, leaving about an inch of headspace.
- Seal, label and date, and freeze.

NOTE: For V-8 style tomato juice, follow the instructions above except cook the tomatoes with several ribs of celery, chopped onion, and a little sweet green pepper. Simmer until all the vegetables are soft. Add salt, if desired. Cool and run through the food mill and freeze according to the directions for sauce.

Whole tomatoes:

Small tomatoes or cherry-type tomatoes can be frozen loose in freezer bags. The texture will suffer and they will be too watery for fresh lettuce salads, but they can be added to soups, casseroles, goulash, and spaghetti. Note that the skins will loosen when they are cooked, which is unattractive but can be ignored for everyday home use since they add nutrients.

Large tomatoes can also be frozen. Follow blanching instructions below to remove the skins, quarter the tomatoes, and pack them into freezer containers leaving one inch of headspace. Seal, label and date, and freeze.

EATING TOMATOES

Raw, they can be served sliced, or added to salads. Cooked, they can be simmered into a sauce or soup, stuffed and baked, sliced and broiled, or stir-fried with other vegetables.

PREPARING: Wash in cold water. Remove the stem end and the core as well as any bad spots. Use the tomatoes whole, cut up in chunks, sliced, or diced. Include the skins, if possible, as they contain valuable nutrients. The gelatinous liquid around the seeds actually has the most nutrition of the entire tomato, so include it in your recipes if at all possible.

Tomatoes can be skinned whole by sliding the tip of a paring knife under the skin, anchoring the skin to the knife blade with your thumb, and then pulling it off in strips.

The skins can be blanched off by immersing the tomatoes in simmering water for thirty seconds, then removing them from the hot water and plunging them into cold water for one minute. Puncture the skin and you can pull it off. Repeat if the skin doesn't come off completely or easily.

FLAVORING: Tomatoes go well with basil, bay leaves, celery seed, chives, cilantro, cinnamon, chili powder, cumin, curry, dill, fennel, garlic, ginger, lemon, rosemary, marjoram, mint, mustard seed, nutmeg, oregano, okra, onions, parsley, poppy seed, sage, sesame seed, tarragon, thyme, turmeric, sweet peppers, hot peppers, Italian spice blends, olives, onions, and cheese, especially Parmesan and mozzarella.

NOTE: If you want to cut the acid in cooked tomatoes, do not add sugar, which ruins the flavor. Instead, add a carrot chunk; its sweetness will counteract the acid. If you like, you can remove the carrot after cooking.

COOKING: Methods include grilling, steaming, boiling, baking, broiling, stir-frying.

My Easy Tomato Sauce or Soup

I've made many hundreds of gallons of this recipe for the freezer, and I've used it for everything from sloppy joes and pizza to spaghetti and lasagna, even tomato soup! For every 8 cups of tomato puree, blending together in a food processor:

> 1 medium onion
> 1/4 cup lightly packed fresh basil without the stems or 2
>   teaspoons dried basil
> 2 tablespoons lightly packed fresh thyme without the
>   stems or 1 teaspoon dried thyme
> 1 tablespoon instant chicken bouillon granules
> 1/2 teaspoon garlic powder
> 1/8 teaspoon black pepper

You can follow the instructions, above, for freezing tomato sauce using my recipe, or take my shortcut by pureeing the tomatoes before they are cooked. Instead of measuring the tomatoes, I just coarsely chop the tomatoes until they reach a certain mark on my food processor, then add the rest of the ingredients and puree it all together. Then I empty the food processor bowl into a large kettle and begin my next batch. I start cooking the sauce after the kettle is filled with puree. This greatly speeds up the process. I can quickly puree many batches of tomato sauce and have kettles of it cooking on every burner on my stove, plus I use a hotplate besides!

When you're ready to use this basic sauce, you can make additions appropriate for whatever dish you are making. For tomato soup, heat the sauce and stir in a little cream.

Tomato Salad

1. Wash and slice 4 to 6 tomatoes into wedges.
2. In a food processor, use the pulse button to chop the following:

> 1 cup fresh parsley
> 1/4 cup fresh chives
> 1 garlic clove
> 1/4 teaspoon salt

3. Stir in 1/4 cup olive oil and 2 tablespoons red vinegar. Toss with the tomato wedges and serve.

Broiled tomatoes

Wash the tomatoes, remove the stems (if any), and cut the tomatoes in half crosswise. Place the halves snugly in a baking dish or pan. Sprinkle on herbs of choice (Italian blends work well, or try garlic salt) and place under the broiler for about 2 minutes. Top with your favorite cheese or cheese blends, like mozzarella and Parmesan, and return to the broiler for a few more seconds until the cheese is melted and lightly browned. Serve immediately. For a variation, try adding minced celery with the herbs—great!

Fried Breaded Tomatoes:

Wonderful!

1. Cut ripe tomatoes into 3/4-inch-thick slices.
2. Heat 1/4 cup olive oil in a large skillet on medium-high heat.
3. Place finely ground pork rinds in a pie plate and salt and pepper to taste. (Make crumbs by placing pork rinds, soda crackers, or stale bread in a food processor.)
4. Place 1 egg in a second pie tin and whisk until yolk and white are blended.
5. Dip the tomato slices in the egg and then in the crumbs. Fry the

tomato slices in the heated skillet until browned, about 2 minutes, then turn and brown the other side. Serve hot. Top with a dollop of sour cream or plain yogurt sprinkled with snipped fresh chives, if desired. (Discard any unused egg or breading.)

NOTE: Delicious with breaded fried eggplant, zucchini, and/or onions.

Easy Tomato-Zucchini Soup

In a saucepan, heat together 12 small whole cherry tomatoes, about 1½ cups shredded zucchini, and 1 can cream of celery soup. Do not add liquid as the tomatoes and zucchini supply enough, especially if using frozen. Heat and serve.

Tomato, Egg, and Cheese Bake

This is a small batch serving 2 or 3; multiply it for a family.
1. Chop a meaty tomato to make 1 cup. Stir in:

> ½ cup cream
> ½ cup shredded cheddar cheese (or cheese of choice)
> 1 egg, beaten with a fork
> 2 tablespoons butter, melted
> Salt and pepper, as desired

2. Pour the mixture into a 1-quart casserole dish coated with vegetable spray.
3. Bake at 350 degrees F for 35 minutes or until bubbly and the cheese is lightly browned.

NOTE: When serving this recipe, you might want to provide individual vegetable dishes, in case the tomatoes are extra juicy and cause a little liquid to separate out from the egg. Or, to avoid any separation, just stir in 1 cup crumbled soda crackers.

ZUCCHINI IN THE GARDEN

Zucchini is notoriously productive. My mother used to send me around the neighborhood with loads of zucchini to give away, sometimes directing me to place a bagful on everyone's doorstep, ring the bell, and leave before it could be turned down!

When I became a farmer's wife, I found that an overabundance of zucchini is no problem—the hogs just love the too-large fruit. First they play football with it; then they settle down to devour it with great zest and look to me for more!

Zucchini is another type of summer squash. It originated as a vining plant, but now many bush-type varieties have been developed. You really only need one hill to feed your family—and probably your entire neighborhood—till frost!

Zucchini is about 95 percent water. If you or someone in your family find the dark green zucchinis to be too limp and watery when cooked, be sure to try the climbing Zucchetta Rampicante variety I've listed. It stays firm and has a wonderful flavor all its own! And what a beautiful vine it is!

LOCATION: Choose a spot with good air circulation where no members of the squash family, including pumpkins and cucumbers, as well as melons, grew the previous year.

Although they are usually found in a vegetable garden, bush-type zucchini form mounds of attractive, deep green foliage that could be effective incorporated in the landscape or in flower beds.

To save space, you can grow the vining types on trellises, along fences, over arbors, etc.

NOTE: All squash, summer and winter, can cross-pollinate. This won't affect the current crop, but it will affect the seeds; if you plan to save the seeds to plant the next year, space the varieties some distance from each other or you might have peculiar offspring.

GROWING RANGE: Zucchini grows everywhere. In extremely short-season areas, warm the soil and start with seedlings.

SOIL REQUIREMENTS: Light, well-drained soil. Till thoroughly and mix in well-rotted manure or compost.

MOISTURE: Zucchini likes plenty of moisture, although it doesn't want to sit in standing water.

LIGHT: Plant in full sun if possible, or light shade.

PLANTING SEASON: All squash is a warm-weather crop and should be planted after the last frost date.

HOW TO PLANT: Zucchini is direct-seeded in all but the shortest growing seasons. I've experimented and found that direct-seeded zucchini catch up nicely with the transplanted seedlings (at least in my area), so why go to the bother?

- Thoroughly and deeply till the soil, mixing in well-rotted manure or compost.
- If necessary, warm the soil bed with black plastic.
- Start the planting one week after the last frost date for your area or when the soil temperature is at least 60 degrees F.
- If desired, for easier watering, bury a perforated plastic one-gallon milk jug so all but two inches is in the ground.
- Plant four to six seeds one inch deep in a twelve-inch circle or hill, surrounding the buried milk jug, if you are using it. Space the hills four feet apart.
- Or, plant the zucchini in a row, spacing the seeds twenty inches apart in rows four feet apart. This is my favorite method, and I finish out the row with other types of summer squash.
- Remove the black plastic, if you're using it, after planting and germination have occurred, or puncture it well to allow rain to penetrate.

To start zucchini seedlings:

- Start three weeks before the last frost date for your area.
- Plant the seeds one inch deep in peat pots.
- Harden off the seedlings for one week before transplant time.
- Transplant the seedlings outdoors one week after the last frost date for your area, when night temperatures are above 60 degrees F.

- Carefully bury the peat pot in the soil, disturbing the roots as little as possible or the seedling won't take well to transplanting.
- Follow direct-seeding directions, above, for spacing.

ONGOING CARE:

- **Covering** the young plants if there is a threat of frost. (Full-grown plants can tolerate a light frost.)
- **Thinning** each hill back to two or three plants.
- **Weeding** near the squash will not be necessary once the large leaves have formed, because the ground underneath is so well shaded that weeds are discouraged.
- **Watering**, as needed, directing the water to the roots, not the plants, or water overhead early in the day so the plants will dry out quickly in the sun.
- **Staying away** from the plants when they are wet, to avoid disease.
- **Harvesting** regularly, to stimulate the plant to keep producing until winter. If you allow one squash to stay on the plant, the entire plant might quit flowering.

VARIETIES INCLUDE:

- **Zucchetta Rampicante**, a climbing zucchini that produces enormous yellow flowers and long, curvaceous, pale green–colored fruits. I love this squash because the flesh is so delicious and it stays firm when it's cooked, as opposed to getting limp and watery like regular zucchini can. It also has seeds only in the bulbous tip; the long neck is seed-free. The squash will get over three feet in length, if you let it—but harvest it sooner. This squash has lovely foliage, and it looks great on an arbor, trellis, or trained to climb along a fence—but be aware that it gets Jack-in-the-beanstalk long! This heirloom variety is highly recommended! 58 days.
- **Black Beauty** is a compact, bush-type plant that grows straight, smooth, glossy zucchini that is almost seedless. A perennial favorite. 50 days.
- **Black Magic** plants are one and a half to two feet tall by three to three and a half feet wide and bear dark green fruit with a small seed cavity. 50 days.
- **Jackpot Zucchini** is a very small, bush-type plant that gets only about 30 inches across, yet yields prolifically. 42 days.
- **Roly Poly** is a bush-type plant that produces three- to five-inch round zucchini instead of the usual oblong types. 50 days.
- **Eight Ball Hybrid** is a smaller bush plant two to three feet wide that produces round squash two to three inches in diameter that are great to stuff and bake. 40 days.

YIELD: One hill will give you dozens of zucchini, depending on how often you harvest them and whether you allow them to get huge.

HARVESTING: Check the plants daily, or you'll find yourself overwhelmed with huge numbers of gigantic zucchini almost overnight.

Squash

For best flavor and the most tenderness, harvest the zucchini when they are young; the best time is just after the blossoms drop. This means most zucchini will be under four to six inches, but the Zucchetta

Rampicante variety will be under eighteen inches and still slender the full length. Of course, you can eat the larger squash as well, but it won't be as flavorful and you'll probably have to remove the skin.

Blossoms

If you find you're getting too much fruit and don't have hogs, just harvest some of the blossoms plus about one inch of stem, and eat the whole thing! They're absolutely delectable!

Want to have both the blossoms and the fruit? Harvest only the male blossoms, leaving one or two per plant to pollinate the females. You can easily identify the female blossoms because they are attached to a tiny squash; the males are attached to a straight stem.

Baby squash plus the blossom

This is a real delicacy! Harvest it before the flower turns brown and while it's still attached to the fruit. Saute the whole thing a short time in butter—wonderful!

Zucchini in the Kitchen

STORING: Regular zucchini will keep a day or two on the counter; Zucchetta Rampicante will keep much longer—I've stored it for months at room temperature with little loss in quality. Or refrigerate them—it's not necessary to place them in plastic bags.

FREEZING: Zucchini doesn't freeze well when sliced or cubed. The best way to freeze zucchini is to shred it and place premeasured quantities in plastic bags. This can be used in many ways, by adding it to soups, stews, and casseroles; making it into bread; etc. Seal the shredded zucchini in plastic bags, label and date, and freeze. No blanching required.

EATING ZUCCHINI

PREPARING: Just wash the zucchini and cut it, as desired. There is no need to peel it unless it has gotten too large and the skin is tough.

By themselves, zucchini aren't very flavorful. Zucchini can be shredded or diced and added to bread, cakes, casseroles, etc. Or cut them lengthwise, hollow them out with a spoon, and fill them with a tomato-based meat or rice stuffing, then bake.

FLAVORING: Basil, celery seed, curry, ginger, marjoram, mint, oregano, rosemary, onion, parsley, garlic, Italian spice blends, dill, salt and pepper, butter, bacon, cheese, walnuts. Especially good with tomatoes.

COOKING: Methods include broiling, grilling, steaming, boiling, frying.

Zucchini blossoms

Harvested with 1 inch of stem during the daytime when they're fully open, these are wonderful sautéed whole in butter and eaten stem and all. Or dip the blossoms in batter and then fry in butter or olive oil—it's really delicious! The blossoms can also be filled with a rice or meat stuffing.

Eat the blossoms fresh from the garden; don't try to hold them in the refrigerator. If necessary, you can quickly rinse them in cold water to flush out any insects, and gently shake or blot them dry. The blossoms can be left whole or cut in half the full length, including the stem, and fried.

BATTER FOR THE BLOSSOMS: Stir together ⅓ cup flour, ¾ teaspoon baking powder, and ¼ teaspoon salt. Gradually add 1 cup cream (you can substitute milk, but cream is better) to make a smooth batter.

Zucchini Omelet

Add a handful of chopped zucchini to your favorite omelet, flavored with your choice of other ingredients listed above.

Broiled Zucchini

1. Cut small zucchini in half the long way. Place cut-side up in a broiler rack pan.
2. Brush the zucchini generously with olive oil and sprinkle it with garlic salt, marjoram, and pepper.
3. Preheat the broiler on high heat. Place the zucchini pan 4 inches below the broiler for 3 or 4 minutes.
4. Place Parmesan, American, or mozzerella cheese slices on the zucchini and return to the broiler for about 1 minute. Serve hot.

Fried Breaded Zucchini

Very quick and so good!
1. Clean zucchini and cut crosswise into ¼-inch slices.
2. Heat ¼ cup olive oil in a large skillet on medium-high heat.
3. Place 1 cup ground pork rinds in a pie tin and add pepper to taste. (Make crumbs by placing pork rinds, soda crackers, stuffing mix, or stale bread in a food processor.)
4. Place 1 egg in a second pie tin and whisk until yolk and white are blended.
5. Dip zucchini slices in the egg and then in the crumbs and fry in the heated skillet about 3 minutes, or until the crumbs are browned. Turn slices and fry another 3 minutes until the other side is browned. Serve hot with a dollop of sour cream or plain yogurt, if desired. (Discard any unused egg or breading.)

NOTE: Try a combination skillet by using this recipe with breaded tomatoes and onions alongside the zucchini. Wonderful!

Quick and Easy Zucchini Soup

Outstanding!
1. Mince a medium onion and cook it in a saucepan with 2 tablespoons butter.
2. Dice up zucchini to make 4 cups (about 4 medium zucchini) and add the zucchini to the onion with 4 cups chicken broth. Or, substitute 4 cups water and 4 chicken bouillon cubes.
3. Bring to a boil, then reduce heat and simmer, covered, until the zucchini is tender, perhaps 10 minutes. Add a handful of fresh minced parsley.
4. Using a cordless blender, puree the soup (or put it in a food processor). Add salt to taste.
5. Serve the soup hot or cold, topped with a dollop of sour cream, whipped cream, or plain yogurt. Garnish with a small sprig of fresh parsley, if desired.

Zucchini Skillet

A frequent summer supper dish in our family!
1. Brown and crumble one or more pounds of hamburger in a large skillet. If there is a lot of grease, pour it off.
2. Stir in one minced garlic clove, one chopped onion, one sliced zucchini, and two or three meaty tomatoes cut in chunks. Sprinkle with Italian spices, if desired. Cook, uncovered, until the vegetables are just barely tender.
3. If desired, top with shredded mozzarella cheese and place the skillet under the broiler a few seconds to melt and lightly brown the cheese. Serve hot.

Easy Zucchini Casserole

1. Layer in a baking dish:

> sliced zucchini
> sliced mushrooms
> sliced onion

2. Sprinkle on basil, garlic, and Italian spices, as desired.

3. Top with shredded cheese, mozzarella or as desired.

4. Bake, uncovered, at 350 degrees F for 20 or 30 minutes or until vegetables are tender.

Elaine's Scalloped Zucchini

Use regular zucchini for this recipe.

1. Mix together and place in an ovenproof casserole dish:

> 3 cups shredded zucchini, skins left on
> 2 tablespoons minced onion
> 1 egg, beaten
> 1 cup crushed soda crackers
> 1 cup shredded cheddar cheese
> $1/2$ teaspoon garlic powder (or more, to taste)
> $1/4$ teaspoon salt
> $1/2$ teaspoon pepper

2. Bake 1 hour, uncovered, at 350 degrees F.

Zucchetta Rampicante Casserole

This recipe is specially designed for this zucchini.

1. Mix together and place in an ovenproof casserole dish:

> 4 cups shredded Zucchetta Rampicante zucchini
> $1/2$ cup minced onion
> 3 eggs, beaten
> $1 1/2$ cups shredded cheddar cheese
> $1/2$ teaspoon garlic powder
> $1/2$ teaspoon salt
> $1/4$ teaspoon pepper

2. Bake, covered with foil, 1 hour at 350 degrees F.

Easy Zucchini Jam

Delicious and pretty, too!

1. Peel and shred zucchini to make $2 1/2$ cups. (Peeling is optional but makes the jam more attractive.)

2. Place the zucchini in a large saucepan and add 1½ cups sugar. Simmer until the liquid is clear.

3. Add:

> 1 cup crushed pineapple in natural juice, undrained
>   (8.5-ounce can)
> juice and zest of one lemon
> 1 3-ounce package of apricot gelatin

4. Stir the hot zucchini until the gelatin is dissolved. Cool and refrigerate or freeze.

Easy Zucchini Bread

An old farm favorite!

1. Shred zucchini to make 2 cups. (It's not necessary to peel it.) Place the zucchini in a mixer bowl.

2. Add to the zucchini:

> 2 cups sugar
> 1 cup oil
> 3 eggs
> 1 teaspoon vanilla

3. Mix well and then stir in:

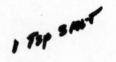
1 Tsp salt

> 3 cups flour
> ½ cup chopped pecans or walnuts (optional)
> 1 teaspoon baking soda
> 1 teaspoon cinnamon
> 1 teaspoon ground ginger
> 1 teaspoon ground cloves
> ¼ teaspoon baking powder

4. Pour into 2 bread pans coated with vegetable spray. Bake at 325 degrees F for 1 hour or until a toothpick inserted in the center of the bread comes out clean. Serve with butter or fruit butter, if desired.

SOURCES

Books

Garden Seed Inventory is an annual, comprehensive sourcebook for 7,300 nonhybrid vegetables available from U.S. and Canadian mail-order seed catalogues, including contact information. A must have! (You also might want to consider joining their fine organization or visiting their test gardens.) The book is available from:

Seed Savers Exchange
3076 North Winn Road
Decorah, IA 52101
www.seedsavers.org

Equipment and Tools

Mantis Tiller is the very best portable tiller on the market. Their claims are not exaggerated. If you don't agree, you can return it within one year for a full refund. Call 1-800-366-6268 for free information or check their Web site, where you can also find composters, sprayers, and other useful equipment:

www.mantistiller.com

Gardener's Supply Company has great equipment and tools for the gardener.

Gardener's Supply Company
128 Intervale Road
Burlington, VT 05401
800-427-3363
www.gardeners.com

Garden Tools by Lee Valley also has excellent equipment and tools for the gardener.

12 East River Street
Ogdensburg, NY 13669
www.leevalley.com

Harris Seeds Home Gardening Catalogue has top quality light stands and other seed starting equipment and supplies.

355 Paul Road/P.O. Box 24966
Rochester, NY 14624-0966
800-514-4441
www.harrisseeds.com

Cuisinart makes wonderful time-saving food processors, cordless hand blenders, and electric ice cream makers, as well as quality stainless steel pots and pans. These products are available in stores and catalogues nationwide, or you can visit the Cuisinart Web site at:

www.cuisinart.com

Organizations

The **Hobby Greenhouse Association** is worth joining, even if you don't own a greenhouse!

Hobby Greenhouse Association
8 Glen Terrace
Bedford, MA 01730-2048
www.hobbygreenhouse.org

The Seed Savers Exchange is a nonprofit organization dedicated to maintaining our plant diversity by saving heirloom fruit and vegetable varieties from extinction. You can visit their gardens on 18,000 acres near Decorah, Iowa, or attend informational gatherings. For more information, contact:

Seed Savers Exchange
3076 North Winn Road
Decorah, IA 52101
www.seedsavers.org

4-H is a program for youth in cooperation with the Extension service. It originated in a small Iowa community and has become an international organization. For more information, contact:

National 4-H Council
7100 Connecticut Avenue
Chevy Chase, MD 20815
301-961-2800
www.fourhcouncil.edu

Products

Gardens Alive! Environmentally Responsible Products That Work is a mail-order company that provides everything from all-natural fertilizers to fruit sprays, pest and disease controls, even a safe product that prevents weed seed from sprouting. Their catalogue is well illustrated to help you identify your problem and tells how to implement the solution. I am very happy with the products from this company and recommend them highly. To get a catalogue:

Gardens Alive!
5100 Schenley Place
Lawrenceburg, IN 47025
Customer Service: 812-537-8651, Mon. to Fri., 8 A.M. to 5 P.M., E.T.
www.GardensAlive.com

Dalen Products, Inc. has inexpensive plastic fencing that is great support for climbing peas.

1110 Gilbert Drive
Knoxville, TB 37932-3099
800-747-3256
www.gardeneer.com

SEEDS AND SEEDLINGS
FROM MAIL-ORDER CATALOGUES

W. Atlee Burpee and Co.
300 Park Ave.
Warminster PA 18991
Free catalogue, many vegetable varieties.
www.burpee.com

Harris Seeds Home Gardening Catalogue
355 Paul Rd./P.O. Box 24966
Rochester, NY 14624-0966
800-514-4441
Free catalogue.
www.harrisseeds.com

Henry Field's Seed and Nursery Co.
415 North Burnett St.
Shenandoah IA 51602
Free catalogue, many vegetable varieties.
800-235-0845
www.henryfields.com

Gurney's Seed and Nursery Co.
110 Capitol St.
Yankton SD 57079
Free catalogue. "America's Most Complete
   Seed and Nursery Company"
800-824-6400
www.mySEASONS.com

J.W. Jung seed Co.
335 S. High St.
Randolph WI 53957-0001
Free catalog. "Quality Seeds, Plants, Garden
   Gifts & Bulbs"
www.jungseed.com

Mellinger's Inc.
2310 South Range Rd
North Lima OH 44452
Free catalogue, many fruits and berries.
330-549-9861
www.mellingers.com

Miller Nurseries
5060 W. Lake Rd.
Canandaigua NY 14424
Free catalogue.
800-836-9630
www.millernurseries.com

Park Seed Co
1 Parkton Ave.
Greenwood SC 29647-0001
Free catalogue.
800-845-3369
www.parkseed.com

Seeds of Change
P.O. Box 15700
Santa Fe NM 87506-5700
www.seeds of change.com

INDEX